The Food of Love

The
Food of Love

PRINCESSE EDMOND DE POLIGNAC
(1865–1943)
AND HER SALON

Michael de Cossart

HAMISH HAMILTON London

FIRST PUBLISHED IN GREAT BRITAIN, 1978
BY HAMISH HAMILTON LTD,
90 GREAT RUSSELL STREET, LONDON WC1B 3PT

ISBN 0 241 89785 8

COPYRIGHT © 1978 BY MICHAEL DE COSSART

PRINTED IN GREAT BRITAIN BY
WESTERN PRINTING SERVICES LTD, BRISTOL

'*If music be the food of love, play on;*
Give me excess of it, that, surfeiting,
The appetite may sicken, and so die.
That strain again; it had a dying fall:
O, it came o'er my ear like the sweet south,
That breathes upon a bank of violets,
Stealing and giving odour.'

Act I, Scene I,
Twelfth Night,
William Shakespeare.

Contents

List of Illustrations

Between pages 116 and 117

Acknowledgments

While responsibility for any views expressed in this work must rest with me alone, I acknowledge my debt of gratitude to the following people for their practical help:

Professor Quentin Bell, Mademoiselle Nadia Boulanger, the Marquise de Casa-Fuerte, Monsieur Hugues Cuénod, Mr Robert Heber-Percy, Winnaretta Lady Leeds, Miss Rosamond Lehmann, the late Hon. Nancy Mitford, Mr Raymond Mortimer, Sir Oswald Mosley, Monsieur Nicolas Nabokov, Mr Peter Pears, Prince Louis de Polignac, Princesse Mary de Rachewiltz and Mrs Vera Stravinsky.

I am also particularly indebted to the Marquise d'Argenson, Sir Lennox Berkeley, Madame Brucker of the Fondation Singer-Polignac, the Duc and Duchesse Decazes, Monsieur Jacques Fevrier, the Duchesse de la Rochefoucauld, *née* Fels, Mr James Lees-Milne, the Comte Jehan de Noue, Monsieur Henri Sauguet and Mr Virgil Thomson.

My gratitude to Monsieur Doda Conrad and to Mrs James Lees-Milne, who, as the Hon. Mrs Anthony Chaplin, succoured the Princesse de Polignac during her declining years, is immeasurable. And a special word of thanks must go to Dr Robert Orledge and Dr John Rogister for their invaluable help and professional advice.

The drawing on p. 181 is from *For Whom the Cloche Tolls* by Angus Wilson and Philippe Jullian and is produced by permission of Philippe Jullian.

MICHAEL DE COSSART

Chapter 1
Singers as a Family
(1865–1878)

On 8 January 1879 a special performance of Beethoven's Quartet, opus 131, was given at the Duchesse de Camposelice's house at 27 avenue Kléber in Paris. If most people still found Beethoven's late string quartets, more than fifty years after their composition, almost completely incomprehensible, the duchess was not among their number: she was a great music-lover whose tastes were considered very advanced for the day. But on this occasion she had not chosen the music. Her daughter Winnaretta was celebrating her fourteenth birthday and, when asked what she would like as a birthday treat, she brushed aside suggestions of a watch from Boucheron's or a fan decorated by Chaplin, one of the most fashionable painters, and insisted instead on hearing a performance of Beethoven's Fourteenth Quartet. Her mother wondered at her choice but said nothing. There was something slightly intimidating about the girl. Her clear blue eyes had a determined look and her incredibly straight nose and slightly jutting chin added to her air of almost masculine aggressiveness. She was adamant: she found the music moving; the opening bars, she said, were a source of inspiration and comfort to her. She knew what she wanted from life and was already beginning to pursue it with a clarity of mind and singleness of purpose that remained with her throughout the rest of her life.

Madame de Camposelice's daughter Winnaretta was destined to become one of the most famous patrons of music in modern France. She would achieve a unique position in French social and artistic life—although there was little about her early background that made this seem likely. She was, in fact, the second of six children borne by the duchess to her first husband Isaac Merritt Singer, the creator of the Singer sewing-machine. Winnaretta Eugénie Singer first saw the light of day in Yonkers in New York on 8 January 1865, just as the Union armies came in sight of victory: three months later, on 9 April, the surrender of the Confederate side to General Ulysses Grant at Appomattox effectively brought the Civil War to an end. Winnaretta's father, Isaac Singer, had played no active part in the fighting. Indeed, within months of the outbreak of hostilities in 1861 he had left America and spent two years in Europe. But he did make one contribution to the North's war-effort: he gave a thousand sewing-machines to the army. If the effect of this homely gift upon the course of political events is not easy to calculate, there is no doubt that as an advertising venture it was very productive: through it the rapid success of the machine and the prosperity of its inventor were confirmed as facts of American life.

Success had not come easily to Isaac Singer. Poverty and failure had characterized his earlier years. Born at Oswego, New York, on 27 October 1811, he had been brought up by his parents, German immigrants who had fled from a Europe suffering from the exigencies of the Napoleonic Wars. Isaac absorbed a basic education at a local elementary school up to the age of twelve when he ran away from home and found work for himself as an apprentice in a machine-shop in Rochester. He learned his trade well and returned to it periodically during the years between 1830 and 1850 when most of his time was spent touring America with his own troupe of actors, the Merritt Players. The stage always fascinated Singer: although his own troupe's efforts were not brilliant and only just provided the actors with their subsistence, the fantasy world of the theatre appealed to a strong romantic streak in his nature. During the periods when no theatre-work was available Singer had to return to his old trade as a mechanic. But he did not allow frustration and hardship to dull his mind. Instead he used to divert himself by trying to improve the machines that he was employed to maintain or mend and in the process he invented two new devices, a rock-drill and an ingenious carving-machine. He patented them but neither achieved much success.

One day early in August 1850, while working in Boston, Singer was shown one of the sewing-machines which Lerow and Blodgett had invented some years earlier. It was a primitive contraption that stitched so crudely that it provided no really viable alternative to sewing by hand. Singer immediately put his mind to the problem of improving the machine and, overnight, he produced a design for a new instrument. But, if he had ideas, he had no money or facilities for putting them into practice. Nothing daunted, he persuaded some of his work associates of the importance of his brain-child and they responded, one by lending him forty dollars, another by letting him use his workshop for making the prototype model. For eleven days Singer worked continuously, taking very little food and practically no sleep. And at 9 o'clock on the evening of the eleventh day the model was at last assembled and ready to be tested. It was a failure: the machine's stitching was slack and almost as poor as the Lerow and Blodgett machine's efforts. Singer despaired. His helpers gave up and deserted him. Only one, George Zieber, who had lent the original forty dollars, remained with him. Eventually about midnight they locked up the workshop and walked dejected back to the poor hotel where they were staying. Still they discussed the machine and, by chance, Zieber remarked that it was only the top row of stitches that caused the trouble: only they were slack. In an instant Singer realized what had happened. He rushed back to the workshop and, by the light of Zieber's lamp, he tightened up a tension screw, which he had overlooked when assembling the machine. He tested the model again and it stitched perfectly.

However, only the first difficulties had been overcome. For some time Singer struggled unsuccessfully to interest potential backers in his invention. Moreover, as soon as he patented it in 1851, he was presented with a claim for twenty-five thousand dollars by Elias Howe, who said that Singer had infringed one of his own patents. In fact, he had. In 1846 Howe had taken out a patent on the eye-pointed needle incorporated by Singer into his machine and, although Howe had not actually invented the device himself, as patent holder he was in a position to proceed against him, despite the fact that the new machine was otherwise entirely different in form and the only one able to sew effectively. But Howe litigated implacably against Singer for three years, until in May 1854 a settlement was agreed whereby he received a royalty on all Singer machines produced. That could have well sounded the death-knell of the Singer sewing-machine if a friend of the inventor, Edward Clark, a rich and successful lawyer, had not stepped in. He had already lent Singer money to establish a factory in New York. Now he took over much of the business side of production and, with equal shares in the venture, Clark and Singer managed to solve the problems together—the one a scrupulous and practical business-man, the other an imaginative but rather unrealistic inventor. While Singer refined his machine, inventing and patenting a series of improvements, Clark ran the manufactory. But a personality clash was almost inevitable, and one did come to the surface about 1860. However, a compromise was again reached. Singer withdrew from active participation, and in 1863 agreed to put production into the hands of an incorporated company, the Singer Manufacturing Company, in which he retained a forty per cent share.

By this time Singer was a very rich man. Despite his problems he had seen his invention accepted by most people as a house-hold necessity. It received the gold medal award at the Fair of the American Institute as early as 1851. In 1855, when it was already in general use, it received a prize at the Paris Exhibi-tion, as a result of which the French government began to use it for making clothes for the army. Within years the sewing-machine was known throughout the world. There were, how-ever, some who deplored its invention because they imagined that it would put seamstresses out of work. Singer himself witnessed some of the reaction: sitting in his office one afternoon, he was confronted by an uninvited caller, a tall woman, dressed in black, gesticulating angrily at the sewing-machine on show. 'Are you the inventor of this machine? Yes? Then you ought to be hanged!' And she left the office as abruptly as she came. In fact, the sewing-machine, far from causing unemployment, provided new work for machine operators and at the same time increased the status and the wages of hand labour in the clothes manufacturing industry. But seamstresses' material prosperity cannot be compared with that enjoyed by Singer himself. He was soon in the position to be able to move into a house in New York's fashionable Fifth Avenue. He could now indulge in a mildly extrovert way of life. He had himself driven round the city in an enormous yellow coach with a capacity large enough for a small orchestra. But war-torn America was not the best place for a care-free existence and so in 1861, even before the incorporation of the sewing-machine company, he set sail for Europe.

At the age of fifty Isaac Singer may well have felt that he deserved to relax and enjoy the pleasures of life. Second Empire

France was especially alluring. But there was another pressing reason for wanting to leave America for a while. Since 1860 he had been relentlessly pursued by Maria Haley, an ex-mistress, or rather a common law wife, by whom he had two children. Although their relationship had ended some time before, Maria Haley, as Singer became rich and famous, put forward a claim that she was legally married to him. Singer denied this, but before he put the Atlantic between them, he seems to have paid her a substantial sum to leave him in peace. However, if Maria Haley was the most troublesome complication in his personal life, she was certainly not the only one. Singer, in his early days when he was living on his arts had had countless passing affairs with women and, in addition to Miss Haley, had had three mistresses with whom he had lived on a more or less permanent basis one after the other up to 1861. In New York Mary Walter had lived with him for a time and borne him a daughter. Mary McGonigal of San Francisco had lasted longer—long enough to have five children by him. The third, Mary Ann Foster, surpassed this by being mother to eight more. To have fathered sixteen children without benefit of clergy, before adding those legitimately conceived later in life, was something of a domestic feat in itself. But Isaac Singer seems genuinely to have enjoyed having children about him. He openly acknowledged all his offspring and later provided for them lavishly in his will, at the same time insisting that they should all bear the name Singer.

As an egocentric and exuberant romantic, he enjoyed domestic life only so long as it imposed no limitation upon his freedom. And, when he turned towards Europe in 1861, he was again motivated as much by an impulse to explore a whole new world of experience as by a desire to escape from the past.

Although by the 1860s the weaknesses in Napoleon III's foreign policy were beginning to be more apparent, and the world was starting to take him less seriously, France continued to act as though she were still on the crest of the European wave. A studied gaiety could conceal signs of political weakness and governmental corruption. French society reoriented itself to changing social and economic conditions. Money became increasingly a determinant of social status. Even the high aristocracy no longer ignored the advantages of associations and alliances with the rich. In an industrial age an income from sources other than land was becoming acceptable. Thus Isaac

Singer found little difficulty in gaining acceptance in the better,
if not the best social circles in Paris. He was moreover extrovert
and lively; he was interested in the arts, if a little crude in
manner; he was rich and, despite his years, was still a bachelor
—after a manner of speaking. He mixed with the comfortable
section of the middle class and hovered on the fringes of the
aristocracy. He frequented their places of pleasure and entertainment. He was to be found in their salons. He was introduced
to their unmarried daughters, suitably chaperoned.

During the summer of 1862 Singer met a young and very
beautiful Parisian woman, called Isabelle Eugénie Boyer, and
was immediately attracted by her. Although only twenty years
of age—thirty years his junior—she turned out to be a stimulating companion. Singer certainly enjoyed being seen in society
with someone as generally admired as the striking Isabelle
Boyer but he liked her mainly for her wit and intelligence. Her
main passion in life was music and, although he was drawn
much more towards literature and the theatre, they did appreciate each other's interests. Possibly Singer also admired her for
retaining an aloof dignity against a background of unsettled
family life. Her parents, Louis Noël and Pamela Boyer, had
enjoyed an easy middle-class existence together at the family
home in the rue de Monceau and in course of time Mme Boyer
had borne five or six children. But also over the years a quarrel
had developed between them, mainly about religious matters.
Pamela Boyer's mother, an Irish Protestant, had brought her
up in her faith; Louis Boyer was a Catholic. As their children
grew up the problem of religious differences became more
acute. The simple French solution whereby daughters of mixed
marriages were brought up in the mother's faith and sons in the
father's apparently was not an acceptable compromise. Eventually tension in the Boyer household became so great that
Louis Boyer abandoned the family to his wife's care and went
to spend the rest of his life with a strictly catholic sister in the
provinces. Isabelle did not become much involved on either
side: she saw practically nothing of her father and remained
coolly detached from her mother. She was strong-willed and
intelligent enough to know her own mind.

Her attachment to Isaac Singer possibly resulted from disillusionment with her parents: she shared his attitude towards
individual freedom; she may also have regarded him as a

father-figure, a substitute for her own father. Almost inevitably
their relationship developed, and by the autumn of 1862 she
had become his mistress. The results—at least according to
Singer's past experience—were inevitable. By spring of the
following year Isabelle could no longer conceal the fact that she
was pregnant and so, to avoid scandal, from which even money
was not immune, Singer decided to return to America and take
Isabelle with him. For some reason he considered it expedient
for her to enter the country using the name Summerville, and it
was as Isabelle Summerville that she was installed in his New
York house at 14 Fifth Avenue and introduced to American
society. As soon as formalities could be dealt with, he made
plans to regularize their relationship, and on 13 June 1863 the
Reverend Edwin Cook, Rector of Saint John's Church in
Hammond Street, was brought to Singer's house where he
married Isaac and Isabelle (still known as Summerville)
according to the rites of the Protestant Episcopal Church. Six
weeks later Isabelle gave birth to her first child, a boy, whom
they called Mortimer. He was Isaac Singer's seventeenth child,
the first to be born, if not conceived in wedlock.

Their second child, a daughter, was born on 8 January 1865:
Winnaretta Eugénie, destined to become more famous, more
notorious even, than either of her remarkable parents. As if
foreseeing that she was marked out for an extraordinary career,
her father chose or invented the unique name of Winnaretta
for her. He had had flights of fancy before when naming some
of his illegitimate children—for example Isaac Augustus and
Jasper Hamet—but 'Winnaretta' was unheard of, though it was
reputed to be of Red Indian origin. At least the names of her
two younger brothers, called Washington and Paris after the
cities in which they were born, were familiar to the ear, even if
rarely encountered at the baptismal font. As a godfather the
Anglo-American artist Edward May, one of Thomas Couture's
pupils, was chosen. In 1865 he was on a visit to America, and he
turned out to be a very appropriate choice. He remained close
to Winnaretta until his death in 1887, and in her adolescent
years was something of a mentor to her.

Winnaretta spent only the first two years of her life in America.
After the birth of her brother, Washington, in 1866, the
Singers decided to return to France and in 1867 took up resi-
dence in a spacious apartment at 83 bis boulevard Malesherbes,

at the heart of Haussemann's newly reconstructed Paris, near
Mrs Singer's former home by the Parc Monceau. However, if
the Singers came to Europe to avoid witnessing the slow process
of America's recovery and readjustment after the War of
Secession, the political situation which they found in France
was also not very happy. Napoleon III's prestige was rapidly
diminishing. Outwitted by Bismarck during the Seven Weeks
War in 1866, and in March 1867 compelled to withdraw French
military support for Maximilian of Mexico, his shame seemed
complete when Maximilian suffered a tragic death at the hands
of Mexican insurgents. Nevertheless French society went its own
way, turning its back on its ailing emperor and covering up
reality with a façade of carefree brilliance. The Great Exhibition
of 1867, designed by Napoleon as an epic celebration of French
peace and prosperity in a world of progress, attracted more
attention to Parisian society than to the bedraggled emperor and
his *entourage* of sycophants. The Singers, as American citizens,
were scarcely concerned with the political situation. They were
interested only in the Paris of the Exhibition, in Feydeau,
Offenbach, Gounod and Flaubert. The only Bonapartes who
concerned them was the Emperor's cousin, the Princesse
Mathilde. Besides, the Singers had family preoccupations: the
arrival of a new baby was an annual event. By 1870 two sons,
Paris and Franklin, and a daughter, Isabelle Blanche, had
brought the Singers' children up to their full complement of
six.

However, by the middle of 1870 relations between Napoleon's
France and Bismarck's Prussia could not but cause general
concern. A friend advised Isaac Singer that Paris was no place
for his young family. On 16 July he drew up a long and
picturesque will, making provision for all his numerous progeny.
On 19 July war was declared. In August a series of defeats
brought the French army to its knees. On 1 September the
Prussians rounded off their victory at Sedan by taking Napoleon
III prisoner. But before they reached Paris on 19 September and
laid it under siege, the Singers had fled across the Channel to
England.

While waiting for peace to return, Singer bought a house in
London at 32 Grosvenor Gardens, just behind Buckingham
Palace, and for a year it served as a refuge for his family while
they waited, watching events in France with ever dwindling

hope: the proclamation of the Third Republic, the siege of Paris, drawn out until 28 January 1871, and then the Paris Commune, lasting from March until its terrible collapse during the *semaine sanglante* at the end of May. By this time Singer's health was beginning to deteriorate, and London's winter weather did not improve it. Since a move to the South of France was for the moment out of the question, the Singers decided to stay at what was considered the mose clement spot in England, Torbay, on the south coast of Devon. Winnaretta, an impressionable six-year-old at the time, was overwhelmed by the beauty of the place: this was the first time she had lived in anything like rural surroundings. Her father was also impressed by the countryside and climate, and decided to remain there. The house he began building at Paignton was designed to fulfil every domestic and social requirement. Indeed it turned out to be a building of palatial proportions, with over a hundred rooms and a small theatre. Having lavished half a million dollars on its construction, he gave it the quaintly simple name of The Wigwam, even if it had more in common with the Petit Trianon than anything in an Indian encampment. Nor was The Wigwam to be just another stopping-point in Singer's hitherto almost nomadic life. As his health worsened during the next four years, he remained in Devon, hastily putting finishing touches to his mansion and lavishly furnishing it. One of his main concerns during his last illness was to make provision for its completion as a home for his family. On 14 July 1875 he made a final addition to his will to that effect, and nine days later he was dead. In a real sense Torbay became his last resting place: he was buried in Torquay cemetery in a newly created vault, on top of which was erected an enormous tombstone, a simple catafalque in shape but intricately carved in a fashion typical of the period. And there Isaac Merrit Singer remained, like a patriarch waiting to gather round him again the children whom he so richly endowed with originality of spirit— and money.

Winnaretta was ten years old when he died, but apart from the fact that she had lost a father who had dominated her life and whom she in turn had loved, for the next few years her life continued much as before. Even the fortune which she inherited (a twelfth of her father's many millions) had little effect upon her, since it was kept in trust until she came of age. She was still

very much under her mother's tutelage. The elements of an
education thought suitable for a girl in her position continued
to be instilled into her by governesses. In the formal sense her
intellectual training was rudimentary, but there were three
influences that helped to cultivate her mind. Her father had
taught her to appreciate American literature: having cut her
teeth on Harriet Beecher Stowe as a girl, she later went on to
enjoy the works of Mark Twain, Henry David Thoreau and
their contemporaries. Painting and drawing were part of the
classroom curriculum, which involved trips to the countryside
and sea. Thus almost instinctively she found herself observing
nature and analysing it in terms of balance and contrast in
form and colour. She loved the rolling landscape around
Torbay, with its elegant ilex trees, the rich red soil and rocks,
the summer flowers and the soft blueness of the sea and yellow-
white sand within sight of the house.

The third influence was a musical one. Marriage had allowed
Winnaretta's mother to give full rein to her passion for it. She
had found herself able to surround herself with the best players,
and had made a special study of old instruments, piecing
together a double quartet of priceless Stadivarius instruments
for use in her own salon. Despite its limitations of life in Devon,
Winnaretta became used to hearing the more sophisticated
works in chamber music repertoire. Mrs Singer probably did not
care how indigestible her children found her choice of music
(and most of them did) : her prime concern was her own enjoyment. Winnaretta was left to make her own responses to it.
Otherwise her only formal musical guidance came in the form
of piano lessons. But she preferred to lose herself in a crowd of
guests at her mother's musical evenings and listen to the music
without having to articulate her thoughts about it—no one
expected her to do so.

However, within a few years of her father's death, Winnaretta's quiet life in Devon abruptly changed; her horizons
were suddenly widened. With the rest of the family she returned
to Paris early in 1878 to find a very different city from the one
she had left at the age of five. Mrs Singer had grown restless
with the comparative inaction of Paignton, and had begun to
hanker after the excitement of city life. She had also decided to
remarry. This time the man whom she—and her fortune—
bewitched was Victor Nicolas Reubsaet, a member of the

Luxembourgeois nobility, who bore the unfamiliar but impressive titles of Vicomte d'Estenburg and Duc de Camposelice.

As soon as she installed herself in Paris as the Duchesse de Camposelice, she bought a grand house at 27 avenue Kléber and turned it into a centre of musical activity, indeed a focal point of social attention. Almost every week a concert of the highest quality took place in her salon. The greatest chamber works of Mozart and Schubert were heard there, along with all the quartets of Beethoven. The duchess also attracted the attention of artists. At the age of thirty-six, with six children to her credit, she was still extremely beautiful; she looked refined and was always elegant in appearance. When she returned to Paris, Frédéric Bartholdi was on the point of beginning his famous statue *La Liberté éclairant le monde*, intended as a secular counterpart of the Basilica of Sacré Coeur, not so much as an act of expiation for past mistakes but as a defiant proclamation of the enlightenment for which, it was hoped, the Third Republic stood. Bartholdi chose to model the head of his statue on the features of the Duchesse de Camposelice and, although he stylized them to suit the clean-cut, heroic nature of the work, few were in doubt, when he exhibited the sculpted head at the 1878 Exhibition, about the identity of the model. Yet when the Statue of Liberty was finally completed in 1886, it was scarcely realized that the massive sculpture dominating New York's water-front owed something for its inspiration to the wife of one of America's famous sons.

Winnaretta's reactions to her mother's new way of life were mixed. While she revelled in the musical opportunities which the salon—and Paris in general—offered, there is no doubt that she became more and more of a stranger to her mother. When not distracted by her many social activities, the duchess tended to spend most of her spare time with the other children, particularly the boys. Winnaretta always appeared to be an independent creature: if she ever needed attention, she did not demand it. Besides, she was too similar to her mother in temperament to be her friend. They were both very self-assertive; and Winnaretta was none too happy about the Camposelice marriage. She disliked the way her mother became the centre of male attention, and considered her lacking in respect for her father's memory. Increasingly she turned to an aunt, Jeanne-Marie Boyer, for the affection she lacked. Her grandmother also took a keen interest in her and, when Jeanne-Marie had to spend less time in Paris after her marriage to an elderly Irish baronet, Sir Robert Synge, in 1884, old Madame Boyer took over her daughter's role as Winnaretta's mother-substitute.

During the years of her youth Winnaretta was to need all the moral support and sympathy she could find.

Chapter 2
Youth
(1878–1887)

One of the effects of her return to Paris was that, at the age of thirteen, Winnaretta suddenly discovered new artistic perspectives. In Devon music had been a fact of life but, as far as art was concerned, scope for its enjoyment and study had been very limited. Paris presented an enormous contrast. Fascinated by the Musée du Louvre, she spent hours there studying paintings and, without much guidance, formed firm ideas about their quality. Art exhibitions intrigued her and, when she first visited the Salon at the Palais de l'Industrie in the autumn of 1878, she was impressed by the canvases selected for official recognition, but not entirely uncritical of them. And, since she showed such an interest in art and was considered to have a facility for painting and drawing Winnaretta's family decided that she should pursue art as her special interest. She had no need of a profession, but it was felt that a cultivated artistic talent would be a social asset in the world in which she would be expected to move in a few years' time. Winnaretta was not consulted on the matter: the adults in the family took the decision on her behalf. For one who was later to become so closely associated with the musical avant-garde of her day, the choice of painting as her *métier* was slightly ironical. But the reason is not hard to find. At this stage music was still very much of a secret passion for her. Certainly she caused raised eyebrows in January 1879 when she asked for Beethoven's Quartet, opus 131, as her birthday 'surprise', but nobody stopped to analyse her motives. Besides, her interest in painting was much more apparent; indeed, it was quite genuine. And so, at the age of fourteen, she was sent to the studio in the rue de Bruxelles where Félix Barrias worked and instructed a few selected pupils.

By conventional standards of the day Barrias was a successful painter. Since winning the *Prix de Rome* in 1844 at the age of twenty-two, he had gone on to receive prize after prize: his paintings, frequently depicting romanticized classical scenes, appealed to the taste of a middle-brow public. But as far as Winnaretta was concerned, his value, apart from his friendship and personal charm, was his competence as a teacher of technique. As for the aesthetic side of art, she went her own way from an early stage. And she had not been involved with art in Paris very long before she came to the conclusion that the type of painting that found favour in conventional circles was dull and frequently uninspired, slavishly conforming to the academic standards of the day. She thought the obligatory colour-schemes that were used were particularly depressing, the heavy browns and ochre tints only adding an unwholesome or lifeless pallor to basically rather stilted compositions. So, when she discovered the Salon des Refusés and saw some of the paintings exhibited there, something of a personal revelation took place.

For almost two decades the small group of Impressionist painters had been struggling to have their ideas accepted, but popular disapproval had been clearly reflected in the reluctance of the jury of the official Salon to exhibit more than a mere handful of their canvases, and these were always so swamped by the thousands of conventional works that they were passed over without much comment. Instead, they had tended to show their paintings in the Salon des Refusés, which had taken place in makeshift buildings beside the Palais de l'Industrie ever since 1863. By the end of the 1870s Impressionist paintings were still the object of critical vituperation and the butt of the general public's scornful laughter. Winnaretta visited the Salon des Refusés, and was very moved by the works of Manet, Sisley, Boudin, Monet and their friends. Their paintings provided her with a thrilling insight into the world around her. Her new sense-perception of visual objects gave fresh meaning to life itself. In reality what Impressionist art did was to focus already quite clear concepts of the nature of colour and light. She could not understand how the derisive crowd could mock artists who painted violet shadows into their landscapes: her eyes were not blind to reality.

This time Winnaretta was not afraid to make her opinions known. She voiced her unequivocal admiration for the new school and all that it stood for. But her family thought her unreasonable and dismissed her enthusiasm as adolescent perversity. Her fellows in Barrias's painting class regarded her views as a joke and seldom let her forget how ridiculous they thought her taste. Her godfather Edward May, by now an almost permanent resident in Paris and a familiar figure in her mother's salon, was dismayed. Although he and Winnaretta remained firm friends, he strongly disapproved of her interest in the Impressionists, and deplored the particular fascination that Manet held for her. May had been a pupil of Thomas Couture's at the same time as Manet and felt nothing but contempt for him. The entire painting class under Couture had heaped ridicule upon him; *le Michel-Ange du mauvais*, they called him: someone who used colours and chose to paint the subjects he did was despicable, possibly slightly mad. May still stuck to these views so many years after his student days, but that did not impress Winnaretta. If her family and friends refused to see what pleasure she got from Impressionist art, the least she could do was to make a stand by remaining faithful to her convictions.

During her adolescent years Manet became an object of hero-worship, although, among all the contemporary artists whose work she admired, he was practically the only one whom she never met. The nearest she came to doing so was when she plucked up the courage to go to his studio in the rue d'Amsterdam. But, when she found that the master was out, she contented herself with persuading the concierge, an Indian by the name of Aristide, to let her have the visiting card that had been nailed to Manet's door, and for many years she treasured it like a relic.

Winnaretta was eighteen when Manet died in April 1883. Regarding this almost as a personal loss, she was heart-broken, although his death did have some agreeable side-effects. Her teacher Félix Barrias took the opportunity to move into Manet's vacant studio at 70 rue d'Amsterdam because it was so much larger than his own. For Winnaretta the attraction was that it was permeated with the atmosphere of the genius who had so inspired her. On a more practical level it afforded her further opportunities for picking the concierge's brains. She questioned him incessantly about all aspects of Manet's life and work. She even persuaded him to sell her a pencil drawing that Fantin-Latour had made as one of the preliminary sketches for the portrait of Manet which he painted in 1867. And, not satisfied

with that, Winnaretta decided to buy a painting by Manet as
soon as possible.

The chance came a few months later when Ernest Duez, a
painter of established reputation who frequented her mother's
salon, explained to Winnaretta how to obtain one of Manet's
works. While visiting Manet's widow with John Sargent, Duez
had been shown Manet's *La Lecture*, a composition depicting
his wife Suzanne and her son Léon Koëlla-Leenhoff. Although
Suzanne Manet had often sat for her husband, she had—
probably wisely—not taken much interest in his art and now,
after his death, was more than willing to part with *La Lecture*,
despite all its personal associations. Duez had immediately
thought of Winnaretta, and before long had negotiated the
sale for her; and so she acquired a picture which at the time no
one else wanted and which most of her friends regarded as a
waste of money, even for the quite insignificant 2,000 francs it
cost her. She kept the painting until she died and watched with
faint amusement how attitudes changed with time: her early
eccentricity came to be regarded as one of the legendary *coups*
of the art-dealer's world. But as far as she was concerned the
painting always had a value beyond the money she paid for it
and what it came to be worth. As a source of inspiration in her
own work it was quite significant. The style of painting that
she began to develop, once she had freed herself of some of the
intellectual restrictions of Barrias's tutelage, was close to
Manet's, although she was too original a painter to become a
mere imitator: she learned from the best of all artists' works and
made of it something distinctly her own.

Nonetheless, the Manet influences were strong, especially in
the paintings which she produced in the decade after 1883. The
first picture which she offered to the Salon and had accepted in
1885, *Les Graves à Villerville*, shows this clearly. And a full-length
self-portrait, which she executed in the same year, when she
was twenty years old, also has distinct traces of Manet: the
bold use of shadow, contrasts of light and colour have a touch
of the master in them. But the canvas was very original in its
own way and, when judged by the Salon jury in 1886, it was
not only given wall-space but was also illustrated in the official
catalogue. As long as she cared to submit paintings to the Salon,
they were accepted. She followed her success of 1886 by
exhibiting another portrait, this time an anonymous one,

entitled simply *Sur un balcon*, among the 1887 collection. And in 1889 she achieved the distinction of having two canvases accepted, *Printemps* and the *Portrait de Madame la Marquise de M* . . . Still a clear feeling of Manet persisted in them. At times this could lead to confusion. Many years later Winnaretta had the interesting experience of discovering at the Impressionist specialists' gallery, Bernheim Jeune, one of her own paintings put up for sale as a Manet. She was flattered by this, although her own style was not so close to his as to be indistinguishable from it. If one glances at some of her other paintings from the late 1880s—for example, the portrait which she painted of Félix Barrias, standing at his easel, palette in hand—one finds something much closer to Monet than Manet: the whole composition is more rough-hewn, the pigments bolder and purer than anything one would ever find in Manet. When this portrait of Barrias was exhibited at the Salon of 1890 alongside a companion-piece painted by Barrias himself, a portrait of Winnaretta at her easel, his work looked rather insipid and old fashioned, while hers had a freshness and vitality similar to that of an early Monet.

But it would be wrong to imply that Winnaretta had only a narrow range of interest within the Impressionist school. She was also fond of Berthe Morisot's work. Possibly the feminist in her approved of a fellow woman-artist's professionalism; and, as Edouard Manet's sister-in-law, Berthe Morisot had an additional appeal. But the work of an individualistic painter like Degas interested her just as much. One of her more enlightened companions from Barrias's class, Madeleine Fleury, took her to Degas's studio while she was having portrait-sittings with him. Winnaretta sat in silence, amazed at the artistic opinions expressed by Degas. His ideas on colour came as a shock to her at first. Imbued with the beliefs of the *école du plein air* about painting directly from nature, she was surprised to find Degas taking his colour-scheme for the portrait-sketches from a Persian rug that lay on the floor of the studio. Surprise changed to admiration, as she watched him paint and examined the hundreds of sketches and sepia drawings that he showed her. Winnaretta absorbed everything in awe-struck silence. But Degas was not impressed and later asked Madeleine Fleury what sort of half-wit Winnaretta was. She was disconcerted when she was told of Degas's comment but did at least learn two valuable lessons from the visit. First, to understand genius in its fulness she would have to have a flexible and unbiased mind: preconceptions could be obstacles in the way of true appreciation of it. And, second, even the most self-assured genius likes to have his work praised; even the least word of critical appraisal can have a fertilizing effect upon great talent.

The Degas incident is all the more remarkable because at the time Winnaretta was mixing quite happily with some of the best-known artists of the day. She was a close friend of the lithographer Jean-Louis Forain, who was as renowned for his acidly witty tongue as for his art. She worked with him in his studio without any qualms and frequently accompanied him to the Louvre when he went there to examine and restore the Old Masters. He was as much a teacher of technique to her as Barrias, and in the process helped her to develop a rational aesthetic sense. In 1882 when the Louvre authorities wanted someone to prepare the English catalogue for the museum, Forain had enough regard for Winnaretta's technical knowledge and sense of discrimination to recommend her for the task. Apart from having an equal command of French and English, she was particularly suited for the job because, while holding distinct views about what interested her in art, she was always careful not to judge other people's ideas too subjectively. Any individual's taste should be accorded some respect. One should try to judge it from a morally neutral standpoint. She firmly believed in Hippolyte Taine's view that a person's environment and general circumstances should be taken into account when assessing his conclusions about the purpose and effect of a work of art.

But, despite being so involved in the world of art during her youth, Winnaretta always regarded this as secondary to her musical interests. Though designated as the painter in the family, she was irresistibly attracted by anything musical that went on in her mother's house. Musicians, executants and composers, were familiar figures in the reception rooms. However, what absorbed her even more was, when in summertime the family went off to her mother's château at Blossville on the Normandy coast of Villerville, near Trouville, they joined forces with a small community of artists, musicians and painters, who gathered there for the season. Here, in early 1880, Winnaretta first met Gabriel Fauré. He used to spend his sum-

mers in Normandy with Marie Clerc and her family, and continued to do so until his marriage to Marie Fremiet in 1883,
and so was almost automatically drawn into the Duchesse de
Camposelice's circle. How he reacted initially to the enthusiasm
of a girl of sixteen, twenty years his junior, is not known, but he
soon came to see that Winnaretta's interest in his work was far
from superficial and immature. She admired his early chamber
works and songs and in particular the piano works, with which
he was preoccupied at that time—she considered them as
inspired as anything written by Schumann or Chopin, being
especially fond of the Piano Quartet which he had composed a
few years before in 1879. Her effusive praise for it may have
contributed something to his decision to write another work of
the same genre, the Second Piano Quartet, which he completed
in 1886. Certainly by that time she had become something of a
confidante to him. She was to remain so for at least another
decade, providing him in times of difficulty or stress with moral
support and occasionally, though discreetly, with material help.
Her relationship with Fauré probably never involved the same
intensity of emotion or intellectual dependence as those he had
with Marie Clerc and Marguerite Baugnies (the Mme René de
Saint-Marceaux of later years). After all, they were women
much more mature in years than Winnaretta. Yet, his friendship
with her was remarkably close and over the years it produced
some unique artistic offshoots.

During the same period Winnaretta also became involved in a
musical world of a very different kind. Her mother first took her
to the Bayreuth Festival in 1882, at a time when the French
contingent there was very small—Bayreuth had not achieved its
standing as a criterion of snobbism by then. But fashion never
mattered much to her. She loved Wagner's music from the
moment she first heard *Parsifal* during that visit, and remained
devoted to it through times when musical taste and nationalistic
feelings caused periodic reactions. Bayreuth became the object
of a regular annual pilgrimage for her, while Munich, as the
second capital of the Wagnerian world, was also of special
interest to her. In August 1884 Vincent d'Indy, passing through
the city, broke off his walking tour of Germany to watch
rehearsals of the *Ring* at the Opera. When they finished, he was
taken by Robert de Bonnières and Charles Lamoureux to join
the artists gathered at the Café Maximilian opposite the theatre.

There was Winnaretta, sitting among singers, writers, journalists and conductors; the young composer Georges Huë was also
there. Their conversation was intense. The merits and demerits
of the *Ring*'s interpretation were discussed with a passion which
at times bordered on the acrimonious. Winnaretta took some
part in the arguments; she was too committed to Wagner's
music to say nothing at all; but generally she kept silent and
just listened, happy to witness the birth of the Wagnerian legend.

Although Winnaretta was allowed to mix freely in artistic
gatherings of this sort, her full participation in the social life of
Paris and Europe's other big cities was still restricted. Her
mother had no objection to her dining with the Forains or
meeting Fauré for long conversations or visiting the studios of
Ernest Duez, Roger Jourdain and José-Thomas Errazuris, the
Chilean artist—there was almost a homely air about their way
of life—but she prevented her from attending the great literary
salons of Paris; even some of the predominantly musical ones
were forbidden for the time being. As a result Winnaretta led a
rather restricted life, largely cut off from the mainstream of
intellectual society, because she was still too young. She was
isolated even in the domestic situation because no one else in
the family, apart from a heavily preoccupied mother, shared her
interests. The guests who came to the duchess's salon, at most
once a week, must have been welcome company. Until she had
been suitably married, whatever her own feelings on the subject,
her social activities were necessarily limited. As an heiress with
an immense fortune she had to be guarded against adventurers.
As the daughter of a mother with serious social pretensions she
had her part to play in the process of integrating the Singer
family into the top ranks of French society.

1a An anonymous portrait
of Isaac Merritt Singer

1b The Singer family tomb in Torquay Cemetery

2a A Self-Portrait by
   Winnaretta (detail),
   1886

2b A portrait of Winna-
   retta as the Princesse
   Louis de Scey-Montbé-
   liard by John Singer
   Sargent, 1889

3a A portrait of Winna-
retta by Félix Barrias,
c. 1889

3b A portrait of Félix
Barrias by Winnaretta,
c. 1889

4a   *La Lecture* by Edouard Manet, acquired by Winnaretta
in 1885.   4b   *Les Dindons blancs* by Claude Monet

5a   *La Barque à Giverny* by Claude Monet

5b   *Le Champ de tulipes* by Claude Monet

6a   Winnaretta's *hôtel particulier* at the corner of the avenue
      Henri-Martin and the rue Cortambert in Paris.
6b   The Palazzo Polignac on the Grand Canal in Venice.

7 Winnaretta with friends, 1899: (first row) Hélène de Caraman-Chimay, Abel Hermant. (Seated, second row) the Marquise de Monteynard, Winnaretta, Anna de Noailles. (Standing, back row) Prince Edmond de Polignac, Madame Bartholoni, Chateaubriand's god-daughter, Marcel Proust, Prince Constantin de Brancovan, Mlle Jeanne Bartholoni and the pianist Léon Delafosse

8a An oil-sketch of the Princesse Armande de Polignac by Winnaretta, *c.* 1900

8b Santa Maria della Salute, Venice, by Winnaretta, *c.* 1902

Chapter 3
A Marriage of Inconvenience
(1887–1892)

Prince Louis de Scey-Montbéliard was the man chosen as a suitable husband for Winnaretta. He certainly came from a very old aristocratic family, even though his princely title did not stand up to very close scrutiny. As the third son of the Marquis de Scey de Brun, he was more correct on occasions when he called himself the Comte de Scey-Montbéliard. There was only a slight justification for his use of the princely style: in medieval times, when France had yet to develop its national identity, his ancestors, the Counts of Montbéliard, had been princes in all but name in their strategically placed sovereignty, nestling in the south-east corner of Franche-Comté. Since there was no such thing as a French prince below the rank of prince of the blood, all non-royal princes to be found in France derived their titles from non-French sources. This does suggest that Louis de Scey-Montbéliard's title was simply the product of an anachronistic view of what his status would have been in a pre-national age. But the fact remained that he did have an impeccable, if slightly faded, pedigree. However, as a third son, he was not endowed with enough money to live up to his princely aspirations but, as far as the Duchesse de Camposelice was concerned, that did not matter: Winnaretta had money of her own and the match itself would pay dividends in social prestige.

The marriage, which took place on 27 July 1887, may have pleased her mother but it also pleased Winnaretta, if only because it emancipated her from her custodianship. Finally, at the age of twenty-two, she could do what she wanted. She was socially acceptable as a married woman; she had an establishment of her own; and she alone had control over her money. The only trouble was that her husband's idea about the nature of their marriage differed radically from hers. It was very soon clear that they were not conjugally compatible. He could not understand the situation and was cruel to her. After a brief period they separated and only came together again to effect a civil divorce in March 1891. Winnaretta completed the dissolution of the marriage by petitioning the Vatican for an annulment. Having received sufficient evidence of her domestic infelicity, in February 1892 the Roman Curia declared the marriage null in the eyes of the church. The episode with Louis de Scey-Montbéliard, though brief in itself, was far reaching in its consequences. Winnaretta would never again put herself in a position in which she might find herself dominated in any way by another human being.

At the time few people knew the real reason why the Scey-Montbéliard marriage ended so abruptly. The truth was that Winnaretta had developed strong Lesbian tendencies some time before 1887 and marriage, in its fullest sense, was something which she had not seriously considered. Louis de Scey-Montbéliard was unable to accept that she, having laid down no preconditions, should then act as though theirs were simply a *mariage de convenance*. It goes without saying that, if she had lingering doubts about being Lesbian before this episode, certainly none of them survived it. She never looked back.

It is rather pointless to speculate why she was homosexual. All the reasons that suggest themselves are negative: her mother's lack of real interest in her that made her turn to other women for affection; or her father's extrovert, dominating character and his legendary flamboyant sexuality that could have made her reserved about and even afraid of heterosexual relationships. But, if her Lesbianism was the product of any negative environmental influence, possibly what played as much part as anything was the fear that men might want her for the wrong reason, her money, and would not treat her as physically and intellectually equal to themselves. This was a significant point. Because of her unusual background and education, she had acquired an incisiveness of mind and a directness of approach which, she knew, in women of her day were considered too aggressive and masculine. But she had no desire to have this altered in any way. More important, she was extremely sensitive to all forms of beauty and the fact that she, like any discerning male, could see and appreciate it in women did not seem unnatural to her. In the initial stages it was just another aspect of her aesthetic approach to the visual world. However, the corollary of this was not true because the only man for whom she is said to have had any physical admiration was Comte Boni de Castellane—and he was so effete that he certainly constituted no sexual threat.

No matter how traumatic an experience in itself, the great advantage of her marriage was that it gave her social standing. As the Princesse de Scey-Montbéliard, she now appeared in the well-known salons of her day. She took her place at table for the Baronne de Poilly's weekly literary dinners. The baroness and her daughter-in-law Corisande de Brigode, the Duc de Gramont's sister, did their best to attract illustrious and colourful guests, renowned academics such as Professor Robin and Professor Dieulafoy and Elme Caro, the Academician-philosopher, the composer Léo Delibes and the playwright Emile Augier. The eccentric and dandified novelist Jules Barbey d'Aurevilly often came to the dinners and kept the conversation alive with witty, often rather blunt comments. One day in 1889 Professor Robin arrived late with the solemn news that Augier had just died. To the general exclamation of 'It's an irreparable loss!' Barbey d'Aurevilly rejoined: 'In effect it is an irreparable loss for French ridicule—because he was adept at foolishness.' But what Barbey d'Aurevilly regarded as ridiculous in others in himself became an individualistic expression of artistry. He would appear dressed completely in eighteenth-century clothes and covered with jewels, greater in quantity than quality. The young and successful novelist Paul Bourget, though casting himself in the rôle of apologist of the new decadence, could not help being amused by the fading dandy. One evening, Bourget confided to Winnaretta, he had made some admiring comment to Barbey d'Aurevilly on the beauty of the elaborate costume he was wearing and had received the cold reply: 'I am simply well-groomed.' But he was not an amusing figure in Winnaretta's circle for very long: before the year was out, he followed Emile Augier to the grave.

Madame Georges Aubernon also held an important *salon* but, despite her own aristocratic origins as Lydie de Nerville, it was considered to be rather bourgeois. Nonetheless, it did rank more highly than Madame de Poilly's: her guests were certainly kept under better control. Madame Aubernon, with all the imperious authority of an established *grande dame*, used to regulate conversation at her table by ringing a little hand-bell. Guests attempting to interrupt the flow of a discussion were

abruptly silenced until the conversation reached a natural
conclusion. Occasionally Madame Aubernon discovered too
late that a silenced guest might only have wanted a second
helping of food. Winnaretta took part in the Aubernon salon in
the rue d'Astorg but, although it could be stimulating from the
intellectual point of view, she kept aloof from the company of
at least one of its members. Madame Aubernon, usually so
strict, allowed too much licence to her cousin the Baron Jacques
Doasan, whom she all but supported. He was outrageously
homosexual. He had ruined his reputation, as well as lost his
fortune, pursuing an egocentric Polish violinist with whom, all
Paris knew, he was completely infatuated. As with another of
Lydie Aubernon's *habitués*, the amateur poet Comte de Montesquiou, elements of Doasan's character re-emerged later in
Proust's Baron de Charlus, although these two men had only
one thing in common with Charlus. Winnaretta drifted away
from the Aubernon set about the same time as Montesquiou.
They both agreed that, whatever kind of life one cared to lead
in private, discretion was often the better part of wisdom.
Doasan's besetting social sin was indiscretion—and, besides, as
far as Montesquiou was concerned, he was far too interested in
his own *ami particulier*, Gabriel d'Yturri, for comfort.

For the time being Winnaretta and Robert de Montesquiou
became firm friends. He felt some affinity for her and she
admired him for the originality of his taste in objets d'art and
décor, if not unreservedly for his verse (which was far from
original). And his friendship came at an opportune moment
because she had just bought a large house at the corner of the
avenue Henri-Martin and the rue Cortambert and wished to
reconstruct it on a grand scale in the eighteenth-century
French classical style but with the addition of all up-to date
conveniences. The young architect Grand'Pierre, whose houses
designed for Jean-Louis Forain and the singer Jean de Reszke
had earned him acclaim, was engaged to do the basic job of
reconstruction. He immediately set about removing a central
decoration of enormous wild animals cast in bronze, elephants,
rhinoceroses and the like, from which water gushed down
elaborately constructed flights of stairs. This was replaced by a
simpler *escalier d'honneur*. And the rest of the building soon saw
the last vestiges of the worst mid-nineteenth-century taste
disappear to be replaced by more restrained and elegant

decorations. The grand salon was arranged so that mirrors filled in almost all the gaps of wall between its classical pilasters. The mirror-backed shutters, when closed, produced the effect of a miniature *galerie des glaces*, more perfect even than the Versailles original. Several decades later, just before the war of 1914, Winnaretta was persuaded to let the Spanish artist José-Maria Sert paint over the pilaster capitals a set of rather grotesquely baroque murals, in which reclining female nudes, worldly *putti* and an assortment of animals, from monkeys to eagles, mingled with one another as strange bed-fellows—on the whole, not a very successful addition to the décor, although the stark and unremitted black and gold of the paintings went well enough with the dark silvery perspectives of the mirrors. More purely classical in spirit was the small adjoining dining-room but even here a baroque touch was provided by an almost altar-like console table of overwhelming dimensions. From these a more subdued public room, constructed as a library and decorated in colours conducive to contemplation, led out through its French windows into a miniature first-floor garden snuggling in an angle of the house and protected, almost smothered, by tall neighbouring residences. The final addition to the public rooms was a ground-floor music-room or studio, built onto the rue Cortambert side of the house. Low ceilinged and simple in design, entirely lined with oak panelling, it had an almost homely feel about it after the severe dignity of the grand salon. It was designed specially for the less formal of Winnaretta's musical parties. And here she had installed the organ at which during the next fifty years she spent hours alone, playing the works of Bach.

While the house was being completed, she constantly consulted Montesquiou about details of interior decoration. He introduced her to Paul Helleu, the painter and virtuoso engraver, and together they induced him to do some work for her. But he did not allow himself to be easily persuaded. She had first to buy one of his paintings, *Les Barques à Cowes*, which she liked for its English associations, and to commission an album of etchings from him. And that caused a sensation in itself since the album was to contain the portraits of all her closest women-friends. All Paris buzzed with the news, although no one was quite sure what was more amazing, the revealing nature of the commission or Winnaretta's grand gesture in paying Helleu to destroy the plates afterwards so that she could possess a unique work of art with as much intrinsic as sentimental value. This gave Helleu a glimpse of the quality of her patronage and made him eager to collaborate with another of Montesquiou's protégés, the sculptor Jean Carriès, in the decoration of her house. Carriès's contribution was remarkable: a huge ceramic tabernacle built in an extravagant Ludwig II style to house a Wagner manuscript, recently acquired by Winnaretta and revered as though it were a sacred relic.

From the outset of their friendship Montesquiou was also associated with Winnaretta in the world of music. If she depended upon him for advice on the intricacies of domestic decoration, he was often guided by her on questions of musical taste. This had significant results. Introduced to her friend Fauré in 1887, it was Montesquiou who first revealed to him the musical possibilities of Verlaine's poetry. Although already a song-writer of considerable stature, with his Verlaine settings Fauré began a new phase, in which his songs achieved not only a greater spiritual intensity than before but also a much more intimate union between the vocal line and the piano part. At Montesquiou's suggestion, the first Verlaine poem tackled by him was *Claire de lune* and the result was a magical evocation of a *commedia dell'arte* atmosphere in the setting of a Watteauesque *fête galante*, a recurring theme in later years. In 1888, after Fauré had orchestrated *Clair de lune*, the new version was given its first performance at a special concert in Winnaretta's house: for, in addition to it, new works by Ernest Chausson and Vincent d'Indy were also heard and a great deal of attention was lavished on some music by Emmanuel Chabrier.

Chabrier, that effervescent character who worked during the day as an official at the Ministère de l'Intérieur and wrote sparkling compositions in his leisure hours, first came to know Winnaretta in the mid-1880s about the time that he composed his opera *Gwendoline*. Of all his works this one particularly interested her because it was closest in spirit to Wagner's music, for which they shared an enthusiasm. *Gwendoline* had been performed at the enterprising Théâtre de la Monnaie in Brussels in April 1886 but had had to be withdrawn after only two performances because of the director's bankruptcy and, since then, the music had not been performed. The Paris Opéra refused to mount the work. As always sensitive to fashionable taste, the management was not convinced that the general public was sufficiently interested in 'Wagnerian' music for it to risk mounting a costly production of it. So Winnaretta decided to intervene. She suggested that a concert version of *Gwendoline* might be given in her salon. Two performances were arranged for 8 and 15 May 1888, the first consisting of the more important sections of *Gwendoline*, along with the new works by Fauré, Chausson and d'Indy, the second comprising an integral performance of the opera with soloists, chorus and a reduced orchestra. On her advice, Chabrier recruited twenty-four resident members of the Opéra's chorus and well-known soloists so that, if his re-opened negotiations with the Opéra came to anything, the singers would be ready to step into their parts at a moment's notice. These two performances were very successful. The audience was moved by the work and impressed by the performance. It was certainly an extraordinary occasion and not only because of the music: among the orchestra Fauré could be seen at the harmonium and Chabrier himself at the piano, while André Messager and d'Indy were the percussion players. Gabriel Marie, himself a composer of great originality, was the conductor. But the enthusiasm of friends was not enough to convince the management of the Opéra and Chabrier had to wait until December 1893 before *Gwendoline* reached its stage, although in the meantime more than five German opera houses mounted performances of it.

Chabrier appreciated Winnaretta's help, however unsuccessful in achieving its primary objective, and grew closer to her. A relaxed and informal friendship developed between them. She found him so light-hearted and entertaining that, whenever his behaviour became mildly outrageous, she could only laugh at him. A short time after the salon performances of his opera, Chabrier came to dinner with her and, as some asparagus was being served, he leaned forward and confided to her in a stage whisper: 'You take some of that, Madame, and it will give you a foul urine!' She was taken aback—but not badly enough to prevent her from repeating the story frequently throughout her life. She soon learned never to be surprised at anything he might do. He could sit at the piano and play through a complete act of an opera before joining her at the dinner table and scarcely finish the meal and smoke a cigarette before rushing back to the piano, exclaiming: 'It's ages since I played some music!' He would then play for another hour or so, singing all the vocal parts with *bravura* and making the piano reproduce all the colour and richness of an orchestra. Or, if he were listening to some stimulating dance music, a waltz or a polka, he might suddenly seize a female guest and dance round the room with her. Even when music was only a subject for discussion, he could be just as unpredictable and just as entertaining. Since he had a great command of colourful language, he would bubble over with enthusiasm and wit about anything he liked, or he would work himself up into a state of dramatic anger at anything he disliked and pour torrents of verbal scorn on it. Music divided itself into two categories, he would say: 'There is music; then music which . . . is not worth the effort.'

If Chabrier never went so far as to sweep Winnaretta off her feet as a dancing partner, he did insist on her partnering him when he played piano-duets. Some of his most scintillating compositions for this *genre* were inspired by this desire to involve others in his enjoyment of music-making. He could always see the lighter side to even the most serious subject and he seldom hesitated to criticize any aspect of even the most admired work that might displease him. As devoted Wagnerite he was second to none but he would not let his admiration cloud his judgment. In July 1889 Winnaretta took him to Bayreuth to hear *Tristan*, *Meistersinger* and *Parsifal*. They gave him immense pleasure, although he had his reservations about *Parsifal*: its religious aspects were irksome and he left convinced that it would be the first of Wagner's music-dramas to become dated. Yet he did express great admiration for the Prelude and, while it was being played, he suddenly sighed: 'For more than ten years I have longed to hear that A-flat on the 'cellos, and now at last I have heard it.' Indeed, this was the first time he had heard an orchestra play *Parsifal* since at that time it was seldom performed anywhere outside Bayreuth. Chabrier's robust enjoyment of the festival, the music, the social life, the German food —he ate enough for four people, he admitted—they all convinced Winnaretta that 'the appetite for life, great works, beauty of art or nature cannot be bought at any price, and that the Cook's tourist highbrow millionaires who thronged to Bayreuth in later years, if they did not lack Chabrier's appetite for things, certainly missed all his enjoyment and fun'. She was profoundly distressed when in the following years Chabrier

began to show signs of severe melancholia and near manic
depression prior to his death in 1894. But it only made her
appreciate his earlier joie de vivre all the more and convinced
her that, because of it, his music would last long after his death
and would influence succeeding generations of composers.

Winnaretta and Chabrier had been accompanied to Bayreuth
in 1889 by her mother. As a widow now, the duchess found her
useful as a chaperon while travelling. In turn, she acted as one
for her daughter, who was regarded as being the all-but-
widowed Princesse de Scey-Montbéliard. The disaster of
Winnaretta's marriage, the reasons for which her increasingly
individualistic social activities were making more apparent,
was something of a family embarrassment. When possible, a
careful eye was kept on her. At this point it was particularly
desirable because in 1888 the duchess's second daughter,
Isabelle Blanche, had married the Duc Decazes. The Decazes
family had suddenly achieved distinction, after centuries of
provincial existence as members of the legal nobility, when
Élie Decazes had attracted the attention of Louis XVIII.
Decazes's ability and personal charm had captivated the aged
monarch, who had come to the throne too late to enjoy either
the social life at court or the exercise of power. As a form of
substitute he indulged his favourite. He allowed him to rise to
ministerial rank in 1818 and maintained him in power until
forced to dismiss him in 1820—but not before Decazes had been
given the Danish Duchy of Glüksbjerg and then a French
peerage with ducal status. From 1820 the family avoided the
pursuit of power until in 1873 Decazes's son the second duke
joined the Duc de Broglie's administration, in which he served
with great flair: he was as brilliant, if not quite so strikingly
handsome as his father. It was his son the third duke, Élie
Decazes, who married Isabelle Singer in 1888. Although this
regilded the Decazes blazon with Singer millions, it did also
bring much more social prestige to the Singer family than
either the Camposelice or Scey-Montbéliard matches had and,
moreover, it had been firmly cemented by the prompt birth
of a male heir in February 1889. So the Duchesse de Camposelice was intent on keeping a weather eye on Winnaretta in
case she might cause some awkwardness as she prepared to shed
her own aristocratic husband. But, as matters turned out, it
was she herself who caused some turmoil within the family and

a moment or two of disquiet in French society. Having gained
a fortune by her first marriage, a title by her second, the
duchess apparently decided that, even in her late fifties, she
was not too old to embark on a third one, this time purely for
love. Her choice fell upon a young man called Paul Sohège,
who had little to recommend him but a gentlemanly manner,
good looks and an interest in music; he was quite accomplished
as a violinist. That was enough. In the early 1890s the duchess
courted him with sweet words, won him and married him. Her
children were furious but had to accept the situation. In the
long run it had its advantages because their mother was less
able to bring moral pressure to bear upon them in their own
private lives.

Despite her own ambiguous position Winnaretta managed to
maintain a social presence without appreciably compromising
herself or her ideals. She made friends effortlessly with the great
or notorious if she discovered that she had anything in common
with them. At the time of the 1889 Exhibition she met Ignacy
Paderewski and at once their mutual passion for music forged
a bond of friendship that lasted for years despite all the vicissi-
tudes of political and social change. About this time she became
more closely acquainted with John Singer Sargent (who,
despite his name, was not related to her). They felt a certain
sympathy for each other's ideas and style of life. Although
Sargent stayed less in Paris since losing patience with the French
public after the storm of protest that greeted the exhibition of
his portrait of a very *décolletée* Madame Pierre Gautreau at the
1884 Salon, he was often entertained by Winnaretta whenever
he did visit the city. He came to Paris in the spring of 1889 and,
in between sitting on the jury of the Salon and spending some
time with Monet at Giverny, he executed a commission to paint
her portrait. This turned out to be a most impressive picture,
full of natural grandeur: a full-length representation of her,
dressed in a white evening gown, a figure of great majesty, she
was depicted as very much the Princesse de Scey-Montbéliard
of its title.

It was probably about this time that Sargent first interested
Winnaretta in Italy as a cradle of civilization. He had spent
most of his boyhood in Florence and was still a frequent visitor
to Italy, although now he tended to stay in Venice with his
distant cousin Daniel Curtis and his family at the Palazzo

Barbaro, their residence on the Grand Canal. In 1890, shortly
after exhibiting their 'artist-portraits' of each other at the
Salon, Winnaretta took Félix Barrias and his wife for a short
holiday in Italy and, while there, they paid a fleeting visit to
Venice. She was enchanted by its unique beauty; she was
captivated by the peace and tranquillity of the canals and
lagoon. Venice was the city where painters from Pisanello to
Longhi had flourished; it was the home of great composers,
Gabrieli and Monteverdi, Albinoni and Vivaldi; and it was
where, more recently, Liszt and Wagner had lived and worked.
And Winnaretta left, vowing to return.

Early in 1891, about the time of her civil divorce, her
youngest brother, Franklin, married an American girl and so
she suggested that they should rent a house together in Venice
for four months during the late spring and early summer. A
Russian Count Wolkoff, who enjoyed some fame as a writer
and photographer, agreed to let them have his little *palazzo* on
the Grand Canal, the Casa Wolkoff. Once settled there,
Winnaretta was able to invite a succession of friends from Paris
to stay with them. Amongst others her artist friends Ernest
Duez and Georges Clairin came. Together they whiled away
the time, painting scenes of Venice from a boat on the lagoon
or copying Old Masters in the Galleria dell'Accademia just two
steps from the Casa Wolkoff. A highly-thought-of exercise,
copying improved her technique. She produced some accomplished paintings, her copies from Carpaccio's Sant'Orsola
Cycle being particularly fine. Nonetheless, it had little effect
upon her own distinctly impressionistic style: it remained fluid
and unstilted; and, during her stay, she did many paintings
from life in the city itself or in the large studio at the top of the
Casa Wolkoff, since it afforded a panoramic view not only of
the Grand Canal but also of the Zattere and the Giudecca
beyond.

Another of her visitors was Gabriel Fauré. Since 1888 she
had maintained and strengthened her friendship with him.
Whenever his works were performed in public, she would be
there. She frequently had them performed in her own salon,
particularly the songs, for which Fauré himself usually played
the piano part, and, in appreciation of her interest, he had
dedicated his songs *Larmes* to her in 1889. Jean Richepin's
verses from *Le Lac*, which Fauré used for it, were quite the most

impassioned he had ever set and his music matched their
emotional intensity. Why he should have dedicated to her such
a strong exhortation to weep is not clear. Perhaps he imagined
that her restlessness was a result of her unhappy marriage. But
by 1891 it was Fauré himself who was in low spirits. Harassed
by his demanding work as an inspector of music-teaching and
bitterly disappointed at being refused the chair of composition
at the Conservatoire, he was tired and depressed. And so
Winnaretta persuaded him to join her for a holiday in Venice.
On 18 May 1891 he arrived in the city which had already inspired
him to write the *Barcarolles* and the Venetian *Nocturne* from Shylock—without him ever having been there. He was thrilled by the
sights and sounds of the place and, as he said, he filled his eyes
with its marvels in order to store up in his head a thousand
charming memories. In fact, the city itself was such a sense-
experience for him that he scarcely ever used the quiet little
study which Winnaretta set aside for him to work in. Instead,
Fauré, who seldom composed away from his piano, was to be
seen at the Café Florian on the Piazza di San Marco, scribbling
music, Schubert-like, amid the noise and bustle of the Venetian
throng. And in the process he wrote the song *Mandoline* and a
substantial part of *En Sourdine*, to which he subsequently added
three others, *Green*, *À Clymène* and *C'est l'Extase*, to make up the
song-cycle *Cinq Mélodies de Venise*. The title is slightly misleading: none of the Verlaine poems used have any Venetian
elements in them, except perhaps for *Mandoline* with its *commedia dell'arte* atmosphere of a nocturnal serenade and *À
Clymène* with its barcarolle rhythm. *Mandoline* was the only one
to be performed in Venice during the 1891 visit. After dinner
Winnaretta often used to take her guests out on to the lagoon
in a large fishing boat to make music with a few instrumental-
ists. She took with them a little portable yacht piano so that
Fauré could accompany Madame Duez while she sang his
songs.

As a song-cycle, the *Cinq Mélodies de Venise* was masterly. As a
stage in Fauré's musical development, they were significant:
they provided a further example of how sensitive he was as an
interpreter of Verlaine's poems. They took up from where he
had left off in *Clair de lune* and *Spleen* and inspired him with
confidence enough to go on in the following year to compose his
monumental *Bonne Chanson*, one of the most touching and

sophisticated of the host of settings of Verlaine's verses. But what had that to do with Winnaretta? The holiday she gave Fauré in Venice restored his health and his spirits. Since this gave him fresh inspiration and a new will to work, the *Cinq Mélodies de Venise* were in a real sense a Venetian creation. And Fauré, recognizing this, gave the songs their distinctive title and dedicated them to Winnaretta as an expression of gratitude for her kindness at a difficult time. They were also intended to be an indirect form of consolation-prize, almost a token of apology.

About the end of 1890 Winnaretta decided that for the inauguration of her new house in Paris she would commission a new and original work. She had in mind something similar to Chabrier's *Ode à la musique* but wanted Fauré to compose the music: he had apparently expressed some interest in tackling a lyric work of this nature. The man to write the libretto, she decided, was Paul Verlaine. He might be induced to provide Fauré with verses along the lines of *Les Uns et les autres*. And in January 1891 she broached the subject with him through their common friends the poet Stephane Mallarmé and the journalist Robert de Bonnières. Soon Verlaine was writing from his bed of sickness in the Hôpital Saint-Antoine directly to Fauré. What type of work was wanted? What period should it be set in? Should the libretto be a mixture of prose and verse or not? And apparently Verlaine took seriously the suggestion of a work reminiscent of the atmosphere of the *fêtes galantes* because he soon drew up a plan for a scenario based upon a scene from the Italian Comedy, set in a hospital ward where the traditional characters Pierrot, Columbine, Harlequin and their friends discuss their views on love and life in general. Winnaretta approved: the idea could be developed into a neat lyric work entitled *L'Hôpital de Watteau*, but Fauré was less pleased and refused to consider the subject. But neither Verlaine nor Winnaretta let the matter drop. For one thing the 300 francs which she had advanced him and her promise to give him credit with his tailor and other tradesmen made him feel obliged to help her.

Early in April 1891 Verlaine was again in correspondence with Fauré, this time about the possibility of writing a libretto for a lyric cantata, entitled *La Tentation de Bouddha*, which Winnaretta had put forward as an alternative suggestion. But

when two months passed without any tangible results coming
from Verlaine, Fauré began to grow restive. Perhaps it had been
too long since the poet had dealt with an oriental theme. By the
end of May 1891 Fauré was enjoying his Venetian holiday with
Winnaretta and probably felt that he should make an effort to
find a suitable libretto. He wrote to Paris to seek the advice of
Maurice Bouchor, whose volume of poems entitled *Les Symboles,*
published in 1888, had revolved round the theme of ancient
religions. But because he was too occupied with work on a
libretto entitled *La Légende de Sainte-Cécile,* for which Ernest
Chausson was writing a score, Bouchor declined to help. He
possibly did not want to offend the other poet. And certainly,
by September 1891, Verlaine was becoming worried about
losing the commission and—more important—the balance of
his fee because he tried to revive his collaboration with Fauré.
However, by this time the composer was beginning to find the
whole business irksome.

Nonetheless, by late December Fauré was still allowing himself to be pressed to write a lyric work and a new librettist had
been found. When approached, the young poet Albert Samain
had jumped at the chance of working on the project. On 2
January 1892 Winnaretta invited Samain and Fauré to her
house and over dinner worked out the details with them. The
subject was to be the same *Tentation de Bouddha* which had
caused both Verlaine and Maurice Bouchor to think twice. But
not so Albert Samain. Before long he had sketched out an
acceptable scenario, which was shortly followed by a complete
text. Consisting of at least 750 verses, it was substantial enough
to be the libretto of a full-length opera. Certainly Fauré seems
to have taken one look at it and quickly abandoned any
thought of writing music for it. Samain's verses remained useless
and unpublished while Fauré temporized. As late as December
1893 many of his friends still imagined that he was quietly
working on the *Bouddha* project but, in reality, he probably
could not bring himself to disappoint Winnaretta by confessing
the truth.

Why he had finally balked at the task is not hard to imagine.
With Samain the project had developed too monumental
proportions. In any case, from the beginning Fauré had not
seemed very happy with the chosen subject (something which
would have appealed more to a Debussy or a Ravel). He prob-

ably only considered the project to oblige Winnaretta and knew
that, even if completed, there would be little guarantee of
success. However, the episode was not wholly unproductive.
Having disappointed his patroness-friend and the poets concerned, he was at pains to mollify them. In some measure his
dedication of the *Cinq Mélodies de Venise* to her late in 1891 was
as much a form of interim appeasement as an expression of
thanks for her concern to help him. They also served to keep
Verlaine happy and, when Fauré used his poems for the *Bonne
Chanson* in the following year, he was well content, since the
royalties from the song-cycle more than compensated for what
he lost through failing to write the *Bouddha* text. As for Albert
Samain, there is reason for thinking that Fauré returned to his
poetry in 1896 and set *Pleurs d'or* as a work for mezzo-soprano
and baritone because he wanted to compensate him in some
way for the disappointing failure of their earlier collaboration.
But, as with Verlaine, Fauré was happy enough to use Samain's
delicate, aesthetic verses even when he had complete freedom
to choose what he wanted from them: they were well suited to
the subtleties and colour of his music. Fauré certainly did
not turn away from Samain after writing *Pleurs d'or*. He used
his poetry for *Arpège* in 1897, for *Soir* in 1900 and for *Accompagne-
ment* in 1903 when, three years after his death, the poet needed
no earthly appeasement.

Winnaretta learned at least one lesson from her attempt to
influence the creative life of two established artists such as
Fauré and Verlaine, both her superior in age by twenty years.
In future, when commissioning any work, she was careful not
to force preconceived notions upon the artist concerned but,
drawing up rough guidelines, she would wait patiently while
ideas took form unforced in the creative mind. The artist must
always believe that the thoughts elicited retain the original
stamp of his own genius and even that they were his in the first
place. The lesson served her well in the years to come.

Chapter 4
Two White Wood-Pigeons
(1892–1894)

The year 1892 was one of the most problematical of Winnaretta's life. At the time no one could tell what direction it
would take. She was fairly well established in Parisian society
by then. She was beginning to gain a reputation as the guiding
spirit behind an increasingly avant-garde salon. She was to be
seen at all the cultural events in the capital. She became the
object of some attention at the Société Nationale concert on 2
April when the tenorino Maurice Bagès gave the first public
performance of Fauré's *Cinq Mélodies de Venise*. There was her
name linked, through the dedication, with one of the leading
anti-establishment composers of the day and with the poet who
was fast becoming the patron saint of decadence. But what was
her name? Since the Vatican set the final seal upon her
annulment on 1 February 1892, many were at a loss to know
what to call her: Madame de Montbéliard, the Princesse de
Scey were still possibilities; she was frequently referred to
simply as Madame Singer. And she herself was vague and
evasive about her present position as she was about her future.
She put off thought of it by preoccupying herself with artistic
manifestations of sight and sound, which Robert de Montesquiou begged permission to put on in her newly constructed
studio. To have her attention distracted by the problems of
installing an electric lighting system which would provide the
effects required by the count-poet in his feasts of aestheticism
was entertaining in itself: it was all very artificial and contrived, rather like stepping into the world of Huysmans's Des
Esseintes, no matter how vehemently Montesquiou denied the
analogy.

The summer of 1892 Winnaretta spent energetically travelling from place to place in Europe, at times indulging in the
luxury of romantic escapism. After a routine visit to London,
she sailed to Stockholm and from there set off to explore the

remotest corners of Norway. Then, having seen the natural beauty of the midnight sun, she made straight for the social comforts of Marienbad and ended up amid the discomforts of Bayreuth enjoying the atmosphere of the Wagner cult. When she returned to Paris, Montesquiou—in between indulging in artistic extravagances at her place—engaged her in serious conversation about her social position. Having recruited the help of his fascinating cousin Elisabeth de Caraman-Chimay (since her marriage to the Comte Greffulhe, as rich as she was beautiful), he tried to persuade Winnaretta that her position as a divorced woman was a social liability, much worse than being a widow. She must marry again, they both insisted. But, in view of her first marital fiasco, she was not eager to risk a second, although she could see the advantages of a suitable match: her position was very tenuous; with nothing but the prestige of her industrial riches to rely on her movements in the more stimulating circles of French society were already restricted.

The Comtesse Greffulhe and Montesquiou decided that the ideal husband for her would be the Prince Edmond de Polignac. He had all the right qualifications: he was one of the most scintillatingly witty men in all France; he was artistic to a degree, his cultural tastes being very much in line with Winnaretta's; he came from one of the oldest aristocratic families in Europe; and, more important, he would not trouble her in the way Louis de Scey-Montbéliard had because he was notoriously homosexual. Besides, since he was almost fifty-nine years old, even the most innocent-minded observer might have expected his sexual demands to be limited. But Winnaretta hesitated and not until the autumn of 1893 did she finally decide to go through with proposed marriage. By that time she had become better acquainted with the prince and had begun to appreciate what immense social advantages he could bring and realize how acceptable he was as a companion. A *rapport* of deep sympathy and mutual respect grew up between them, despite the fact that, even before they ever met, they had had a mild *contretemps*. One day Prince Edmond had gone to an auction to buy Claude Monet's *Le Champs de tulipes à Haarlem* but he was outbid by an American woman, whom he watched with impotent rage carrying off the coveted canvas. The 'American woman' was none other than Winnaretta. But, as he later commented, once he had married her, he could sit and look at the painting to his heart's content.

But who was the Prince Edmond de Polignac? According to French law he did not exist, since his birth in 1834 took place under rather unusual circumstances. His father Prince Jules de Polignac was the son of Marie-Antoinette's beloved friend Yolande, Duchesse de Polignac, from whom he inherited a devotion to the House of Bourbon. He had reaped the reward of his fidelity by being made head of Charles X's government in 1829 and as such he had been the man charged with implementing the King's famous Ordonnances of 25 July 1830, which, by attempting to suspend the constitution, provoked the revolution that led to Charles X's downfall and the emergence of Louis-Philippe as the King of the French. While his master fled to the safety of Great Britain, Polignac was arrested and sentenced to death. But because of considerable international pressure, the sentence was not carried out; instead, Prince Jules was confined in the dismal fortress of Ham on the Somme marches where he remained for more than six years until he was finally allowed to go into exile in Bavaria. During the period of his captivity the prince's English wife Charlotte Parkyns had insisted on living in a house close to the fortress in order to see as much of her husband as possible and in April 1834 their son Edmond had been born while his father was still in this legally anomalous position. After early years of deprivation in the shadow of the prison-fortress Edmond's period of exile with his family on their estate at Wildthurn in Bavaria was a welcome change. King Ludwig I went out of his way to treat them generously and in 1838 honoured Prince Jules by adding a second princely title to the one which he had received from Pope Pius VII in 1820.

With the death of Prince Jules in 1847, the Polignacs returned to Paris and took an apartment in the rue de Berri. Here Prince Edmond grew to manhood and prepared himself to enter his chosen career as a naval officer. However, with time, his developing academic interests began to oust that idea. He was fascinated by mineralogy but eventually it was music that turned out to be his great passion in life. Having begun his musical studies in Munich he continued them in Paris under Alphonse Thys and then under Reber at the Conservatoire, where in 1865 he gained the third prize for composition and in 1867 the first. In 1869 he submitted his entry to the opera

competition instituted at the 1867 Exhibition. His opera on
the approved subject, *La Coupe du roi de Thulé*, came fifth among
the forty-two entries. That was an achievement in itself because
among his rivals Massenet only won second prize and Bizet
was placed two below Edmond in order of merit. The reason
why the prince came no higher than fifth was that the jury
thought his instrumentation unnecessarily complicated: his use
of two bass clarinets was considered outlandish.

Prince Edmond was not always Bizet's rival. As a founder-
member of the Cercle de l'Union Artistique, known as the
Cercle des Mirlitons, he had been one of the first to commend
the *scherzo* of his latest symphony when it was played to them
in 1861. This was, incidentally, the same year in which the
Mirlitons had gone against the grain of fashion by supporting
Wagner enthusiastically after the fiasco of *Tannhäuser*'s French
première at the Opéra. Gounod, Berlioz, Auber, Catulle
Mendès and Edmond de Polignac immediately rallied round
him and pressed him to join their club. Wagner seems to have
taken some interest in Edmond. He sought him out for lunch
one day and told him how impressed he had been by his
brother's translation of *Faust*. Wagner was also impressed by
Edmond's compositions, though less so by his attempts to
expound his theory that the last movement of Beethoven's
Seventh Symphony was a programmatic representation of all
the phases of a shipwreck. That certainly showed some originality of imagination, which, if misplaced in this instance, served
the prince well in his own compositions: they frequently contained some element of fantasy or novelty. His *Lamento* for
humming chorus caused something of a sensation in his day.
His experiments with new scales were regarded as astonishing:
he invented a modified whole-tone scale, which he used in his
Echos de l'Orient judaïque in order to produce a certain hardness
of sound. In his *Jeu de Robin et Marion*, written in the mid-1880s,
he made use of the so-called Chinese scale before the vogue for
orientalisms gripped other French composers as a result of the
stir caused by pavilions from the Far East at the 1889 Exhibition. There is good reason for supposing that his ideas on
tonality and rhythm had some influence upon Satie and
Debussy, whom he first met in the 1880s. And his musical
inventiveness was not confined to composition: he was one of
the first to pioneer a method of combining music and spectacle

by accompanying a score with pictures projected from a magic lantern as an early precursor of Satie's *musique d'ameublement*. He also caused some excitement when he insisted that some of his music should be played in the open air in the woods by the Comtesse Greffulhe's house at Varengeville, near Dieppe; and, when this idea worked, he organized a performance of Gluck's *Orphée* there, making the chorus and ballet of the Paris Opéra appear against a natural background of sea, pines and serene moonlight. The painter Pierre Puvis de Chavannes, in whose honour this spectacle was arranged, was suitably impressed.

Edmond de Polignac's flamboyance extended beyond musical matters. His sparkling wit and intelligence made him a welcome figure in society and he tended to play up to his image as a socialite. Although basically of a philosophical bent and extremely sensitive, he had no objection to posing as a fashionable dandy and in James Tissot's picture the *Balcon du Cercle de la rue Royale* (1868), he is depicted among the aristocratic young-men-about-town with whom he mixed: the Marquis de Lau, the Comte de Ganay, the Baron Hottinger, the Marquis (later général) de Galliffet, Gaston de Saint-Maurice and the figure who transfixed Marcel Proust so many years later, Charles Haas. Yet, although Polignac could be eye-catching to the point of eccentricity, artistic motives were seldom far beneath the surface of what he did. The way in which he and a young Robert de Montesquiou went off to Bayreuth to hear Wagner's music, soon after the festival's institution in 1876, was considered rather affected but their interest was in music not in social point-scoring. In 1885 when he and Montesquiou were joined by Dr Samuel Pozzi on an expedition to London to do some artistic browsing, their ultra-aestheticism caused some comment in a Parisian society that had not yet adjusted itself to Pre-Raphaelite attitudes. Through John Sargent, Prince Edmond introduced his two friends to Henry James, who in turn agreed to introduce them to Whistler, although he reeled psychologically at the rather too blatant homosexual overtones in their manner. Whistler was less concerned and willingly showed his famous Peacock Room to the three Frenchmen. He was pleased to see how their Pre-Raphaelite idols, Rossetti and Burne-Jones, by comparison began to diminish in stature. And many who heard the story of Swinburne's introduction to the prince at Lady Brooke's saw in his reactions a wittiness that for once was not intended: Swinburne greeted him as a cousin because, he believed, he was related to the Polignac family on the distaff side. Edmond replied: 'Believe me that of the two the one more honoured by this cousinage is myself!'—and he was quite serious.

However, to picture Edmond de Polignac as simply an extrovert socialite, no matter how artistic, is misleading. Much of the time he was very reflective and almost oversensitive about his relations with others. As Proust remarked, he was always youthful but from his youth he had had the face of an old man. Yet, if the face of an old man indicated wisdom, it was a wisdom that had come partly through suffering. And Edmond suffered most from his inability to reconcile an inbred sense of obligation to humanity as a whole with a distinct feeling of unease in the company of others. He had a horror of not being able to control his emotions. For him the most humiliating thing in the world would be, as he quaintly put it, to find oneself weeping like a calf on the waistcoat of a complete stranger. He taught himself to endure stoically the exigencies of life. He usually suffered in silence but, if ever pressed to explain his feelings, he invariably expressed them in terms of his relations with his fellow beings. Once, having endured the rigours of a country house party in England—the local gentry, the indifferent food and wine and the banal conversation—he summed up the experience in his diary: 'Decidedly, I don't like the others.'

It was possibly this mixture of faint pessimism with the feeling that one had no right to be misanthropic, no matter how one felt, that prompted him to become involved in the Boulangerist movement between 1888 and 1889. He had some sympathy for Général Boulanger's views on the need to cleanse the Third Republic of political corruption so that there could be fair and effective government at home and prestige for France in international affairs. Prince Edmond went so far as to stand as a Boulangerist candidate for the third constituency in Nancy in the 1889 elections for the Chambre des Députés. But, beginning to see what a tarnished idol Boulanger really was, he took the opportunity to resign his candidature in favour of Maurice Barrès, whose political views were much more anti-liberal than his own. The irony of the situation was that both Polignac and the new deputy Barrès, while antagonistic towards corrupt government, were very much associated with artistic decadence:

the prince was one of the original aesthetes and Barrès with his
novels on the *culte du moi* soon became notorious for his fondness
for erotic and sensationalist literary themes. They both contributed their share to the new Decadence which left an
interesting mark upon French civilization but which at best
was seldom regarded with more than mild tolerance by society
in general and at worst with open hostility.

In November 1893 when Winnaretta announced her intention of marrying this distinctly individualistic figure, the Prince
de Polignac, there were some predictable reactions. All his
kinsmen who could not understand him assured Winnaretta
that she was marrying an unbearable maniac. Those with more
insight thought that a touch of perversity had affected the
couple's decision. More generally, comments were made about
their difference in age: his fifty-nine years compared with her
twenty-eight. When the artist Jacques-Emile Blanche, like
themselves a friend-for-the-time-being of Robert de Montesquiou, told his mother about the engagement, she commented
drily that this would not be the sort of wedding at which
Mendelssohn's march from *A Midsummer Night's Dream* could be
played. And Prince Edmond, to humour her and 'prove' that
he was still marriageable, ran along her terrace in his checked
trousers and Second Empire alpaca jacket and jumped with his
two feet together over a chair. Madame Blanche was still not
convinced: the marriage of the sewing-machine and the lyre,
she murmured. No, the marriage of the dollar and the *sou*, he
countered; with Winnaretta's good taste and money they would
both enjoy themselves having his music performed. And then
Blanche steered his mother off the topic of conversation before
it became more involved: an examination of the prince's
motivation in life might give too much insight into his own
propensities.

Once Winnaretta had decided, as she confided to the Comtesse Greffulhe, that this marriage was the only appropriate
way of assuring her a life of peace and right to work as she
wished, she was eager to embark on it as soon as possible. Once
Prince Edmond had sorted out the problem of his legal status
(or lack of it), the marriage took place on 15 December 1893
in the Chapelle des Carmes, before witnesses and guests drawn
exclusively from the families of the bridal pair. Even the Abbé
de Broglie, who conducted the nuptial mass, was a distant

kinsman of the Polignacs. As was appropriate for the marriage of a papal prince, Pope Leo XIII sent his special blessing to the couple. Apart from that the external world did not obtrude itself for the time being. An anarchist's bomb may have exploded in the Chambre des Députés six days before but the authorities were dealing with that; if anything preoccupied the minds of the newly married prince and princess, it was the thought that the Opéra's long delayed première of Chabrier's *Gwendoline* would take place in five days' time.

No matter how quiet the Polignacs tried to keep their wedding, their matter-of-fact attitude towards it soon caused a ripple of comment throughout society. A failing Edmond de Goncourt was curious enough to arrange to visit them on 18 April 1894. Pessimistic at the best of times, the impression of their situation, which he confided to his journal, was not flattering. Referring to them as *mes bibelots*, he commented that Prince Edmond had 'the air of a drowned dog' and Winnaretta had 'a cold beauty, distinct, cutting, the beauty of the daughter of the inventor of the sewing-machine'—whatever that meant. And he continued, repeating a fragment of gossip: 'It is said that the marriage between these two was concluded on the condition that the husband does not enter his wife's room, on the payment of a sum of money which might permit him to mount his music which the opera houses do not want.' An unpleasant mixture of cynicism and jealousy, Goncourt's assumption that the Polignacs' marriage was one of convenience was fair enough but his other comments contained unjustifiable implications—and no one had to look far to find the source of the trouble. Robert de Montesquiou, from being a close friend of the couple, had quickly turned into an implacable enemy. Having effected the formal introduction between them and suggested the idea of marriage, he was unsubtle enough to imagine that this gave him some special right of consideration in their union. By the middle of January 1894 the Comtesse Greffulhe had taken it upon herself to tell them that Montesquiou was furious at not being invited to the wedding. Prince Edmond hastily wrote a note of explanation: the person charged with sending out the invitations must have made a mistake because his name was certainly on the guest-list. But this only increased Montesquiou's anger: he, as well as anyone else, could read the *Figaro* report that invitations to the ceremony had been strictly limited to members of their two families. And he was not the person to miss the implication that his distinctive presence at that already rather unusual occasion might have been considered embarrassing. With his facile tongue, he would not have resisted the impulse to turn out epigrams on the subject. The man who had once exclaimed after a concert paid for with Winnaretta's money: 'Now we are going to have supper prepared by little sewing-machines!' might be expected to say anything: what, for example, would his comments have been on the fact that the bride's step-father, Paul Sohège, was young enough to be her husband's son? However, having avoided a momentary awkwardness, the Polignacs had mortally offended Montesquiou. Relations between them cooled to freezing point and until the end of his life the count took every opportunity to vilify them, particularly Winnaretta, who, he thought, should have been more grateful for being supplied with a faultless husband who would guarantee not to object to her girl-friends.

Although there may have been some truth in what he said, what Montesquiou was slow to realize was that their marriage was not nearly such a cold business-arrangement as he imagined. From the beginning Winnaretta and Edmond took an almost child-like pleasure in each other's company, eager to share the pleasures of life and exchange ideas on artistic matters. She wanted him to share all that she had, her experiences as well as her material prosperity. One thing that she insisted on doing was to take him to Venice as soon as the summer of 1894 came. He was as stunned by his first sight of the city's spectacular beauty as she had been. He liked the international society that congregated along the Grand Canal during the summer season. The atmosphere was altogether less fraught than that in Paris.

During their stay the Polignacs were invited to lunch by Mr and Mrs Daniel Curtis, very rich Americans whom they had met through their cousin John Sargent. Sargent himself still frequently stayed with them in the Palazzo Barbaro by the Accademia bridge and, on occasions, enticed Henry James to accompany him (in fact, James was later inspired to use the *palazzo* as a setting for Milly Teale in *The Wings of a Dove*). But on the occasion of the Polignacs' lunch the topic of conversation centred not so much upon artists and writers as upon the grape-coloured Palazzo Manzoni-Angaran directly opposite on the other side of the canal. The Polignacs were enchanted by it. Next day Winnaretta went off to see an estate agent, who supplied her with the interesting but disappointing information that the palace was not for sale because a rich South American was living there in practically connubial bliss with a friend. They had no intention of leaving. Yet, as Winnaretta commented, human emotions can be unpredictable: a few months later the same agent came to her in Paris with the information that the lovers had quarrelled and parted. The palace was up for sale. By Christmas 1894 the beautiful Lombardesque building was hers and she presented it to Prince Edmond with its new name, the Palazzo Polignac. It had started life in the fifteenth century as the Palazzo Contarini and had changed into the Contarini-dal Zaffo, then into the Montecuccoli and afterwards into the Manzoni-Angaran, so why not, finally, the Palazzo Polignac? The Polignacs, past and present, were as illustrious as any of the Venetian patriciate. Montesquiou seized upon this as an opportunity for being offensive. The frightful Polignacs had just bought the former Palazzo Montecuccoli, or rather, as he insisted, the Palazzo Montecuculli—the repeated syllable was most fitting. And he attempted to gild his surprising vulgarity by chanting a piece of doggerel, in which he likened the Polignacs' activities to the antics of two wood-pigeons:

> *Sur les coupoles de Venise*
> *Deux ramiers blancs aux pieds rosés,*
> *Au nid où l'amour s'éternise,*
> *Un soir de mai se sont posés.*

There was a world of difference between this stanza and the heady, exotic poem *Effusions* that had appeared with a dedication to Prince Edmond under the section *L'Autel des parfums* in the collection entitled *Le Chef des odeurs suaves*, which Montesquiou, at his Des Esseintes best, had published just over a year before.

Chapter 5
A Touch of Mauve
(1894–1895)

One of the most disconcerting things about Winnaretta was her physical appearance. She always gave the impression of being reserved and cold, and this could intimidate those who did not know her well. Moreover, her majestic profile and determined jaw, her clear ice-blue eyes gave her an indomitable look. She had the habit of observing everything in silence and then, when she spoke, it was in a dry perfectly neutral voice, whose accent always retained an un-French timbre, despite the fact that (perhaps because) she had been bilingual since childhood. Her way of speaking slowly through her teeth gave what she said a brusque quality. Nevertheless, anyone who came to know her soon learned that her formidable appearance was really only a façade that concealed a basic shyness; it was a form of natural protection against everything that made her feel vulnerable. In France this was thought to be a very Anglo-Saxon characteristic and she was half-admired for it. Those who could not penetrate her marble-like impassivity often mistook it for unfriendliness and reacted accordingly.

And yet, whatever personal reactions were, nobody denied that she possessed a real sensitivity in cultural matters, if not always in social affairs. She was clearly very talented. She was vastly intelligent and so eclectic in her interests and tastes that there seemed to be nothing in which she was not interested or which she was not capable of understanding. Her main interest was always music; listening to it, playing it and composing, she derived immense spiritual elation from it as an abstract art. But on occasions when music could combine the best of itself with the best of another art-form her pleasure was all the more keen: for instance, the use of Grillparzer's poetry in Schubert's *Ständchen* or, for that matter, Fauré's settings of Verlaine's words added considerably to her intellectual stimulation. One of the first things that attracted her to Debussy was his treatment of

Rossetti's poem in his early master-work *La Damoiselle élue*. In fact, the Pre-Raphaelite movement in general had considerable appeal for Winnaretta because its syncretic approach to forms of art, literature, philosophy, history and religion, came near to reflecting ideas of her own on life. While most of society called such beliefs effete, decadent or even depraved, for her and a few others they represented one possible form of intellectual existence. Yet in the 1890s Winnaretta was most closely associated in the public mind with only one art-form, painting, and with one particular school of art, not the Symbolists but still the Impressionists and their more immediate successors.

With Edmond de Polignac to help her now, she pursued any Impressionist paintings that came on to the market. Since, even by the mid-1890s, only the more recherché collectors were seriously interested in the Impressionists, Winnaretta did not encounter very serious opposition. In May 1895, for example, when Monet put up twenty canvases for sale at Durand-Ruel's gallery, twelve of them remained unsold. Even the efforts of Sargent to sell them to rich American acquaintances were not very successful: once Winnaretta had carried off the rose version of the Rouen Cathedral series, interest had waned. Nonetheless, despite the comparative failure of the cathedral paintings, the price of Monet's canvases was just beginning to rise. In the previous year, when he put up *Les Dindons blancs*, Monet found that instead of a hoped-for eight or ten thousand francs, Winnaretta had been willing to pay twelve thousand francs for it. It was certainly an extraordinary painting. The idea of using a flock of white turkeys, strutting through the grounds of the Château de Montgeron, virtually as a decorative design, reminiscent of a Japanese print, did not have immediate popular appeal. Yet, Winnaretta liked it and was willing to pay more than its market-value to have it. About the same time she managed to buy Monet's *Les Pommiers en fleur*, his *Une Femme assise sous un arbre* and his *Au Bord de la Seine*. The delightfully tranquil canvas that Monet painted of his step-daughters and entitled *La Barque à Giverny* was also acquired by her. She added a portrait of Jeanne Samary by Renoir to her collection about the same time.

Winnaretta later bought a number of Old Masters to swell her collection but in the 1890s the non-contemporary works of art in which she was most interested were objets d'art that could

be used decoratively in her newly constructed house. A Renaissance tapestry was hung in her bedroom and some Louis XVI
wainscotting, doors and panel-friezes were acquired and used
to enhance the period-atmosphere of her library. Though of a
later period and very utilitarian, Coromandel screens of fine
quality were installed in the Paris house. The decoration
of the Palazzo Polignac in Venice was less classical because
alterations to the interior of the building had to be done in an
appropriately Lombardesque style and therefore some modern
imitation work was unobtrusively done on it. She preferred to
restore what already existed rather than alter and so spoil the
character of the building. At times this could cause unexpected
complications. One day workmen, restoring the pavementing
of one of the ground-floor rooms, found a human skeleton of
some antiquity. No one ever discovered whose remains they
were. Years later, repeating the story, Henri de Régnier
declared that this must have been a victim of Renaissance
Venice's system of anonymous denunciations. But what did it
matter? Under Winnaretta the Palazzo Polignac had become
such a famous centre of musical activities that it was now
haunted by nothing except great musicians.

For the princess, art in the domestic situation had another
side to it. Throughout the 1890s she held annual exhibitions of
paintings in her Paris house. For one thing it afforded her an
opportunity to exhibit her own canvases; it also let the work of
artist-friends reach a public which otherwise would be closed
to it, either because it was unsuitable for the established salons
or not voluminous enough to warrant one-man shows. Her
exhibition was famous for attracting remarkable consignments
of paintings each year. This, however, did not make her turn
her back on the official Salon. And the thought of her winning
commendations at it used to provoke Montesquiou to jealous
fury. He hated to hear of her success in anything but he could
do nothing except dissipate his feelings by writing crude verse
about her. In his *Vinaigrette*, from the *Quarante Bergères*, what he
described as a satirical portrait but in fact no more than a
slanderous canard, he accused her of using any means to gain
her ends: she makes an artist show her where to put the colours
on the canvas; signs it herself and then sends it to the Salon. She
gains a medal after many a try. But is she satisfied then? No,
she complains about being placed low down the table at the

official dinner. Those at the head have put her there out of their line of vision in case the sight of her should sour their stomachs and spoil their dinner. Vinaigrette continues to grumble. In the end what does she want? To be given consideration? Good God! as what? But, if Montesquiou refused to see why she should be given consideration, others were not slow to recognize her qualities.

The sign of one's acceptance among the 'civilized' in Paris was an invitation to the salon which the sculptor René de Saint-Marceaux and his wife (formerly Marguerite Baugnies) held every Friday in their apartment in the boulevard Malesherbes. Nobody who was not a creative artist of some sort or a scientist was admitted; mere social personalities, no matter how culturally inclined, were strictly excluded. Moreover, since everyone there was assumed to spend their days in productive work, Madame de Saint-Marceaux insisted that there should be complete informality about dress: to appear in one's working clothes was a mark of distinction—or rather of individual distinctiveness. Though not in working clothes, Winnaretta came invariably dressed in a high-necked gown which, everyone said, somehow made her look indestructible. She represented the talented young. Prince Edmond at her side was among the talented old but regarded as young in spirit and mind, despite his age and increasingly old-mannish habits—he was inseparable from a beige *vicuña* shawl that protected his shoulders from draughts which no one but he could feel. He would sit, sunk in a sofa and, listening to the music, would produce a pencil from nowhere and begin doodling. Old and young mingled at the Saint-Marceaux salon without regard for fame or position. At the select dinner beforehand Winnaretta might encounter Madame Alexandre Dumas, the writer Jean-Louis Vaudoyer, Paul Mathey and his intensely musical daughter; Chausson, Lalo, Vincent d'Indy and Paul Dukas might also be there. Afterwards a more general fathering could include Sargent, sometimes accompanied by Monet and André Messager. Henri Gauthier-Villars added his presence to the company and in 1893, a little before Winnaretta's own marriage, began to bring his new wife, a young Colette, a frail, overshadowed creature. Maurice Ravel, learning to conform before he could surprise, counted an invitation to Madame de Saint-Marceaux's a great honour. More casual were the inseparable poet and musician

Pierre Louÿs and Claude Debussy. Fawn-like with black, curly hair and short beard, a slightly retroussé nose and dark, deep-set eyes, Debussy gave Winnaretta the impression of being an Italian model: his swarthy complexion and the small hooped gold earrings which he sometimes wore added to his Latin image. Fauré, one of Marguerite de Saint-Marceaux's closest friends, was invariably there.

Having gathered together a company of such variety, the hosts would launch them into a discussion on some artistic topic, a piece of music, a painting or perhaps a newly published book, and they would talk, often straying from the subject as related ideas occurred to them, sometimes until dawn. Frequently the evenings were taken up with music, the performers being drawn from the guests. Edouard Risler would play for hours, astonishing the audience with the lightness of his fat paw-like hands on the keyboard. Songs by Brahms, Schubert or Fauré were sung by Maurice Bagès or by Marguerite de Saint-Marceaux herself. Indeed, Fauré had given her the first copy of the *Cinq Mélodies de Venise*, with precise instructions how to sing them; and *Après un rêve*, which was dedicated to her, was first performed at one of her early salons. Sometimes Messager would play piano duets with Debussy or, more frequently, with one of the other composers present, while Debussy—judiciously, it was felt—confined himself to turning the pages. Occasionally the guests were marshalled into a choir with soloists and the evening was spent singing Bach cantatas.

In many ways the Saint-Marceaux salon provided Winnaretta with inspiration for her own salon, which became a Parisian institution in years to come, although hers did not take place on a fixed day of the week and was always organized on a more professional basis. Madame de Saint-Marceaux's gatherings were unusual in that they were slightly Bohemian; Winnaretta's were regarded as more sophisticated and startling. Nonetheless, the Saint-Marceaux lesson was profound, if only because it taught Winnaretta that what could be said or heard in a salon should be, even though it might initially surprise one or hit at one's most cherished principles. Nothing brought this home to her more than when, among the *salonniers'* voices proclaiming a by now fashionable enthusiasm for Wagner, she heard Debussy and a very young Ravel insist that his music left them unmoved. They found the clearer, more delicate works of the Russian nationalist composers much more stirring. Winnaretta appreciated their love of Russian music but failed to see why that should invite invidious comparisons with the Wagnerian school.

Possibly this impartiality of Winnaretta's was what gave her own salon the reputation of being one of the top quartet of academic salons—the others were those of the Vicomtesse Alix de Janzé, Madame Beulé and, of course, Madame Aubernon de Nerville. The word 'academic' was used to signify that here was a forum for ideas on anything connected with civilization. Everything from art to politics was given an airing there at the highest possible intellectual level without any suggestion that partisanship of any sort made much difference to one's acceptance in the princess's circle. This was something of an achievement in that troubled decade, the 1890s, when feelings ran very high over the claims of different schools of art and over sociopolitical questions, especially once the storm of the Dreyfus Affair broke. Without sacrificing any of her own principles, which were strong and well thought out, Winnaretta did not hesitate to welcome to her salon people of opposing persuasions. In this respect she differed markedly from hostesses such as Madame de Saint-Marceaux and the Baronne de Poilly. Unlike many leading a way of life requiring some social tolerance, she never countered intolerance with intolerance. By now few were unaware that the Polignac salon was presided over by two homosexuals. Many were shocked by that fact alone and regarded their salon as being *per se* immoral. But that did not restrict the Polignacs. They were adequately discreet in their private lives and in their public lives as intellectually honest as they could be without causing open offence. And to a large extent this was possible: public reaction against the increasingly overt activities of the more tortuous-minded devotees of Decadence was not yet strong enough to make a significant difference. Besides, the Polignacs were associated primarily with music and this did not immediately lend itself to criticism of that sort.

However, even on the musical side, some of their activities caused raised eyebrows. Like Winnaretta, Edmond was devoted to baroque music, which, except for a few notable exceptions was played very little in late nineteenth-century France, and so in 1895 they organized a major enterprise under their aegis

—the only performance of Rameau's opera *Dardanus* to be given in the nineteenth century. Since its composition in 1739 it had only been revived three times, the last being in 1784. And the Polignacs' production made a great impression upon intelligent musicians, such as Debussy, and upon young *littérateurs*, such as Marcel Proust. But *Dardanus*, of all Rameau's operas the one which expressed the most radical sentiments, disturbed more listeners than it impressed. Yet, it did inspire the Schola Cantorum to give a concert performance of it some twelve years later in 1907.

The forces of soloists, choir and orchestra, assembled for the Rameau, were also frequently engaged to perform the music of his equally neglected contemporaries, Handel and Bach. If Madame de Saint-Marceaux's amateur experiments with Bach cantatas were unusual, Winnaretta took her interests much further, exploring the extent of the eighteenth-century German repertoire much more fully and indulging a passion for Handel that was considered rather too English to be palatable in France. Edmond de Polignac took advantage of the same musical resources and had many of his own works performed properly for the first time. His *Imprecations* for choir, organ and brass was heard at last in the studio in the rue Cortambert and his two oratorios *Le Christ de Gethsémani* and *Pilate livre le Christ*, scored for bass recitative, choir and orchestra, were given in the grand salon. Early in 1895 a very impressed Debussy came away from one of these performances and commented to Pierre Louÿs that, although he had missed a recent performance of Hervé's *Chilpéric*, hearing the music of Edmond de Polignac was some form of compensation. Some of the same forces were used to perform Fauré's works in Winnaretta's salon. The *Requiem* was a particular favourite of hers and *Madrigal*, in its version for choir and orchestra, was also performed there.

There was one unfortunate side-effect of Winnaretta's desire to have played works requiring musical forces larger than those usually employed in private houses. She had to invite a sufficient number of guests to balance the mass of musicians and frequently the level of appreciation decreased in inverse proportion to the numbers invited. Critics and social commentators were alternately annoyed and amused by the flock of elegantly hatted princesses and forgetful dukes who shuffled their chairs, clattered their teaspoons in their saucers and gossiped noisily

while the musicians struggled manfully against this acoustical
background reminiscent of an aviary.

Winnaretta's ability to engage large musical forces for her
salon-ventures was the talk and envy of Parisian high society,
however inattentive. Yet, it was not this but her interest in
having small-scale chamber works performed that earned her a
reputation as a discerning patroness of music. Other rich
melomanes existed at the time. The musical ventures of the
Comtesse de Béarn, Madame Gaston Ménier, Madame
Edouard André and the Baronne Alphonse de Rothschild were
remarkable, as were those of her mother Madame Paul Sohège,
but Winnaretta's stood out from among them. She was very
much younger than these formidable women; she required
excellence as an essential prerequisite from executants; and,
above all, she was much more adventurous in her musical
pursuits than the others. She constantly had Beethoven's
chamber music played, especially in the late quartets, which
were still generally unpalatable and had another two decades
to wait before becoming *chic* in 'Proustian' circles. French taste
in the *Belle Epoque* extended little beyond certain categories of
nineteenth-century music; but music of all periods, stretching
back to the late Middle Ages and Renaissance was to be heard
at the Polignacs. Just as unusual for the day, Prince Edmond's
harpsichord was used when performances of baroque music
required it. The harpsichord was practically unknown in other
musical circles because in those pre-Landowska days it had
virtually been relegated to the scrap-heap of obsolescence; and,
when Ravel, very much of a habitué of the Polignac salon,
produced his *Deux Epigrammes antiques* in 1898, his apt scoring
of the second song, entitled *D'Anne jouant de l'espinette*, for possible
harpsichord accompaniment was considered extraordinary—as,
indeed, it was.

Possibly more significant than the gems of pre-classical music,
the latest, most advanced chamber music was already a feature
of Winnaretta's salon offerings, particularly Fauré's small scale
works. Although his music was becoming much more acceptable
and Fauré himself was well on the way to becoming a Conservatoire professor, many still found his compositions difficult to
digest. Few manifested even as much sympathy as Albert
Samain, whose poetic imagination could not fail to appreciate
his exquisite music: one finds him sighing for the theatrical

romanticism of Bellini and complaining bitterly about the music which Fauré and his colleagues on the committee of the Société Nationale de Musique, Chausson and d'Indy, insisted upon foisting on the public. Why was their music so modern? Winnaretta did not agree and consistently tapped the rich flow of instrumental music that flowed from Fauré's pen during that period. The instrumental piece for piano with flute, violin or violoncello, the Verlaine songs, the latest piano pieces, *Barcarolles*, *Nocturnes*, *Valses-Caprices*, the *Thème et variations* and the unexceptional *Dolly Suite*, were played for her select audiences, Fauré's admirers, who were gradually growing in number. Society music-lovers, such as the Princesse Bibesco, Mme de Maupeou, Mme de Guerne and the Princesse de Brancovan, herself an excellent pianist and notable Chopin exponent, bore with dignity the Cottardesque nickname '*les serpents-à-sonates*' and continued to be seen in drawing-rooms where music of the best quality was to be heard, 'particularly the Polignacs'.

Another interesting, if less formidable person who haunted Winnaretta's salon was Marcel Proust. Robert de Montesquiou had been introduced to him in March 1893 by the flower-painter and enthusiastic party-giver Madeleine Lemaire and through him he had entered the much more exclusive world of the aristocratic salons. Just before their marriage, both Winnaretta and Edmond de Polignac were introduced to Proust by Montesquiou, eager to share his latest discoveries with them. With the skill of the non-committed, Proust managed to survive the split between Montesquiou and the Polignacs and straddled the ever-widening gulf between them without choosing between one side or the other—only at the expense of not rising significantly in the estimation of either. Early in 1894 Proust found himself sitting at the end of the Polignacs' dinner table, transfixed by the sight of Prince Edmond's old crony Charles Haas and, although he did not deign to glance at him, far less speak to him, from that moment the gestation of Swann had begun.

For the next decade Proust came to the Polignac salon and laid up store upon store of impressions, which reappeared thinly disguised in his works. In a short story, '*La Mort de Baldassare Silvande*', published in the *Revue Hebdomadaire* in October 1895, he based the character of Silvande upon elements of the lives of various acquaintances but the musical characteristics were modelled upon the life of Edmond de Polignac, with an additional touch or two taken from the career of Proust's composer-friend Reynaldo Hahn. Both the Polignacs were the focus of attention in the article which Proust published in *Le Figaro* on 6 September 1903, under the title of '*Le Salon de la Princesse Edmond de Polignac*'. His treatment of this theme was slightly injudicious and the consequences were unfortunate. He was more subtle in the references made to Prince Edmond in *À la Recherche du temps perdu*. He appeared in person when Proust mentioned Tissot's painting of the Cercle de la rue Royale in *La Prisonnière*. And elements of the prince went into the making of Bergotte. Sitting muffled in shawls and plaids like someone on a train journey, Prince Edmond would sigh a quotation from Anaxagoras: 'After all, life is a journey.' The comment ended up in the mouth of the dying Bergotte. Proust's impressions of the funeral of Prince Edmond re-emerged for the burial of Robert de Saint-Loup at Combray. The black curtains draping the church door and the princely coronet surmounting the single initial 'P', in Polignac's case, and 'G', for the dead Guermantes, signified to Proust that death gathers one back into the family fold: by shearing away the initials indicating Christian names, it deprives the individual of all personality other than that as the scion of a princely family. When Proust added that 'the feudal turret, emptied of its books, had become warlike again', he was still thinking of the dead Edmond de Polignac. His scholarly interests died with him but he remained a Polignac. In *Sodome et Gomorrhe* Proust made another reference to Prince Edmond's erudition: the Baron de Charlus, purposefully bent on flattering the attractive Victurnien de Surgis, commented upon his unrivalled knowledge of Balzac but affectedly checked himself to add: 'No, I'm wrong. There are also a Polignac and a Montesquiou.'

But in the 1890s these Proustian memories were still in the making and, for the most part, far from their re-incarnation on paper. For the time being Proust was observing and learning. In the salon he seldom expressed opinions or feelings that might offend or reveal a lack of sophistication, though Winnaretta was the last person to worry about that. And the only occasion upon which he expressed genuine delight was when Victor Cucheval, his old schoolmaster from the Lycée Concorcet, arrived at a Polignac reception. But even then his delight was tinged with embarrassment as the butler turned to Prince Edmond and

asked if it might be more delicate not to announce someone
with a name that lent itself to obviously obscene interpretations.

Winnaretta's salon was indeed a place where social lessons
were learned. Proust's musical tastes were very largely cultivated and pruned under her roof. The Polignacs infected him
with their passion for all music from Gregorian chant onwards.
Their concert programmes influenced his own choice of music
when, for his soirées at the Ritz, he maintained a fine balance
between Beethoven, Chopin and Schumann and less popular
composers, such as Couperin at one end and Fauré at the other.
In fact, Proust's love of Fauré's music grew because he heard it
performed so often at Winnaretta's. The Vinteuil Sonata,
which enjoyed a certain vogue in Madame Verdurin's drawing-
room, was at least in part inspired by his hearing Fauré's
Violin Sonata at Polignac concerts. If Proust was amused at the
sight of the aigrette in the Comtesse d'Haussonville's head-
dress swaying in time to the music, as if to indicate that she was
familiar with every note of it, he himself knew it just as thoroughly: the Princesse de Polignac had given him every opportunity for learning it note for note.

If Proust had entered the Polignacs' circle as a result of one
of Montesquiou's last friendly acts towards them, about the
same time they introduced one of their friends to him, Claude
Debussy, the haughty neo-Bohemian, who during the 1890s
remained a faithful member of their salon. Despite differences
of opinion over the merits and demerits of Wagner, he and
Prince Edmond maintained a close friendship based upon
mutual respect. They often went to the Lamoureux concerts
together with Pierre Louÿs and there quarrelled amicably
about the music. If Polignac and Louÿs sided against Debussy
on the subject of Wagner, Louÿs and Debussy joined forces
against the prince when he enthused about Richard Strauss,
after hearing a performance of *Also sprach Zarathustra* in January 1899. But it is not surprising that the music of Strauss and
the sentiments of Nietzsche did not appeal to the two younger
men, who had made their own ideas clear when they collaborated to produce the enchanting and unequivocally Sapphic
Chansons de Bilitis of 1897 and 1898. Performed in the Polignac
salon, they amounted to an elaborate compliment to the
hostess, even though not formally dedicated to her. But Winnaretta was not interested in Debussy's music simply because

some regarded it as verging on the anti-social. In the 1890s she had many of his small scale chamber works performed in her salon, usually very soon after their composition. She watched his progress with interest, even when in 1911 her introduction of the composer to Montesquiou bore belated fruit in the form of *Le Martyre de Saint-Sébastien*, that joint collaboration with Ida Rubinstein and Gabriele d'Annunzio that was designed to shock and entertain the public with its ambiguous treatment of the story of the most effete of all Christian saints.

But by that time Montesquiou was far beyond being counted among the Polignacs' friends. By the end of 1894 relations between them were hopelessly strained. During that year Montesquiou and Maurice Barrès organized a small scheme to help an impoverished and ailing Verlaine. They addressed themselves to a circle of sympathizers in the hope of raising enough capital to pay the poet a pension of 150 francs. Contributions from friends, including the Comtesse Greffulhe, Léon Daudet and Octave Mirbeau, fell short of the required sum and so Montesquiou urged Barrès to write to the Comte Henri de Saussine and the Polignacs. Saussine ignored the request but apparently money was forthcoming from Winnaretta, who through Prince Edmond was said to have contributed one hundred thousand francs. Whether the cheque that came into Montesquiou's hands was as large as that or not, according to him, it made no difference. He boasted that he kept the money himself and compensated Verlaine by giving him a very fine scarf from Charvet's. That ended any lingering regard that Winnaretta had for her former boon-companion. Thereafter, what friends they had in common made sure not to invite the Polignacs and Montesquiou to the same social events. If this worried the Prousts of the world of snobbism, with time it made less difference to Winnaretta, as she watched Montesquiou cross one after the other of their acquaintances off his visiting-list, as he quarrelled with them and adamantly withheld his forgiveness. She was just as sensitive as he was but, whereas his near-paranoiac neurosis condemned him to an increasingly solitary existence, where he nurtured imaginary wrongs to bolster up his self-esteem and assuage his jealousy, Winnaretta countered social opposition by living the life she wanted to live, paying only the merest lip-service to conventions which otherwise might have stunted the growth of her spirit.

Chapter 6
A Climate of Social Change
(1895–1900)

During the second half of the 1890s French society was not quite as carefree as in the early years of the decade. The *Belle Epoque* was becoming less beautiful, less integral as an age. The mauve 'nineties were fading from over-exposure to the light of day. Reaction and social change were affecting all Frenchmen in one way or another. Ironically, the first signs of change were noticed not in France but in the England of Oscar Wilde. Wilde had been a frequent visitor to Paris in years past and Paris had loved him. Here was a writer with as much literary flair as a Huysmans but with very much more style and panache. Sarah Bernhardt and the Duchesse de Richelieu, Heine's niece, took him to their hearts. Lady de Grey and the tenaciously Pre-Raphaelite Baronne Deslandes fawned over him. Jacques-Emile Blanche and Marcel Schwob imitated his dress and manners. When he appeared in Paris in the spring of 1894 with the beautiful Lord Alfred Douglas, he had caused a sensation. Only Robert de Montesquiou and Marcel Proust, who could not endure to recognize anything of themselves in him, shunned him, shuddering at what they claimed was the wasting disease of degeneracy infecting the pleasantly intellectual spirit of Decadence. Winnaretta was not of that opinion because, probably more than most, she could see through the extravagance of Wilde's manner to the poet and writer of near genius. She associated with him in public and entertained him and Lord Alfred in her home. For her they were as much a symbol of growing social acceptance as they were harbingers of disaster for Montesquiou. And for once Montesquiou was right.

In the following year, 1895, Wilde—his Antinöus of the horrible—shook the foundations of society not because of his homosexuality but because of his lack of discretion. As Wilde disappeared from sight behind the walls of Reading Gaol, the shock-waves hit the aesthetes' world. The British middle-classes used the Wilde scandal to whip up antagonism against an unmanly style of life and way of thinking that could undermine the constitution of a hardy imperialistic race. Something similar happend in France. The blame for social ills and political ineptitude was laid on a defenceless scapegoat in the form of a movement that openly associated itself with decadence and symbolist introversion. In May 1895, about the same time as the Wilde case, Octave Mirbeau lashed out against the aesthetes in an article in *Critique*. Many of the Decadents abruptly called a halt to the more public of their activities; some even pursued respectability as though it were a new cult, while others turned round and violently attacked what they so recently had held dear. Rachilde produced no more books of the *Monsieur Vénus* and *Marquise de Sade* genre. Maurice Barrès, claiming to have exhausted the literary possibilities of his *culte du moi*, turned wholeheartedly to the patriotism and ultra-nationalism to which his Boulangerism already inclined him. Paul Bourget tried to obliterate memories of a blatantly homo-sexual youth by echoing Barrès's nationalistic sentiments and making the Académie his goal in life, the epitome of respec-tability. Jean Lorrain, still incorrigibly homosexual, found it difficult to disguise his image as a tawdry imitation of Wilde but even he turned his wicked pen on the aesthetes and slated the values of his own past. The mock Gothicism and pseudo-Assyrian cult of the Rosicrucian Joséphin Péladan died a more gradual death, mainly because most people regarded it, how-ever pleasantly diverting, as too childish to be dangerous. But even Sar Péladan made efforts to deflect suspicion away from himself: conspicuous by his absence at his 1896 Salon of Rosicrucian Art, he made sure that the public knew where he was—in Venice on his honeymoon.

Winnaretta's attitude towards the change was one of sorrow, not because she had ever been as forthright about her tastes as others. She had never deliberately set out to shock the shockable, since that had little to do with art and even less to do with one's private life. To certain extent her marriage to Edmond de Polignac had been an acknowledgment that society's most sacred convention—appearances—must be respected. However, after 1895 she stratified her life a little more strictly than before into public and private. Decades later

André Germain, the amateur writer whose inability to cope
with marriage to Lucien Daudet's formidable sister Edmée left
him with a love-hate fixation about homosexuals of either sex,
used this as an excuse for venting his neurotic spleen on
Winnaretta. She was a hypocrite, he said, and accused her of
living her life not just on two but on three levels, those of the
social comedy, the intellectual and artistic life and the world of
nocturnal activities. Although there may have been an element
of truth in his claim, Germain failed to see that the structure
of her life still allowed for some overlap between its spheres
and he also failed to recognize that a well-structured life was,
in her case, a purely practical necessity, unlike his own, which
was the result of a schizoid mind. He repeated the retort which
she once directed at someone who was unsubtle enough to
speculate on the nature of the famous friendship between
Marie-Antoinette and the first Duchesse de Polignac: 'To think
that anyone could dare to misinterpret that innocent friendship! To think that one could dare attribute such practices to
my grandmother!' Germain was incapable of detecting the
tongue-in-cheek tone of her protest. He could not reconcile it
with her confidential admission to him that she had found Oscar
Wilde charming. And her additional comment: 'What a
terrible middle-class we have in England!' only emphasized
her real sympathies and, to Germain, her hypocrisy. But what
he forgot was that she had not been afraid to entertain Wilde
during his years of 'exile' when, dying beyond his means in
Paris, he needed material as well as moral support. Germain
certainly did not appreciate the concessions to tact made by
almost everyone living in the late 1890s, even those most above
suspicion. For instance, Jean-Louis Forain, who had little to
worry about, began to tone down his stories of the period when
he had shared rooms with Verlaine and Rimbaud. He had
witnessed many of the squabbles which characterized their
relationship but, he said, there was never any evidence to
suggest that their relationship was homosexual, as everybody
assumed. When Forain told Winnaretta this, she made no
comment: that was one concession to convention which, as
Verlaine lay dying, was unworthy of a friendship that had
produced the *Romances sans paroles* and *Les Illuminations*.

If Germain imagined that Winnaretta restrained the exuberance of her nocturnal hours at this point, he had no cause for

complaint about the panache with which she went about her social and artistic activities. Her cult of Wagner's music was reaching new heights as French taste at last caught up with her. Each summer, institution-like, she took up residence in Bayreuth, usually renting the former summer residence of the margraves of Bayreuth, the Schloss Fantasie, for the duration of the Festival. In 1896, as always, she invited friends to join her there. An overworked Fauré, for one, welcomed the opportunity to escape from the cares of city life and spent ten days enjoying the peaceful forested dales and beautiful vistas of the Fantasie estate. Haunted by the music of the *Ring*, he exclaimed that Wagner should be played nowhere except in Bayreuth. Nothing could match it as a setting for the music-dramas. No one should think of imitating his work: it would always fall short of the original.

But, if Winnaretta had any hope of seeing Wagnerian influences creep into Fauré's music, she certainly gave no hint of it. Eight years before, in 1888, she had sat with Fauré at Bayreuth and seen how moved he had been by the last scene of *Meistersinger* but the sentiment left his own music untouched. Rather she seems to have been eager to use the gathering of musical *cognoscenti* at Bayreuth as an opportunity for propagandizing Fauré's music to an international audience. She had also invited the pianist Edouard Risler to stay, as well as a singer from London, Miss Palisser. A violinist from Paris, Fridrich, joined them. And, having requisitioned two other players from the string section of the Bayreuth orchestra, she organized them into various ensembles to play music by Fauré. She had some of the songs sung in the *schloss* before a small audience of friends; these were followed by a piano-duet version of the music from *Shylock* and of the *Allégro symphonique*, played by Risler and Fauré himself. Then in Bayreuth itself on the afternoon of Saturday, 8 August, a select gathering heard another programme of his music, including the two Piano Quartets and the Violin Sonata. That was followed in the evening by an appearance at Cosima Wagner's weekly reception. However, by that time, Fauré was becoming restive: the German guests were too naïve or unsubtle to be stimulating and Cosima Wagner was an unsympathetic creature. He was certainly pleased to have his music played outside France and enjoyed the change of air but soon he was hankering after the

sparkle and lightness of Paris life. And he left the Polignacs to
continue the worship at the Wagnerian shrine.

But later in the year Winnaretta was again involved in
spreading Fauré's reputation abroad. He accompanied her to
London in December to attend a concert of his music, with
which Frank Schuster inaugurated his new music-room in Old
Queen Street. The vocal and orchestral works played, especially
the *Madrigal* and the *Pavane*, were a great success and Fauré
was overwhelmed by the praise of new admirers, as well as of
old friends such as Henry James and Sargent. Lady Randolph
Churchill and her sister Lady Leslie also showered compliments
on him. Fauré was pleased at his success, even if a little out of
pocket after the trip. It led to further, more lucrative successes.
A year later in December 1897 more concerts of his music were
given in London and the following March he visited England
to discuss detailed points about music which he had been commissioned to write for the first London production of Maurice
Maeterlinck's play *Pelléas et Mélisande*. According to Mrs
Patrick Campbell, who was to play Mélisande, Fauré obligingly
wrote the music to her own specifications. But she was probably
only concerned about questions of vocal range, tempo and
rhythm in a little song which she had to sing at one point. The
rest of the music was very Fauréan, dream-like, entirely suitable
for Maeterlinck's 'disembodied' play.

Despite contrary predictions, *Pelléas et Mélisande* achieved a
remarkable degree of success when it opened at a matinée in
the Prince of Wales Theatre on 21 June 1898. Even the time
of day and the appearance of great actors such as Forbes
Robertson, Martin Harvey and Mrs Campbell herself, in very
uncharacteristic rôles did not affect the warmth of its reception,
much of which reflected on to Fauré, who had been present to
conduct his music. And Winnaretta was also there, behind him
in the audience, sitting flanked by the Earl of Wemyss, still
spritely and enthusiastic, despite his considerable age, and by
Sargent, who marked the occasion by sketching Fauré in the
theatre. She was delighted when Fauré subsequently arranged
the *Pelléas* as a suite and published it with a dedication to
herself. This was his way of thanking her for her help and
support. The first performance of the suite *Pelléas et Mélisande*
at a Lamoureux concert in Paris on 3 February 1901 must
have afforded her particular satisfaction and all the more in

succeeding years when Fauré's *Pelléas* music retained its fascination despite rival musical interpretations of Maeterlinck's
drama, although the scores produced by Debussy, Schoenberg
and Sibelius, all distinctive in their own way, may well have
helped to maintain public interest in the *Pelléas* theme in spite
of its rather unfashionable symbolist nature.

About this time Winnaretta's friendship with Fauré had
another 'English' side-effect of a rather different kind because
through him she met the composer Frederick Delius. In March
1899 the Polignacs were invited to a select musical evening at
the Paris home of Adela Maddison (a rich London lawyer's
wife and a talented amateur composer, with whom Fauré had
a lengthy love-affaire) and at it he and 'a few of the best young
French musicians' played through Delius's opera *Koanga*.
According to the composer himself, the audience received it
with enthusiasm. However, despite Adela Maddison's continued invitations to Delius to meet the Polignacs, not to mention the efforts of his mistress the Princesse de Cystrie, Delius
was not drawn into the mainstream of Parisian musical
activity, although in subsequent years some of his music was
given a public airing at Société Nationale concerts. He made
no attempt to associate himself with any of Winnaretta's
musical ventures. Yet, they did keep up their acquaintance for
years to come.

By contrast, another off-shoot of the Polignacs' friendship
with Fauré bore more fruit: Maurice Ravel became closely
involved in the life of their *salon*. Earlier Winnaretta had had
passing doubts about him because of his untempered anti-
Wagnerian views but, as a pupil in Fauré's composition class
at the Conservatoire, after 1896 he became more integrated as
a *bona fide* member of their artistic circle. At this point Ravel
himself possibly felt more at ease in the Saint-Marceaux salon
or in the home of his refined and civilized friends Cyprien and
Ida Godebeski but, as an artistic social-climber, he recognized
that Winnaretta de Polignac's support for his music was the
most valuable available. Yet, he set about the matter in a
curious way. In 1899 he dedicated to her a newly written
piano-piece, the *Pavane pour une infante défunte*. She confessed to
being deeply touched by having her name associated with this
transparently beautiful work with its poignant melodic line
and literary and musical archaisms suggestive of Spain in the

age of Velazquez. It became immediately successful and was being played in Parisian drawing-rooms long before the official *première* given by Ricardo Viñes at a Société Nationale concert on 5 April 1902. Why it was so popular is easy to understand: it was a lovely piece, anyone could tell that, but headed by a dedication to the Princesse Edmond de Polignac, almost notorious for her musical discrimination, it flaunted an unofficial guarantee of quality. Winnaretta, however flattered, was slightly embarrassed. For the moment it did nothing to make her eager to support Ravel. The works which he subsequently wrote, the *Jeux d'eau*, *Shéhérezade*, the String Quartet and *Ma Mère l'oie*, impressed her much more and by 1905, when he was being excluded from the *Prix de Rome* competition on the grounds that his music was too dangerously innovatory, her esteem increased as he finally emerged as a composer who cherished his ideals more than social approval. She did not voice her thoughts when, soon after Ravel had made an orchestral arrangement of the *Pavane* in 1910, he acknowledged that it was an insubstantial work whose faults had become only too apparent to him with the passage of time. She herself came to this conclusion rather more quickly but afterwards valued Ravel more as a friend with whom in later years she found intellectual communication much easier than when she first knew him as a slightly inscrutable dandy in his mid-twenties. She was always vaguely suspicious of anyone who tried too hard to be ingratiating towards her.

In all her artistic activities Winnaretta had the support of her husband. His warmth of personality could be an asset at times when she was too shy or uncertain of herself. Certainly his approach to Ravel was initially much more relaxed and friendly than hers—but then he had less cause to be afraid of men's ulterior motives. With Fauré too his friendship was of the warmest kind. Prince Edmond regarded him more as a fellow-composer with a background of financial and artistic struggle similar to his own. Long before he met Winnaretta, Polignac had known him and had collaborated with him and the Comte Eugène d'Harcourt in concerts in which each composer conducted his own compositions, played by the orchestra of the Société des Concerts du Conservatoire. His marriage to Winnaretta only strengthened his ties with Fauré.

The prince's marriage also gave him a new lease of creative

life. Even in his declining years he was constantly exploring new ideas and artistic combinations that would blur or break down the frontiers between different branches of the arts. This was the period when his experiments with lantern-slide projections, accompanied by music and recitations, caused a mild stir. With his talent for drawing he also turned his attention to the decorative arts and in 1897 and 1898 exhibited some of his designs at the Salon des Champs-Elysées. Tables, chairs and a library, constructed to his specifications, were considered remarkable: they combined elegance with utility. Perhaps Proust was thinking of this as much as of Prince Edmond's scholarly interests when he used the image: 'freed from the books which encumbered it, the feudal turret had become military once more', when meditating upon the death of Saint-Loup.

Prince Edmond's next preoccupation with composite art-forms was possibly his most unusual, some would have said uncharacteristic. In 1900 Isadora Duncan came to Paris after achieving transitory fame for her dancing in London and one of her first friends there was Madame de Saint-Marceaux's son Jacques Baugnies. Impressed by the almost naïve simplicity of the American girl's dancing, he persuaded his mother to invite her to demonstrate her art at one of her salons. She did and Ravel was there at the piano to play waltzes and preludes by Chopin while Isadora executed choreographic poems to them. The audience was appreciative, particularly Messager, who thought her ravishing. As a result of this the Comtesse Greffulhe invited Isadora to dance at her house. She was fascinated by what she imagined was a renaissance of Greek art, although, according to Isadora, the countess's ideas derived more from Pierre Louÿs's *Chansons de Bilitis*, which had a voluptuous significance entirely lost upon Isadora. But more were inclined to share Madame Greffulhe's impressions and eagerly encouraged her dancing. Madeleine Lemaire invited her to her studio where the music of Gluck's *Orphée* inspired the dance. Jean Lorrain saw her and was impressed by her artistry. The Roumanian-born Anna de Noailles, celebrated as much for her brilliant personality as for her poetry, was beside him and was equally impressed—if for different reasons. Yet, on the whole, Isadora was regarded by high-society as a passing diversion from their more serious social or artistic pursuits.

But Isadora's fortune really began to change when one afternoon she opened the door of her studio in the avenue Le Villiers and found Winnaretta standing there, looking imposing and masterful: her face might have been that of a Roman emperor, she thought, except that an expression of cold aloofness protected the otherwise voluptuous promise of her eyes and features. At first Isadora was disconcerted by the forbidding, metallic ring of her voice but the impression quickly changed as Winnaretta began discussing her art sympathetically and she realized that the hard voice and cold manner concealed a real sensitivity and shyness. The princess explained the purpose of her visit in a forthright way. She had seen Isadora's performance at the Comtesse Greffulhe's and had found it interesting but her husband had been particularly fascinated. He would like to meet her and, if she wished, a concert could be arranged for her at the studio in the rue Cortambert. Isadora was delighted and agreed to dance for the Polignacs. Her mission accomplished, Winnaretta left but not before unobtrusively slipping on to the table an envelope containing two thousand francs to help relieve the Duncan family's very evident poverty.

Next afternoon Isadora went to the avenue Henri-Martin to meet Prince Edmond. A close friendship instantly sprang up between them, a near passion for each other as persons and a mutual respect as artists: he, the delicately built aesthete, looking older than ever but radiating vitality; she, the effervescent girl, still very innocent and unspoiled, eager to put on her tunic and explain the theory of her dance-methods with a practical demonstration. Then he played for her on his beautiful harpsichord, which, she could see, he loved from the way in which he caressed it with his sensitive, tapering fingers. Carried away by their excitement, they planned an artistic collaboration: he was to compose music specially for her and she would choreograph new dances that would recapture the spirit of antiquity. No one knows what the result of the scheme might have been. Isadora's contribution would have been predictable; Edmond's work would have been interesting because he was always at his expressive best when writing music with a human source of inspiration. But his failing health prevented their venture from coming to anything.

More important for Isadora's career, the concert which

Winnaretta arranged in her studio was highly successful. She realized that Isadora had not yet achieved wide acclaim because she had always danced before select audiences at private functions, so she threw open the doors of her studio to the public and so attracted much more attention to her dancing than ever before. After that Winnaretta helped her arrange a series of subscription concerts at the Duncans' own studio. Among the audience of twenty to thirty people, the prince and princess were always to be seen. Edmond was invariably so carried away by the performance that he would wave his velvet cap in the air and shout, *'Vive Isadora!'*

Winnaretta was never very explicit about her views on Isadora's art. Although she probably did appreciate it for its sheer expressive vitality, as her husband did, it was not really serious enough for her and it failed to convey the spirit of classical Greece as she conceived it. Unlike the Comtesse Greffulhe, she could see the discrepancy between her own and Isadora's ideas. Such emotional and intellectual scruples did not occur to her husband, who regarded Isadora more as a charming girl than as a woman. Nonetheless, because Winnaretta was willing to indulge the whims of his old age, she did more than anybody else to launch Isadora on her successful career as a dancer who earned a place for herself in the mythology of the twentieth century.

However, for Winnaretta the Duncan episode was one of the lighter, more innocent events of this *fin de siècle* period. In November 1896 her sister the Duchess Decazes died at the age of twenty-seven. This affected Winnaretta profoundly not only because of their blood ties but also because of its rude lesson in human mortality: Isabelle-Blanche had been her junior by four years. There was another sobering aspect to it: two children had been born of the Decazes marriage, the Marquis (later fourth Duc) Decazes and a six-year-old daughter Marguerite. Winnaretta felt some responsibility at least for the daughter who, she thought, might not gain as much from her father, with his single-minded passion for boxing and yachting, as the son might, nor much useful guidance from governesses. And so the young Marguerite Decazes (better known in later years as the irrepressible Daisy Fellowes) became a frequent visitor, if not permanent resident in the Polignac household. The effect upon her of the consequent intellectual stimulation was remarkable, although later it resulted more noticeably in eccentricity than in anything more positive.

The death of Winnaretta's aunt Jeanne-Marie, Lady Synge, less than a year later in October 1897 was, if anything, an even greater blow: it marked the end of one of the happiest associations of her childhood years.

A more disturbing aspect of the period was the Dreyfus Affair. Especially after 1897, the way in which the controversy split society, split families and groups of friends into warring factions profoundly distressed Winnaretta. Many revelled in the bitter dialectic, which gave plenty of scope for destructive criticism of the social, political and religious establishment; just as many felt obliged to defend and counter-attack on a general front in order to protect particular interests. The princess hated this world of scapegoats in which more vicious crimes against humanity were being committed than in the England of the Wilde Case. She believed in Alfred Dreyfus's innocence but she had the greatest difficulty in steering a middle course amid the storm of vituperation that raged round about her. It was difficult to preserve one's pose as a rationalist in a world of irrationalities. Winnaretta was dining with Jean-Louis Forain on 13 January 1898, the day upon which Zola's '*J'accuse*' appeared in *L'Aurore*. Forain had read and been impressed by the article but it was clear to him, as a thoroughly Gallican catholic and nationalist, that the implications of the case were too serious for church and state to allow him any flexibility of principle. He passed the matter off laughingly: he had no choice about being an anti-Dreyfusard because he had drawn so many caricatures of Jews that it would be easier for him to continue to do so. But Forain's quip, though feeble and cynical, was one of the few light sides of the matter. Winnaretta wondered what was in store for everyone when friends of differing opinions began to refuse to sit at the same dinner table.

Of all those in the Polignac circle Marcel Proust seemed to suffer most from the Dreyfus controversy. Over-conscious of his mother at the best of times, he regarded her Jewish blood as a licence to indulge in displays of hypersensitivity. Winnaretta sympathized with him, but not because, as many imagined, the Singers were Jewish in origin (they had been German Lutherans when history lost them in the mists of time). His distress made her unbend towards him more than ever before and she tried to divert his attention on to other matters. When they went to Versailles in March 1898 to hear the first performance of their friend Reynaldo Hahn's opera *L'Île du rêve*, they were to be seen deep in conversation at the home of Reynaldo's sister Maria de Madrazo (step-mother of the artist Coco de Madrazo). The subject of their conversation was Lucien Daudet and his attempts to try his fledgling wings as a novelist. Proust expressed great confidence in his talent; Winnaretta encouraged him in his preoccupation, which she knew sprang more from his love of Lucien as a man than from his appreciation of him as a writer.

At another crisis-point, while Dreyfus was being re-tried at Rennes in September 1899, Proust escaped from the unpleasant tensions of the capital by staying with his parents at Evian on the Lake of Geneva. However, even there, the strain of having to keep his Dreyfusard opinions from his anti-Dreyfusard father, Dr Adrien Proust, was too much for him. He relieved the tension by escaping to the Princesse de Brancovan's Villa Bassaraba at Amphion, where the atmosphere among the guests was distinctly sympathetic towards Dreyfus. The princess's two striking daughters were there, Anna and Hélène, recently married to Comte Mathieu de Noailles and Prince Alexandre de Caraman-Chimay respectively. The brilliant young writer Abel Hermant had joined the party and Montesquiou's pianist-friend Léon Delafosse, fading in favour as well as looks, had been invited to help with the musical activities. The Prince and Princesse de Polignac provided another two distinctive, if different focal points of interest. Since the prince's health was poor, he kept largely to the châlet which had been assigned to him in the grounds of the villa and it was there that many of the other guests used to come to visit him, often with the single purpose of admiring the strength of his convictions and originality of spirit. As Abel Hermant remarked, his sincerity put the younger ones to shame. Yet, serious though the situation was, it seldom clouded his sparkling sense of humour for very long. At the most solemn moments he would turn to Proust and say: 'Well and what's the old Syndicate doing now?'—as if he really believed anti-Dreyfusard propaganda about the existence of a secret conspiratorial society of Dreyfusards, inspired by Jews, atheists and the like. But when the news that Dreyfus's trial had ended with the absurd verdict of 'guilty of high treason but with extenuating circumstances' reached the Villa Bassaraba on 10 September, there was little call for humour. Anna de Noailles stole the stage by sobbing violently and exclaiming: 'What will other countries think, the whole world? How *could* they do it?' Prince Edmond shook his head, at a loss to understand what had come over the judges at Rennes because he knew that his old bosom-friend Général de Galliffet was a man incapable of dishonesty. Winnaretta was more practical in her approach and, with the Princesse de Brancovan, went out of her way to be charming to Proust. But he was momentarily inconsolable. What made matters worse was that the day before Winnaretta had inadvertently mentioned to the Comtesse d'Haussonville while visiting Coppet (where her husband was working on a biography of his ancestress Madame de Staël) that Proust was staying at Evian. He was terrified of being invited to lunch by this outspoken anti-Dreyfusard, whose views on the Affair, Winnaretta reported, had reached the limit of flexibility when she uttered the extraordinary comment: 'I can quite understand foreigners like you thinking as you do.'

The Prince de Polignac attempted to take Proust's mind off Madame d'Haussonville by saying that the climate of adverse opinion was bound to change sooner or later and the princess tried to divert him by taking him out for a walk. Unfortunately she lost her way, with the result that they had to cover a much greater distance than anticipated. Though in good health and free from any asthmatic congestion, Proust was so exhausted that he could not sleep that night. Next day he was seized by fits of nervous laughter, which in his weak condition he was unable to control. The Princesse de Brancovan's habitual eccentricities did not help matters and the more they provoked him to laughter the more he felt embarrassed. He was inclined to blame Winnaretta for causing his nervous condition in the first place, although he knew that her intentions were good. In fact, here was the fatal flaw that was to mar their friendship: she was too robust physically but genuinely sensitive, while he was too delicate physically and at times so extraordinarily unsubtle and ego-centric that often they found themselves at cross purposes. Proust consoled himself by writing to his mother —Winnaretta was the exact opposite of a mother-figure—and distracted himself by discussing the unreliability of using calligraphy as material evidence, as they had with unfortunate results in the trials of Dreyfus. He gave Madame Proust an example: if she were to turn back to page 2 of his letter, where the name Polignac occurred three times in two adjacent lines, she would see distinct variations in the way in which he had formed his Ps.

But that was just another of the uncertainties of life. Change was in the air but no one could tell what would eventually happen. In a society torn by two warring factions the victory of either might lead to reaction which, one way or the other, might impose a social regimentation inimical to the free expression of intellectual, emotional and creative impulses. The Polignacs as well as the Prousts of the day watched with feelings of apprehension as the 1890s drew to a close.

Chapter 7
The Widow Polignac
(1901–1904)

The beginning of the twentieth century found Edmond de
Polignac in very bad health. In spring 1901 Winnaretta
decided that an early trip to Venice was called for: the warm
Italian weather might do him some good. To keep them company, friends from Paris were invited to stay at the Palazzo
Polignac and among them were Henri de Régnier and his wife,
the daughter of the poet José-Maria de Heredia; Anna de
Noailles, for whom Prince Edmond felt a teasing affection,
arrived, languid as ever but enormously stimulating. Reynaldo
Hahn made up the party as musician-in-chief. In fact, the main
cultural happenings of the stay centred round him and the
concerts which he organized on board the princess's gondolas.
Using her yacht piano, he would accompany himself singing
Venetian songs as they sailed across the lagoon by moonlight.

But Prince Edmond's health did not improve. Nonetheless,
back in Paris he still tried to keep up with the social round. On
19 June 1901 he was well enough to attend a dinner-party
given by Proust in an effort to reconcile differences which the
Dreyfus Affair had caused between friends. The party was a
remarkable success: an anti-semitic Léon Daudet, seated beside
a Jewish banker's daughter, moderated his language for the
evening, happily perhaps, because this was one of the last
occasions on which Edmond de Polignac was seen by his
friends. Soon his illness confined him to bed and he had to
cancel the elaborate travel-arrangements made for that
summer. (He had a habit of noting the numbers of favourite
rooms in hotels so that, when booking on subsequent occasions,
he could specify precisely what he wanted.) Winnaretta promised to inform the manager of the hotel in Amsterdam where
they had intended to stay. But that would not do. Edmond
insisted on writing to explain fully why the cancellation had
to be made, in case the manager should think badly of him. And

he wore himself out writing him a dozen pages. But presently his strength ebbed away until even the sight of anything unfamiliar weakened him. He refused to have the English nurse whom Winnaretta engaged to look after him. Maintaining that all Englishwomen looked alike, at the sight of her uniform and white collar, he exclaimed: 'I won't talk to the Princess of Wales at three o'clock in the morning!' Eventually Winnaretta had to sit with him day and night, reading Mark Twain to him and discussing it late into the night in order to divert his attention from his failing health.

Prince Edmond de Polignac died on 8 August 1901. Parisian society heard the news with sorrow tinged with regret because his qualities, notwithstanding his slight notoriety, had made him universally loved and esteemed. Only the implacable Montesquiou had a bad word to say and he directed that at Winnaretta:

> '*La veuve de Polignac*
> '*Viens de perdre . . . son cornac.*'

He clearly had no appreciation of the success of the marriage if he regarded Edmond as an animal-keeper and her as an animal. Their close friends knew otherwise. The prince's family and kinsmen rallied round Winnaretta and all but thanked her for making his last years so pleasant, to which she replied that, on the contrary, he was the one who had brought so much vitality into their lives.

General public reaction to Edmond's death was muted. Two days previously the Empress Frederick had died, so soon after her mother Queen Victoria, and that had diverted the attention of his British and German acquaintances. Prince Henri d'Orléans, Duc d'Aumale, Louis-Philippe's fifth son, died within twenty-four hours of him and the minds of many French loyalists were distracted by that event. No one was in doubt that a poem appearing in *Le Gaulois* under the title '*Un Beau Prince*' was an elegy for the Orléanist, not the Polignac prince. And during the week all other ears strained for news of Italy's colourful ex-prime minister Francesco Crispi as he too went through his death-throes.

Simplicity was the key-note of Prince Edmond's obsequies. After his death-mask had been made—to be cast in bronze later—and his remains taken to lie in state at the Church of

Notre-Dame-de-Grâce in Passy, a requiem mass took place on Monday 12 August and a host of his friends and admirers came to pay their last respects. His brothers the Princes Ludovic and Camille and the Duc de Polignac, the Duc Decazes and Winnaretta's brothers and step-father Paul Sohège along with an illustrious list of mourners, old friends such as Baron Hottinger and the artist Antonio de La Gandara, and young ones such as Hélène de Caraman-Chimay, who shed copious tears, and Isadora Duncan (also crying bitterly), who found herself at the end of the ceremony bewildered at having to shake hands with the prince's bereaved kinsmen and gazing, transfixed, into the eyes of one of them, Winnaretta's brother Paris Singer. Proust came to the service and revelled in the atmosphere of serenity, the black hangings with bands of ermine, the princely coronet picked out in red over the initial 'P' with the exquisitely feudal motto *'Sacer Custos Pacis'* and the beautiful Gregorian plain-chant, sung by the choir of Saint-Gervais. After the mourners had gone, the coffin was placed in the vaults of the church and from there transported to England. On the afternoon of Sunday 18 August a small family group gathered round the Singer vault in Torquay cemetery where, as he wished, the prince's body was laid to rest, awaiting the day when death would bring him and his wife together again.

On her return to Paris one of the first persons who came to see Winnaretta was Marcel Proust. On 31 August he interrupted his afternoon rest to murmur gentle words of consolation to the widow. She told him about Prince Edmond's last days and how she had sat up with him at night. Proust, of course, related this to his own experience and remembered how his mother used to watch over him when ill as a child. The conversation switched to American literature, the last distraction of the dying prince. Proust confessed his own love of the American novel and the discovery of this mutual interest forged a new bond of friendship between them. But it did not last long because the two things brought them closer while in mourning, their devotion to Prince Edmond and this literary interest, were what soon drove them apart.

On 6 September 1903 Proust, using his Shakespearean nom de plume 'Horatio', published in *Le Figaro* his article entitled *'Le Salon de la Princesse Edmond de Polignac: musique d'aujourd'hui; échos d'autrefois'*. The very Proustian sub-title gave a forewarning that although the article aimed at flattering the princess, the dead prince was the focal point of the piece. Proust intended it as a serious appreciation of a man whom he had liked and admired but it emerged as a sickly piece of snobbery of the worst sort. He elaborately listed the family connections of the Polignacs: there were the La Rochefoucaulds, the Luynes, the Mailly-Nesles, the Noailles, the Olliamsons, the Lignes and the Croÿs; and their relationships were divertingly complicated. Was not Winnaretta the aunt of the Duchesse de Luynes, *née* La Rochefoucauld, and the great-aunt of the Duchesse de Luynes, *née* d'Uzès, and of the Duchesse de Gramont? But she was not amused. At the age of thirty-eight she did not like being portrayed as the great-aunt of fully-fledged duchesses. But what really incensed her was his reference to the fact that the prince had hated draughts while she, by contrast, liked plenty of fresh air blowing through the house. That was the only domestic problem they ever had to cope with, said Proust. But he made the mistake of expressing it in these terms: '. . . *elle avait toujours trop chaud, et lui était extrêmement frileux.*' However correct his style, he might just as well have said that she was always too hot—because that is precisely how his readers interpreted the phrase. Winnaretta's reputation as a widow with distinctive interests made comments like that very unwelcome. And a certain coolness subsequently affected her feelings for Proust.

However, dazzled though he continued to be by her connections, riches and intelligence, by this time Proust himself was nursing a grievance against Winnaretta. While planning the *Salon* article, he had met her at the home of Prince Alexandre de Caraman-Chimay and across the dinner table she had casually mentioned that she had made a French translation of Henry David Thoreau's masterpiece *Walden*. She assumed that Proust would have shown some enthusiasm. Instead, he was hard put to it to conceal his dismay because just then he and his friend Prince Antoine Bibesco had been considering undertaking the same task. Why Proust, indeed, why the Princesse de Polignac, should have been so interested in translating a work in praise of a society—or rather a lack of society—that was the very antithesis of the world in which they lived is something of a mystery. Perhaps Thoreau's philosophy of self-sufficiency and respect for the dignity of the individual had a romantic appeal for those who went against the grain of organized society in a

significant area of their lives. For them there was a certain ring
of truth in his words: 'The greater part of what my neighbours
call good I believe in my soul to be bad.' Unbelievably rich,
Winnaretta knew better than Thoreau that, 'if there were
bestowed on us the wealth of Croesus, our aims must still be the
same, and our means essentially the same. . . Money is not
required to buy one necessary of the soul.'

Winnaretta's translation of *Walden* had been made while she
idled away the hours during a visit to the house of her brother-
in-law, Ludovic de Polignac, at Bouzareah in Algeria. And
when she returned to Paris and showed it to Prince Constantin
de Brancovan, he immediately asked to publish it in his new
magazine *La Renaissance latine*. The first instalments, appearing
in December 1903 and January 1904, met with a lively interest.
Previously the French public had only been able to read
excerpts of *Walden* that had been published in 1894 in the
Magazine international by the socialist writer Léon Bazalgette.
Though the Princesse de Polignac was considered an unusual
successor, it was her work on Thoreau rather than Bazalgette's
that fired the imagination of French left-wing intellectuals—
and caused a shiver of excitement to run through high society.
She successfully stimulated an interest in Thoreau's philosophy
among French-speaking writers, particularly C. F. Ramuz,
Charles Vildrac, Henri Pourrat, Jean Giono and André Gide.

Only Proust, though just as interested in Thoreau, greeted
Winnaretta's translation with theatrical howls of annoyance.
Putting down the January 1904 edition of *La Renaissance latine*,
he wrote to Anna de Noailles—the editor's sister—and called
the journal 'the perfidious *Inconstance latine* . . . the ungrateful
Jactance latine . . . the shocking *Inconvenience latine* . . .' but neither
disappointment nor displeasure could cloud his delight in
Walden. His own success as the translator of Ruskin's *La Bible
d'Amiens* gave him no reason to envy Winnaretta for the mark
made by her work on Thoreau.

In reality Proust's mock cries of pain were probably only his
way of counteracting Winnaretta's forthright disapproval of his
Salon article. Whatever the reasons the result was plain enough:
Proust and the princess were very guarded in their approach
to one another after that. Basically she mistrusted him, although
the excuse she usually gave for her antipathy was that he was
an incorrigible emotional hypochondriac. He was always pre-

occupied with some unrequited love and secretly enjoying his misery. It became tiresome after a while. Nonetheless, she admired him as a creative artist, her admiration growing considerably once *À la Recherche* began to appear. She also confessed to being grateful to Proust for suggesting that she should read Baudelaire's exquisite *Poèmes en prose* and Gobineau's *Les Pléiades*. This was possibly a strange work for him to admire but about 1904 he was showing some interest in Gobineau's ideas on the nature and characteristics of races. Arguably the *Essai sur l'inegalité des races humaines* stimulated and matured Proust's thoughts on class and human relationships in general. But his mind also fixed on something specific. Had Edmond de Polignac ever known Gobineau and, if so, could his influence be detected in his ideas? Why Proust should have posed such a question is difficult to understand: except for his brief period of political activity, Polignac had been rather a-political and remarkably liberal in his views; he was as doubtful about Gobineau's concept of integral nationalism as Proust was himself. Yet, Proust must have asked Winnaretta about the matter and at the same time probably discussed *Les Pléiades* with her.

But during these early years of widowhood she was not eager to sit around with Proustian gossips, reminiscing about the only man for whom she ever felt anything. The end of a marriage which had been so unexpectedly idyllic had left her disoriented. For some time she travelled, spending longer periods away from Paris than usual. England, Scotland, the Netherlands, the German states, Algeria and Italy provided healing distractions. The absorbing business of being a citizen of the world, swimming against strong currents of nationalism, could be exhilarating; it provided a sense of purpose, the preservation of civilization as a means of communication between peoples as well as an end in itself. National consciousness was a barrier to intellectual development. In Paris Winnaretta's salon was regarded by the *beau monde* as extraordinary because, along with a small number of fellow hostesses, such as Anna de Noailles, the Duchesse de Clermont-Tonnerre, the Duchesse Gabriel de La Rochefoucauld, the Princesse Murat and the Comtesse Greffulhe, she welcomed foreigners as well as Frenchmen to her *fêtes de l'esprit*. When abroad, she mixed in a society that was international to the point of confusion. Jacques-Émile Blanche, sitting in a London concert-hall, waiting to hear

a recital of music by Fauré and Reynaldo Hahn, espied
Winnaretta. But his attention was soon distracted by the arrival
of the Duke and Duchess of Connaught and Princess Alice,
Donna Vittoria Colonna and the Marquès de Soveral, the Graf
Mensdorf, the Austrian ambassador, and the Duchesses of
Portland, Sutherland and Rutland with the beautiful Lady
Helen Vincent—'Eternal Spring'—, Rodin, Padereweski,
Edmond Rostand, Hélène de Caraman-Chimay and her
mother the Princesse de Brancovan; Sarah Bernhardt made a
grand entrance. Was one in London or Paris? What did it
matter? The bond of friendship ran horizontally on social,
intellectual and artistic plains and took little note of nationalism
and xenophobia. Even at the domestic level the bonds still held:
the Duchess of Rutland decided to sell a series of tapestries on
the subject of Don Quixote so that she could install central
heating in her castle. George Blumenthal of New York was the
man to buy them but he would have to be persuaded. She
consulted Jacques-Emile Blanche. Could the Princesse de
Polignac use her influence with Blumenthal or the Comtesse de
Béarn; or should one rely on the good will of Paul Helleu?

During the Edwardian era Winnaretta spent a lot of time in
England. She enjoyed visiting scenes of her youth in Devon and
found the distractions of London life stimulating. Endless
concerts during the season and an active cultural life at all
times were welcome preoccupations. As a world art market it
was invaluable. For instance, only in London could she get an
opportunity to fulfil an ambition to acquire a painting by her
lately dead friend Whistler. In June 1905 she snapped up his
Three Figures: Pink and Grey (1867–8) as soon as it came on the
market and she carried off this delicate composition of languid
female figures to her Paris home. Eventually the attraction of
England proved so great that she decided to acquire a *pied à
terre* in London. In 1908 she took a fancy to a house in the
King's Road in Chelsea. The owner Sir Louis Malet agreed to
sell it and for the time being Winnaretta managed to avoid the
restricting alternative of having to stay with friends or in hotels.
On a comfortably small scale her house became another focal
point in London's high-society—until the forces of the law
intervened.

Venice, however, always remained Winnaretta's favourite
city outside Paris. Tranquil, the only town where one could

open a window without having to raise one's voice, and, divorced from the world, it still managed to maintain its position as a cross-roads of international society. She loved the place and no one took her seriously when, finding a scorpion in her bathroom one morning, she announced that she would sell the *palazzo* and retire to Scotland. Venice had too many happy memories of Edmond de Polignac to be abandoned so easily. In fact, shortly after his death she used Venice as the setting for a memorial tribute to him. She persuaded the Duca della Grazia to allow her to have music played in the courtyard of his home, the Palazzo Vendramin, where Wagner had died. The Banda Municipale played Siegfried's Funeral March from *Götter-dämmerung*. The houses and palaces nearby had their balconies decked with the colourful hangings reserved for festivals and in the brilliant spring sunlight people crowded the windows to hear the music and watch the fleet of patrician gondolas bear the guests to the palace. Afterwards the duke gave a reception in his *sala grande*. Winnaretta took the opportunity to question him about Liszt and Wagner, his tenants in years past. Did he see much of them? Yes, they sometimes came for coffee after dinner and talked about music or played the piano. Winnaretta enthused. How wonderful to have known such great men! The duke mused lightly: 'Yes, they were certainly two eccentrics.'

A greater degree of sophistication characterized the Venetian society ordinarily frequented by the princess. She was a regular visitor at the Comtesse de La Baume's house, the Casa Dario, where, surrounded by a collection of fine pictures, rare books and priceless musical instruments, she entertained guests specially chosen for their talent and discrimination. That poetic couple, the Régniers, were flanked by the collector Henri Gonse. Anna de Noailles was there, inseparable from her sister Hélène de Caraman-Chimay. Proust occasionally appeared with his friend Léon Daudet, whom Winnaretta admired for his brilliance and style. Together they would dine on the roof-terrace of the house and then listen to a string quartet playing Mozart. Winnaretta knew and socialized with almost all the important visitors to Venice: Lady Layard and the Countess of Radnor, the Curtises and the lovely Miss Muriel Wilson, all welcomed her to their houses in the city. She was to be seen in the company of Horatio Brown and the dress-designer Fortuny; and she visited Sickert in his studio in the Calle dei Frati in

those early years of the century while he was making his studies
of the Ghetto Nuovo and the San Trovaso area and painting
the famous portrait of Israel Zangwill, also an occasional visitor
to Venice.

The guests entertained by Winnaretta at the Palazzo
Polignac were also impressive: at her dinner table the proud
Contessa Morosini would sit, chatting familiarly with the
Grand-Duke Paul of Russia and his morganatic wife the
Comtesse de Hohenfelsen. Lady Helen Vincent, looking like 'a
Reynolds recreated as a Whistler', and members of the illustrious Guerne, Borghese, Meyer and Ségur families brought
additional lustre to such occasions. Yet, for all that and the
grand surroundings, the atmosphere was relaxed and diverting,
as when the art critic Claude Phillips arrived, tottering in too
small shoes, polished and scented like an old tart, the Ségurs,
taking him for the actor Cooper, went into momentary ecstacies;
and after dinner the company sat around with Reynaldo Hahn,
recalling Italian operas they knew and singing and playing all
the rôles, amazing each other with their memories. Or, on
other occasions, the virtuoso pianist Blanche Selva, impressively
grand but incongruously dressed as a shepherdess, might volun-
teer to play Bach's *Chromatic Fantasy*. How extraordinarily
beautiful, thought Reynaldo, so hauntingly oriental, despite its
composer. But the fugue left him cold. No matter what La
Selva did to dramatize it, no matter how much the hostess
revelled in it, Reynaldo could not forget his French veneer long
enough to enjoy it. In fact, his seriousness, for all his social
sparkle and panache, amused Winnaretta. One day she came
upon him overflowing with indignation about a dilettante
acquaintance who had claimed that in Venice the disparity and
unevenness of the architecture produced a bad effect. 'He is no
artist!' exclaimed Reynaldo. 'No,' replied the princess with
studied gravity, 'he is a thinker.'

But delightful though the peace of Venice was in those pre-
war days before the noise of tourist parties and motor-boats
shattered it, Paris was never far from Winnaretta's thoughts.
There was always something to bring her back there. On 30
April 1902 she returned in time to attend the first performance
of Debussy's *Pelléas et Mélisande*. But to what avail? Having an
instinctive feeling for the depth of inspiration in Debussy's
music, she was horrified by the reception the opera received.

Even the unforgettable performance of Mary Garden and Jean Périer did not soften the critics' hearts nor inhibit the scornful laughter of the general public. Why should this work, so transparently sincere, dignified and beautiful, earn the derision of even the most avant-garde? And what made Gabriel Fauré exclaim to her after the performance: 'If that is music, I don't know what music is.' She was at a loss for an explanation. Were there personal reasons for Fauré's attitude? Possibly his own ideas about Maeterlinck's drama were too well-formed to adapt to another musical interpretation of it. Certainly, it was Debussy's treatment of the text as much as his music that the audience found so uproariously funny in places. In reality, though he had written a masterpiece which would weather the storms of public disapproval and passing time, in 1902 the subject matter was about seven years out of date. French taste had changed. The 'crash' of Decadence in the mid-1890s and mounting nationalism very nearly caused *Pelléas* to be still-born.

No one was more aware of the stigma that attached to it than Winnaretta. Though the timing was possibly coincidental, only nine days after the première of *Pelléas*, her mother Madame Paul Sohège had an extraordinary will drawn up. After making a few bequests to friends and protégés and setting aside some small gifts for members of her family, she left the residue of her estate to her husband. That proved to be problematic enough in itself when she died almost exactly two years later on 12 May 1904, since she had enjoyed much of her money only for the duration of her lifetime, and so her children were left with the problem of thrashing out the question of giving Paul Sohège a respectable settlement without letting him have any Singer capital. Years of litigation under the expert guidance of Raymond Poincaré eventually brought the matter to a successful conclusion. But the list of gifts in the will was most revealing. All Madame Sohège's surviving children and their respective spouses were left a piece of jewellery as a keepsake—all except Winnaretta. The omission was very pointed. Though remarkably like her mother in taste, she had always regarded her as an egocentric woman whose beauty she could not hope to match and whose love she had long since given up trying to gain. On the other hand, during the 1890s, Madame Sohège had become increasingly estranged from her daughter because of her uncompromisingly up-to-date ideas and her only barely veiled

Lesbianism. Winnaretta's reputation and how this reflected upon the family was her only concern; in turn, her daughter spurned her as a hypocritical and vain woman. Her death made an indelible impression upon her sons: for years afterwards Paris Singer claimed to be haunted by the sight of her dead face in her coffin. Always the question remained: what is the point of life if it only ends in death? Winnaretta was haunted by her mother in a different way. Madame Sohège specifically directed that she should be buried in the cemetery of Passy in a plot scarcely more than a hundred yards from Winnaretta's house in the avenue Henri-Martin and had set up in her tomb a bust made of herself in her mid-thirties when she was still undeniably beautiful and completely feminine. And it was there that Paul Sohège, the indulgence of her old age, whom Winnaretta regarded as little more than a glorified gigolo, was also buried some two decades later. Her mother's choice of a last resting place and the way in which, even in death, she flaunted her marriage to a handsome youth amounted to a silent reproach for Winnaretta and much of what she stood for.

Chapter 8
Ioanian Twilight and Russian Dawn

(1904–1909)

In the early 1900s nothing encouraged an overt resurgence of homosexual assertiveness in the world of the arts or in high society. Quite the contrary. The example of what could happen to the likes of Oscar Wilde was hammered home in the autumn of 1902 when the arms-king Friedrich Krupp died of apoplexy, which everyone knew was suicide precipitated by fear of exposure. In the following July Paris was rocked by the arrest of Baron Jacques d'Adelsward-Fersen for taking too much interest in schoolboys from the Lycée Condorcet. Few approved of his paedophilia but the French public felt no need to discriminate between the mature and the immature in its reaction to the case. There was nothing unequivocal about the Eulenburg Affair, which broke like a storm a few years later in 1907. The Kaiser's favourite Fürst Phillipp zu Eulenburg and his friend General von Moltke survived criminal prosecution for homosexual activities (though theirs was as much an indictment of their injudicious choice of sexual partners as anything else) but both their political careers were ruined and throughout Europe the homosexual fraternity received a shock to its system. The sophisticated might nickname the prince 'Eulenbougre' and be amused by a recurring piece of graffiti in Parisian *pissotières*: '*Parlez-vous allemand?*'—there was something almost patriotic in it—but the more sensitive viewed the case with morbid forebodings.

However, unlike their male counterparts, Lesbians became increasingly uninhibited, almost aggressive both in private and in public. Lesbianism became almost fashionable among society ladies, married and single alike. The Baronne Deslandes gave up trying to be a Pre-Raphaelite beauty and openly lived with her friend the Comtesse d'Orsay. Colette, abandoning her

unscrupulous husband Willy, took to the music-hall stage and
surprised everyone by appearing there with her bosom-friend
'Missie', the Marquise de Belbeuf. The marquis assumed the
air of an outraged husband; the audience was slightly taken
aback when the two women kissed too lingeringly in the middle
of one number. Colette did not worry and openly went around
wearing bracelets inscribed 'I belong to Missie'. The affaire of
Claudine and Rezi in *Claudine en ménage* was nothing compared
with her own activities; in turn they paled beside the high
style of more uncompromising Lesbians.

Two young American poetesses, Natalie Clifford Barney and
her friend Renée Vivien settled in Paris in the 1900s, after
unsuccessfully trying to found a colony of poetesses at Mytilene
in honour of Sappho. Paris provided a more fertile ground for
their activities. Having produced volumes of unequivocally
Sapphic verse, so Baudelairean as to be out-of-date, Renée
Vivien died in 1909 after a brief life of extreme exoticism,
hastened to her grave by paranoia, anorexia nervosa and too
much alcohol. Natalie Barney survived her by more than sixty
years, having set up her *'temple de l'amitié'* in 20 rue Jacob, a
more accessible centre for Amazon activities than Lesbos, for
all its sentimental associations. She and her friends lived in a
violet-tinted world in which light and perspective were happily
distorted. Anna de Noailles and her sister Hélène de Caraman-
Chimay are said to have explored the Lesbian twilight-zone
when the dominating and demanding English writer Vernon
Lee swept into their lives and offered her services as a guide.
But that was a brief episode and Vernon Lee soon became
infatuated with another *femme de lettres*, Madame Bulteau,
familiarly known as Toche. But that friendship did not survive
long after Vernon made the mistake of preventing Toche from
visiting her separated husband while ill. Monsieur Bulteau died
and Toche, for all her vagaries, was heart-broken, so Miss Lee
received her marching orders. Later in the decade Gertrude
Stein arrived in Paris, with the devoted Alice B. Toklas in tow.
La Stein soon settled down in her ménage and, like a queen-bee,
attracted round her swarms of creative artists. The Princesse
Violette Murat, the Duchesse de Clermont-Tonnerre, née
Elisabeth de Gramont, and Princesse Catherine Poniatowska
pursued their girl-friends with as much discreet flair as their
princely positions allowed; or were in turn pursued. And less

exalted, despite their names, the great courtesans Liane de Pougy, Emilienne d'Alençon and Liane de Lancy were not averse to a little Lesbianism on their days off.

Throughout the 1900s possibly the most extraordinary figure in this world was the Baronne van Zuylen. As enormously rich as she was enormously fat, if she was not cruising the Mediterranean in her yacht, she was in Paris, marrying off her girlfriend Alexandra Ricoy Antokolsky to the cousin of the Duca di Sforza-Cesarini and setting her up in a house in the avenue Henri-Martin; or she was vying with Violette Murat for the wilting favours of Renée Vivien. But the baroness usually went in for more robust activities. Mademoiselle de Bellune (who had abruptly turned into a Portuguese viscountess overnight after sleeping with Madame de Sarmento, whose influence at the court in Lisbon was equal to none) reported to Colette how Madame van Zuylen had appeared in her box at a gala performance in Nice, wearing a white tie and tails and a moustache. Alexandra (who by then had usurped the title of Duchessa di Sforza-Cesarini) was at her side also in tails. The idly curious who had insisted on intruding into the box were sent packing by the baroness with mouthfuls of unfeminine abuse. It was with this woman that the Princesse de Polignac was said to have 'shared the rôle of High Priestess of Lesbos' in Paris.

In many ways the juxtaposition of their names was meaningless. There was none of the outrageous flamboyance in Winnaretta's manner that was apparent in almost all the other leading Lesbians of the time. She was sensitive to public opinion; she was even more careful not to cause her family any open scandal, even after her mother's death. Indeed, her very discretion gave her the air of someone possessed of almost sinister powers. Her influence was felt, but its workings were unseen. She continued to regard her private life as her own business and, though curious, few openly disputed this right. Only Montesquiou, on one occasion, overstepped the bounds of convention. Winnaretta and he, finding themselves face to face at a reception, carefully ignored each other. But he noticed, as she was being introduced to Natalie Barney, how she gave no sign of having met her already, as she had, and he chose that precise moment to tell Madame Maurice Barrès in a stage whisper: 'Lord Alfred Douglas wants to marry her but she prefers Liane de Pougy.' Montesquiou knew that his comment, uttered as their hands touched, would embarrass the princess much more than a young Amazon like Miss Barney.

Almost all other reference to Winnaretta's propensities were made in a more oblique fashion, partly because she was unfathomable, mainly because of her grim discretion. Many suspected, some knew, that Winnaretta though painfully shy with human beings and terrified of animals, hovered on the sado-masochistic fringes of the Lesbian world. André Germain approached the question guardedly. Since she took care to dress correctly on every occasion, he asked, why did she dress up in riding-boots and impeccable hunting costume? In his book *Les Juifs*, where fact mingles promiscuously with fiction, Roger Peyrefitte made what appears to be a reference to this aspect of her life: the (fictional) Baronne de Goldschild 'one day . . . arrived unexpectedly at the house of the Princess de . . . (I forget her name), and through a half-open door saw her whipping one of her girl-friends with all her might, the friend bent over an armchair with her skirts hoisted up.' Though rather sensationalist, the allusion is quite revealing.

However, looked at too objectively, the dramatic character of Winnaretta's love-life can obscure its gentler side. Emotionally disoriented after Prince Edmond's death, she became passionately attached to a young lady as aristocratic as she was ravishingly beautiful. She had an eye-catching style: she would appear in public with postillion's bells sewn on her robe. But for all her panache, she was not happy. She had fallen in love and separated from her husband, at which point she had become involved with Winnaretta. The complications were too much for the young woman, and so she committed suicide. The princess was so stunned that she fled from Paris to the Gironde where she hid herself in a kinsman's *château*. In deep despair, transfixed by the quick transition from love to death, she tried to take her own life but survived to haunt the family chapel, where slowly she regained her composure. Her friends were amazed at her uncharacteristic loss of self-control and, when she eventually returned to Paris, they treated her with a much greater degree of sympathy than before.

It was unfortunate that just about this time Ethel Smyth, meteor-like, collided with Winnaretta's world. In 1903 she arrived in Paris and at once insinuated herself into the society of female sophisticates. Anna de Noailles and her sister became her friends. Madame Bulteau was much taken by her. Winnaretta was very impressed by her talents and more so by her determination to succeed. Ethel Smyth was less restrained: she fell violently in love with her at first sight. Mesmerized by her, she went around calling her adorable and enormously gifted. She was enchanting, well-read and intelligent; she was delightful to talk to and riveting when she played. Ethel's love knew no bounds. In fact, it was so impossibly possessive and uncontrollable that Winnaretta soon grew irked by it and did her best to cool the English woman's ardour. At the best of times Ethel Smyth would not have qualified as her ideal lover: Winnaretta was most attracted by young, beautiful and submissive women; Ethel, seven years her senior and domineering to a degree, caught her off guard. Although she knew the princess's tastes well enough Ethel took the cooling of her sexual response very badly and she went through the routine of trying to upset her with abuse: she was cruel and hard-hearted; she was ill-educated and unreliable, the sort of person who was always fighting the impulse to hit out at anyone who brushed against her in the street. She was unworthy of love because she was incapable of loving. Ethel's was the fury of a woman scorned. She went further and tried to set Winnaretta's friends Anna de Noailles and Hélène de Caraman-Chimay against her. But they knew her well enough to realize that she was not entirely to blame for the trouble. In time Ethel Smyth calmed down and sensibly transformed her insane love into a warm friendship that lasted for another forty years. Her respect for, if not her blind adoration of, Winnaretta returned: Ethel classed her among rare acquaintances, such as Nikisch and Bruno Walter, who were 'capable of estimating the point and value of music regardless of how the faculty judges it'.

Ethel Smyth had to acknowledge that Winnaretta was a discerning music-lover if only because she took a lot of interest in her own music. She was constantly recommending it to conductors and opera-house managers; and she frequently had to mollify people whom Ethel had offended. The princess once met the Graf Seebach, intendant of the Dresden Opera, and, remembering that Ethel had spent long periods in Saxony, asked him if he knew her. Know her? She had harried him so much, insisting that he should produce her opera *Der Wald*, that, he maintained, if he were ever to espy her in the street, he ɔuld leap into the nearest cab, drive to the station and take the next train out of town. Winnaretta was amused and possibly appreciated his feelings, although she was prepared to be more amenable than Seebach. She tried to persuade French theatre-managers to produce her opera *The Wreckers* but met with little success. She then suggested that the Théâtre de la Monnaie in Brussels might be enterprising enough to take it. She knew members of the theatre board and introduced them to Ethel. An invitation to come and discuss the matter sent La Smyth scurrying to Brussels, score in hand. The board was over-whelmed by her solo rendition, reducing the orchestral score at the piano and singing all the vocal parts, so overwhelmed that they apologized for not having the money to give *The Wreckers* the production worthy of it. Ethel Smyth was dis-appointed but secretly impressed by their backhanded compli-ment.

For her own part, despite some reservations about her friend's music, Winnaretta was happy enough to have it played in her salon. If the music was slightly derivative, Ethel's personality as a performer made a great impression. Anna de Noailles, for one, moved by the force with which she sang, exclaimed that she was like the tiger in the zoo at Amsterdam.

But that was not the only dramatic display to be seen in Winnaretta's salon about this time. Early in the decade the brothers Julien and Fernand Osché caused a great sensation by producing some ballets and *tableaux vivants* inspired by the drawings of Beardsley. Winnaretta was quick to take up the idea while still new and mounted similar productions in her grand salon. But the grandiose room altogether lacked the intimacy of the Oschés' house in Neuilly and, without any of the neces-sary fairy-tale illusion, the enterprise was not a success. It was almost sad and dismal. 'It's the funeral for Cythera,' muttered Madame Henri de Régnier. Before the *tableau vivant* had its reputation sullied by the scandalous news of Jacques d'Adelsward-Fersen's essays in the form broke in July 1903, Winnaretta had safely abandoned it and gone back to arranging less effete happenings in her salon.

She was still among a tiny minority of music-lovers who seized the earliest possible opportunity to have the latest compositions of Fauré and Debussy played in her house. After giving a recital in 1902 a very young Marguerite Long was

asked by her aristocratic host if she would play a piece by
Fauré. Completely unfamiliar with it, she had to refuse. She
knew of no pianist whose repertoire included pieces by Fauré:
she had heard that only his songs were ever performed at
recherché salons such as those of the Marquis de Saint-Paul,
Madeleine Lemaire and the Princesse Edmond de Polignac.
Debussy's small scale works fared even worse and would
have been practically ignored but for these few discerning
patrons.

During the 1900s Reynaldo Hahn was another friend of
Winnaretta's whose music she helped to introduce to the public.
Reynaldo was certainly no avant-garde composer but in his
youthful years he caught the public imagination with his very
palatable songs and orchestral pieces. His settings of poems by
Verlaine and Robert Louis Stevenson, his *Études latines* and *Le
Ruban dénoué* had a delightful quality. They were all performed
at Winnaretta's house, he himself frequently taking the joint
rôle of singer and pianist. He did not neglect other composers'
works. Winnaretta was particularly moved whenever he sang
Bizet's *Adieux de l'hôtesse arabe* and Gounod's setting of Byron's
tender love-poem *The Maid of Athens*. But she experienced a
different kind of pleasure when on 11 April 1907 Reynaldo sat
down at the piano in her salon and directed the first performance of his orchestral suite *Le Bal chez Béatrice d'Este*. The piece,
which proved to be Reynaldo's most durable composition, was
enthusiastically received. Winnaretta was impressed: the
implications of the juxtaposition of her name and that of Béatrice
d'Este, one of the greatest Renaissance patronesses, could not
have failed to cross her mind. Marcel Proust made the performance the occasion of his return to a society from which he
had disappeared almost two years before. And, as a result, he
was all the more impressionable. He was fixated by Reynaldo's
playing. At times it was so forceful that it threatened to upset
the candlesticks on the piano and set fire to the paper roses on
the dais. A moment later Reynaldo changed into the conductor
and Proust noted how his hand would flash a signal to the
furthest corner of the orchestra and reactivate a dozing triangle.
But, sitting in this carnival atmosphere, a morose Proust was
plagued by one morbid thought: how all his acquaintances
had aged since he had last seen them! Only he could have
considered time past time lost and he tried to preserve time by

letting details of that première at Winnaretta's re-emerge at Madame de Saint-Euverte's salon in *Du Côté de chez Swann*.

Another musical première of sorts took place in the princess's salon some months later. On 2 January 1908 her friend Blanche Selva played the first three books of Isaac Albéniz's *Iberia* to an audience of distinguished musicians and writers, eager to hear the work because, although the first two books had already been published, this was the first occasion upon which the third book *Eritaña* had been performed. Everyone was very impressed. Winnaretta considered herself honoured by Albéniz's presence at her soirée and undoubtedly their relationship would have developed productively in time had he not died soon afterwards: Albéniz's nose for money was almost as acute as Winnaretta's was for musical genius. Time would prove that the presence in the audience of a new arrival in Paris, an over-awed Manuel de Falla, was more significant. His friendship with Winnaretta would mature into something very fruitful in years to come. But for the moment the invitation to her house afforded the young Castilian his first real taste of artistic faction-fighting that raged in Paris in those post-*Pelléas* days. Entirely unbelligerent himself, nonetheless, he met and became a firm friend of some of the prominent protagonists, such as the composers Florent Schmitt, Déodat de Séverac and Maurice Ravel, the pianist Ricardo Viñes and the poet Léon-Paul Fargue.

Another new arrival on the Parisian social scene of the late 1900s was the young but immensely precocious Jean Cocteau. Almost automatically he gravitated towards Winnaretta's circle, more because of its ambience and *avant-gardisme* than because of his interest in music. He found plenty there to claim his attention. Anna de Noailles fascinated him, almost frightened him because, as he soon realized, her facility with words was even greater than his own. One evening at the end of a concert in Winnaretta's salon, the guests still standing around or seated amid a disorder of orchestral desks and chairs, Cocteau noticed Anna de Noailles surrounded by a group of women. He could only just see that she was going through some bizarre bird-like routine of clearing and exercising her throat. The croaks, coughs and bellows over, she was ready to begin and, shedding Turkish scarfs and strings of beads, she loosed a flood of words, which flowed on and on effortlessly. The audience, clustered round, the more sedate in arm-chairs, the younger ones on the floor at her feet, were spellbound by her virtuosity. Liveried servants crouched behind half-open doors, trying to catch the pearly words that the countess scattered around. Cocteau was carried away, imagining that her voice penetrated the neighbouring houses and stopped men in their tracks or gilded their slumbers. Out in the garden her words whispered from tree to plant and vaporized in the direction of the stars, enchanting them with their beauty. But he returned from this Orphean reverie to note how Winnaretta and Hélène de Caraman-Chimay stood on either side of Anna, like 'ring-attendants in a dream boxing match'.

Yet, there were occasions when Cocteau was glad of Winnaretta as a ring-attendant, particularly when he found himself the worse for wear in a verbal tussle with Anna. In her house at 94 avenue Henri-Martin the countess would surround herself with friends and followers for her select *festins de l'esprit*. In her flouncy house-coat of beige silk, lounging in a Louis-Quinze arm-chair, she would hold court, like a Boucher sultana, communicating to rather than listening to the intellectuals around her: Fernand Gregh, Léon Daudet, Maurice Barrès, Madame Bulteau and Madame de Pierrebourg; her husband the democratic-minded Comte Mathieu with Léon de Montesquiou from *L'Action française*; and Cocteau with Winnaretta. Anna discusses the existence of God: Indisputable! The existence of His temples is proof enough! Cocteau accuses her of being impenetrable like a bust with a marble-like finality, but also lacking legs for running anywhere. The point hits the mark. Anna lashes out at Cocteau with her tongue. He abandons words and flees to take refuge with the poetess's baby son Anne-Jules. Winnaretta is given the task of rescuing and consoling the foolhardy young man.

But, more often, Anna de Noailles was the one who needed consolation. When unwell, highly strung and feverish, she would only allow her friend Madame Argyropoulo near her; she could endure no one but her sitting holding hands and watching over her. But when well in body, the countess knew no greater comfort than the music with which Winnaretta soothed her agitated spirit. Lullabied by the strains of Beethoven or Chopin, Anna would return to her house and work with renewed vigour. Volumes of sparkling poetry, such

as *Le Visage émerveillé* and *Evanouissements*, poured from her
pen.

As the decade progressed a new element of inspiration
entered Winnaretta's life at a time when her spirits were
flagging. Her friend the Grand-Duke Paul of Russia, the Tsar's
great-uncle, frequently invited her to dine with him at his house
in Boulogne-sur-Seine. The company was always delightful: his
morganatic wife, for whose sake he lived in voluntary exile, was
a charming hostess; her cuisine was famous in Paris; and their
musical entertainments were always very good, if never too
daring. Jean de Reszke and Reynaldo Hahn were often brought
along to sing there or a quartet came to play after dinner. One
day in 1906 Winnaretta encountered among the guests one of
the grand-duke's fellow countrymen, a tall impressive aristocrat
with a chinchilla-like white forelock in the midst of his black
hair. It was Serge de Diaghilev, who at the age of thirty-four
already had an international reputation as an impressario and
connoisseur in the world of music, art and the ballet. At this
time he had just startled Paris with his exhibition of Russian art.
Once introduced, Diaghilev and Winnaretta frequently met
each other during that season and, after a momentary hesita-
tion, they became close friends as they recognized that they
might pursue certain common interests without there being any
danger of sexual antagonism. Diaghilev was to provide her
with a unique but divers outlet for her creative urge and she
was to help him to realize many of his enterprises in the next
two decades. Even in 1906 Winnaretta thought that Diaghilev's
genius was self-evident, although at the time neither she nor
anyone else had any idea how profoundly it would affect almost
every sphere of the arts in the years to come.

In 1907 Diaghilev began to stimulate popular interest in
Russian music by mounting a season of concerts in Paris. In
co-operation with his former teacher Rimsky-Korsakov, he
brought such artists as Chaliapin, Scriabin and Rachmaninov
before fascinated French audiences. But this was only a prelude
to his great enterprise of the following year. He mounted
Mussorgsky's *Boris Godunov* with Chaliapin in the title rôle. Its
success convinced him that Paris was ready to experience
bigger, better and more daring productions. Diaghilev had
realized the 1907 and 1908 seasons with the help of official
patronage from the Russian government and with the influence

of the Russian ambassador M. Nelidov and the young French minister of state Aristide Briand but what he planned for the future needed more extensive backing from private patrons.

During these years Diaghilev frequented Winnaretta's salon not only because it was a crossroads in French musical life but also because he met there potential backers for his projects. This was not an easy task for someone as snobbish as Diaghilev: for her salon was one place where, as Degas remarked, talent was welcomed without a tail-coat; one could be the Great Condé himself or only have two *sous* in one's pocket and be treated as an equal. Yet, it was at a party given by Winnaretta on 4 June 1908 that the subject of a full season of Russian ballet and opera was first mooted. The impresario Gabriel Astruc, already famous for taking calculated risks in launching Artur Rubinstein, Wanda Landowska and even Mata Hari, mentioned Diaghilev's ideas to the Grand-Duchess Vladimir. She approved, and, with Astruc and Diaghilev, set about devising how to raise the necessary subsidy of 265,000 francs. They drew up a list of possible patrons: the Princesse Murat, the Comtesse de Chevigné, the Marquise de Ganay, the Grand-Duke Cyrille, the Comtesse de Pourtalès, the Comtesse Jean de Castellane, the Baronne de Rothschild and the Grand-Duke Paul's wife the Comtesse de Hohenfelsen, they were all possibilities but the Princesse de Polignac headed the list as a certain bet, closely followed by another of Diaghilev's original devotees, Misia Edwardes, soon to be Madame José-Maria Sert. Not all the persons suggested did contribute anything but, nonetheless, an adequate sum of money was soon assured and the following May Diaghilev was able to open his ballet season at the Théâtre du Châtelet with a programme that included the dances from *Prince Igor* and *Le Pavillon d'Armide*. A glittering cast of unknowns from the Maryinsky Theatre made such an impression that their names, Fokine, Bolm and Nijinsky, Ida Rubinstein, Pavlova and Karsavina, soon went into household usage. The artistic work of Alexandre Benois and Léon Bakst and the conducting of Nicolas Tchererpine became equally famous during that season.

Winnaretta was fascinated by Diaghilev's energy and will-power, which made everything possible. On a personal level, she felt that a decade which had begun so sadly and progressed without much inspiration was ending with the promise of stimulation and excitement for the future. Diaghilev's ballet was already becoming a focal point of artistic creativity. His almost aggressively assertive approach to sexual *mores* was already beginning to cure much of the neurosis of the post-Wilde era and dispel some of the inbred silliness of Lesbian life of the 1900s. For her own part Winnaretta was beginning to develop a new self-assurance in her love-life.

In 1908, while in London, she was introduced to the immensely rich but chronically melancholic young American artist Romaine Brooks and this tomboyish thirty-three year old beauty fell hopelessly in love with her. Exactly why she did is difficult to tell. Certainly she was impressed by the princess's intelligence and artistic sensibility. She may have seen in her a mother-figure, a substitute for her own half-mad mother, who had rejected her as a child but who, after her death, haunted her in a psyche that remained damaged for the rest of her long life. Romaine was so transfixed by Winnaretta that she pursued her, taking up residence in Paris to be near her and desperately cultivating all the social graces in the hope of impressing her, even though this went against the grain of her own Bohemianism and despite her frank criticism of the princess for forcing herself into the strait-jacket of French aristocratic society. Their relationship was almost a love-hate one, certainly from Romaine's point of view. She expressed her mixed feelings in her portrait of Winnaretta. The beloved's face, which attracted her but also repelled and frightened her, was depicted in profile, 'the lowered eye escaping detection, . . . the nose . . . arched and noble, but the mouth with its protruding lower lip showing strong atavistic ruthlessness ever active in self-defence. . . .'

The affair was doomed almost from the start. Winnaretta had no intention of being Romaine's mother-substitute as well as the butt of her fundamental criticisms and so, while the younger woman found immediate solace in Ida Rubinstein's exotic arms and subsequently life-long friendship in Natalie Barney's more practical ones, Winnaretta cultivated a more congenial and socially dazzling relationship with another woman.

As a child Baroness de Meyer had borne the legal name of Olga Alberta di Caracciolo. She was certainly the daughter of the Duchessa di Caracciolo but, since she had deserted her ducal husband literally at the altar-steps to go and live with her

lover Prince Josef Poniatowowski in semi-exile in their villa
near Dieppe, Olga had no Caracciolo blood in her. Nor, indeed,
was there said to be much of a Poniatowski infusion in her veins.
The Prince of Wales would periodically anchor his yacht at
Dieppe and stay with the unconventional couple as their
house-guest. Almost everybody believed that Olga Alberta was
the British prince's child and, although he confined himself to
the rôle of godfather, his doting indulgence of her as a child
and the favours lavished upon him once on the throne seemed
to confirm popular suspicions. Suggestions that she might have
been his mistress seem to be unfounded in fact, if only because
from an early point she began to show marked Lesbian tendencies. In 1901 Edward VII married her off to his favourite
Baron Adolf de Meyer, who lived happily with her for thirty
years despite—perhaps because—their marriage was known to
be unconsummated. What mattered was that, by the time of
her supposed father's delayed coronation in 1902, she was able
to cut a splendid figure at the ceremony with her husband who,
as the King of Saxony's chamberlain, appeared among representatives of the diplomatic corps. Thereafter, she became an
influence to be reckoned with at Court, in part a beneficial
one: her cultural interests were wide and far from being
confined, as some said, to hanging her bedroom with Sapphic
pictures executed by Condor. In fact, it was because of her
involvement with Diaghilev's ballet that she initially became a
close friend of Winnaretta's.

Their love-affair lasted for more than five years. Blessed by
the indulgent discretion of the Baron Adolf, who benignly
coped with the cross-Channel flutterings of his pretty and pas-
sionate young wife and the faintly masculine and just as ardent
princess. Only the outbreak of war put an end to their relationship. Indeed, it put an end to their love. In August 1914, the
Meyers, as German citizens, were forced to flee to America
where, despite the sequestration of their fortune by the British
authorities, they managed to survive to re-emerge in post-war
Europe, still fêted but now more for the baron's success as a
photographer than for their erstwhile connections with the
British court. Winnaretta alone remained unimpressed and
distinctly out-of-love. The wounds of war had indelibly scarred
her soul and, when she espied the Meyers by chance at one of
Comte Etienne de Beaumont's celebrated but ultra-precious

balls, she surprised those with her by muttering under her breath the uncompromising words, '*Sales Boches!*'

However, those days were still far off. For the moment Winnaretta was blissfully happy exploring the limits of love with her Olga.

Chapter 9
An Era Ends
(1909–1914)

A young French woman, noting Winnaretta's strong foreign accent, patronizingly turned to her and asked: 'How long have you been in Paris?'

'For thirty years, I think,' was the growled reply.

The young ingénue wilted. Unsubtle she certainly was but she might be forgiven for being unable to fit the princess into any preconceived category. For by 1909, when she had indeed lived continuously in Paris for just over thirty years, many still thought of her as unassimilable. Few found it easy to analyse her character. Her inscrutable air inhibited attempts to understand her. By contrast, French people found her very anglicized brother Paris Singer, an extrovert and pleasure-loving man who had little of her sensitivity and none of her self-discipline, much more comprehensible. His 'rediscovery' and pursuit of Isadora Duncan about this time made him an almost sympathetic figure in French eyes. As Isadora surrendered to her 'Lohengrin' and enjoyed all the benefits of his wealth (which she affected to despise), many looked on with good humour. They were almost sentimental about the birth of their child Patrick in 1910 and, when he died, tragically drowned in the Seine with his half-sister and their governess in 1913, public sorrow was genuine. Winnaretta was better able to assess Isadora, although for her brother's sake she occasionally pandered to her whims, as when she organized a Pink and White Ball for her at the height of the Ballets Russes season in 1909.

If Paris Singer was a down-to-earth hedonist, lovable despite, perhaps because of his faults, this helped no one to explain the mystery of his sister. Even close friends failed to fathom the depths of her personality: at a dinner given by the Comtesse Thérèse Murat, Winnaretta watched Anna de Noailles verbally assault the gentle pastor of the aristocratic faubourgs, the Abbé

Arthur Mugnier. Her chosen subject is the nature of love.
Mugnier shares his Master's view and reiterates His comment
on the repentant Madeleine: 'Her numerous sins will be
forgiven her, because she has loved much.'

Anna is not convinced. 'How can priests know about love?'
'They have the confessional,' replies a meek Mugnier.

'Yes, but they sit on the side where nothing happens!'

The abbé pauses and sighs. 'True indeed. Some come to us
with the twilights of love. But few tell us of its dawn.'

Anna, for once, is reduced to silence. And Winnaretta returns
to her sober conversation with the philosopher Henri Bergson,
sitting next to her. They shake their heads and try to explain the
incidence of intolerance and fanaticism in the human being.
What about the antisemitism manifested in recent Russian
pogroms? Bergson, as though willing to shoulder an almost
genetic guilt, says to her: 'I must confess that religious intolerance, fanaticism and exclusiveness come from our Bible, the
Hebraic Bible. These horrible passions were not rife among
the Greeks and Romans.' But that is no real explanation and
the faintly sad atmosphere of reflection remains.

When the party breaks up, the diplomat Maurice Paléologue
stays behind with Thérèse Murat and reflects upon Winnaretta.
She is a strange, baffling creature, slightly pathetic. Her
enigma can only be explained in two lines of Baudelaire:

> 'Faites votre destin, âmes désordonnés,
> 'Et fuyez l'infini que vous portez en vous.'

If Paléologue, for all his wisdom, was not able to understand
the workings of her mind, Winnaretta—far from being pathetic
—pursued self-knowledge as though it were destiny itself.
About this time she decided that no one was equipped to understand the human mind unless he knew the writings of the
Ancients. Nearing the age of fifty she set out to teach herself
Ancient Greek so that she could study the philosophy of Plato
and Aristotle in the original. Friends and scholars alike were
amazed at the rapidity with which she assimilated the language.
One wonders if the impulse to study Greek came from that
chance remark of Bergson's. Certainly, though he was the
greatest French philosopher of his day, she did not accept his
ideas and opinions indiscriminately. Of the two philosophers at
Thérèse Murat's, the theoretical Bergson and the practical

Mugnier, she was less heartened by Bergson's despairing reflections than by the abbé's irrepressible optimism and sophisticated saintliness. In her Greek studies she retraced the steps of the Renaissance humanists to find in the utterances of Socrates the antetype of the primitive Christianity which Mugnier practised with such simplicity and love.

Another person who provided Winnaretta with as much intellectual stimulation as Mugnier and Bergson was Sir Ronald Storrs, whom she met about this time. He was holiday-ing in Venice in the summer of 1911 and used his friendship with Ethel Smyth to effect an introduction to the princess. Ethel's recommendation was—for her—glowing: he was 'the only righteous man'. Without considering Ethel's almost general prejudice, Winnaretta was soon able to make up her own mind. Quickly a strong bond of friendship based upon mutual respect was forged between her and the English diplomat. Whenever he passed through Paris or spent vacations in Venice, she insisted on his staying with her, so that, to the exclusion of all else, they could lose themselves in the realms of the intellect. He encouraged her with her classical studies and helped her to develop and prune her genuinely syncretic philosophy of life.

One offshoot of her involvement with the classics was an interest in numismatics. As years went by she gathered together a remarkable collection of Greek and Roman coins. They had an aesthetic as well as a historical appeal. A similar impulse affected her picture-buying about this time. She acquired two large and impressive paintings by Gian Paolo Pannini, the *Galleria di vedute dell' antica Roma* and the *Galleria di vedute della Roma moderna*. When she bought them from the Duc de Morte-mart's collection in 1912, experts were under the impression that they represented the Cardinal Melchior de Polignac, as Ambassador to Rome, surveying two separate galleries of paintings and sculptures, one of views of ancient Rome with antique sculpture, the other of views of Renaissance and Baroque Rome with sculpture by artists such as Michelangelo and Bernini. The principal personage in Pannini's paintings was later identified as the Abbé de Canillac, the French Chargé d'Affaires in Rome in the mid-eighteenth century. That was of little consequence: despite her regard for the Polignac family, Winnaretta's prime interest in the paintings were their original way of depicting a classical civilization so significant that it had flowered for a second time and was capable of doing so again.

However, her love of art was always wider than the limits imposed by any particular genre. Whenever a work of art that pleased her in any way came on the market, she tried to buy it. A pastel drawing of an unknown man by Latour was added to her increasingly eclectic collection and in 1911 she bought an exquisite drawing of a ten-year-old boy, Félix Leblanc, whom Ingres had sketched during a visit to Florence in 1823.

If Winnaretta always showed great reverence for established masters, she possibly took even more delight in encouraging living artists. In the years prior to the First World War her patronage of artists took on a new lease of life. About this time José-Maria Sert worked on the black and gold murals for her grand salon and for once, restrained by the atmosphere of the place, he executed a work that was markedly less loud than his usual mural creations. The monochrome effect of this distinctive piece of Sert's work almost appears to mock gently the obsessively dark tones, to which Romaine Brooks was addicted. Throughout this period, even after the ardour of their relationship had cooled, Winnaretta helped her as an artist. She helped her to fit into the Paris of the *Belle Epoque*, where she cut a slightly sad figure with her short hair and masculine clothes. She made a point of steering in her direction commissions for portraits more for the diversion they provided than for the fees, which she did not need. Around 1910 she painted her portrait of Winnaretta and it impressed everyone except Robert de Montesquiou. On seeing it, he declared that Romaine had succeeded in representing her as 'a Nero a thousand times more cruel than the original, a Nero not content with giving the Christians to wild animals but who dreams of seeing them pricked to death by sewing-machines.' Perhaps Winnaretta could understand the envy of this professor of beauty-on-a-shoe-string had turned so sour but she ignored him. She introduced Romaine Brooks to a close friend of hers—another of Montesquiou's bêtes noirs—Clothilde ('Cloton') Legrand.

Madame Legrand, who gained immortality as Proust's chic Madame Leroi, knew everybody and had known everybody from Guy de Maupassant to the Prince of Wales. Indeed, Montesquiou became apoplectic at the news that Edward VII had invited her to dine during his last visit to Paris: he could have entertained Anatole France, Rodin or even Sarah Bernhardt but he had to choose her! The portrait of Cloton Legrand, which resulted from her meeting Romaine at Winnaretta's, was something of a reply to Montesquiou's comments on her own portrait. *Madame Legrand au champs de courses*, a portrait study of Cloton returning from the races, is one of Romaine's best works and was recognized as such when first publicly viewed in 1912. Montesquiou was chagrined and, exclaiming that Cloton looked like 'a hard-up Gioconda', contrived to acquire the painting so that he could ridicule it to his heart's content—which he did until a pacifistic Natalie Barney tried to pour oil on troubled waters by buying it from him. But she did not succeed in her ultimate aim of creating peace between Winnaretta's circle and the hypersensitive count. In fact, Montesquiou's exaggerated dislike of them took on such alarming proportions that, when the fiasco of his grand garden-party performance of Verlaine's *Les Uns et les autres* at his Palais Rose occurred two years later in July 1912, he was inclined to point the finger of suspicion at Cloton Legrand. On the day before the party someone sent a forged letter to Madame Estradère, who wrote a social column in *Le Figaro* under the name of the Princesse de Mesagne, announcing that bad weather had caused him to cancel the *fête*. Almost all Montesquiou's hundreds of guests took *Le Figaro*'s information at face value and stayed away. Next day Madame Estradère, by way of explanation, showed Montesquiou the letter written in a skilful imitation of his own handwriting. He pounced on the first words, '*Chère princesse*'. How could Madame Estradère believe what followed such an opening? Montesquiou took the matter no further but retired, deeply wounded, harbouring the suspicion that it had been Madame Legrand who had wrought such a savage revenge on him. But that was just part of his neurosis: Cloton Legrand would have known as well as himself that no princess, real or otherwise, should be addressed as '*chère princesse*'.

In Montesquiou's eyes, Winnaretta only made matters worse in the following year by extending her patronage to another of his former friends Jacques-Emile Blanche. Her friendship for Blanche was all that concerned her and during 1913, while he made preliminary sketches for a portrait of her, she enjoyed

sitting for him, as much because of his witty conversation as for
anything else. The result of this mildly gossipy association,
nonetheless, was the completion in May 1914 of two very
impressive portraits, depicting Winnaretta as a balance
between a figure of social significance and a woman of distinctive individuality and intelligence. At the same time she
bought from Blanche his large painting of Nijinsky in his
costume for the choreographic sketches *Les Orientales*, which the
Ballets Russes had mounted in 1910. Nijinsky and Tamara
Karsavina, dressed in her costume for *L'Oiseau de feu*, had been
photographed by Blanche (supervised by the aesthetic eye of
Cocteau) prior to his making study sketches for individual
portraits of them. Only the Nijinsky portrait got beyond the
early stages and, of course, it was the one most lost for a home
once Nijinsky's unexpected marriage blighted his association
with Diaghilev in 1913. Winnaretta was happy to buy the
picture but, one imagines, she was tactful enough to hang it in a
place unobtrusive enough not to catch Diaghilev's eye when he
visited her house, as he frequently did.

At the inception of Diaghilev's annual seasons of Russian
ballets and operas in May 1909, the princess was one of his
main patrons and she remained his most dependable supporter
until his death in 1929. In the first decade she was content to
make large donations to his funds and leave all the artistic
direction in his hands. Later on she began to finance the
production of specific works in addition to continuing her
general subsidies. So involved financially, she made sure that
she never missed a work presented by him. If at all possible, she
would join the audience for the first performance of new works
so that she could enjoy the excitement of the unknown as well
as encourage the company. She was impressed by the classical
ballets from Russia and the wild orientalism of many of the
contemporary works. In 1909 Rimsky-Korsakov's opera *Ivan
the Terrible*, which re-introduced her to Chaliapin, she found
almost as moving as the previous year's *Boris Godunov*. She took
a possibly more partisan interest when Diaghilev presented
works composed by her friends. In 1912 he mounted Reynaldo
Hahn's *Le Dieu bleu*, a ballet based on a libretto by Cocteau and
Coco de Madrazo. And in the same year Ravel's *Daphnis et
Cloë* was a musical delight, if less successful as a ballet and,
coming as it did a week after the première of Nijinsky's original

creation to Debussy's music *Prélude à l'après-midi d'un faune*, it was rather overshadowed by the storm of outraged protest provoked by the unusual choreography and by some of the fawn's more fetishistic actions. The sculptor Rodin and the newspaper proprietor Gaston Calmette were still hotly arguing out the pros and cons of the ballet when the première of Ravel's work took place.

If in 1912 Debussy's music received more attention than Ravel's, on 29 May 1913 the first performance of Igor Stravinsky's ballet *Le Sacre de printemps* diverted all attention away from Debussy's *poème dansé Jeux*, produced two weeks earlier. *Jeux*'s implications, its hints at a possible compromise sexual triangle were rather too subtle to make much impression upon Diaghilev's audience but Stravinky's music for *Le Sacre* and Nijinsky's coarse-grained choreography caused riot conditions in the Théâtre de Champs-Elysées very soon after the curtain rose. Winnaretta sat through the unforgettable evening, becoming increasingly dismayed as howls, jeers and torrents of abuse and counter-abuse erupted around her and distracted attention from the ballet. At times the cries of protest were so loud that the dancers were forced to stop and the orchestra was reduced to silence. She began to become very annoyed. Full of sympathy for the artistes, she was outraged by the scenes caused by some of the audience, such as the Comtesse Mélanie de Pourtalès sweeping out of the theatre exclaiming that never in the sixty years of her life had she been so insulted. Thereafter, each time *Le Sacre* was repeated Winnaretta was in the theatre to watch as gradually it won approval until by the end of the season Stravinsky had become something of a hero, if a slightly wounded one. She had admired him ever since attending the première of *L'Oiseau de feu* in 1910 and this episode only strengthened her regard for him. A close friendship grew up between them, one based on mutual respect, and it lasted a lifetime.

New friends and new interests did not detract from Winnaretta's other interests. She still kept up her acquaintance with Delius and visited him and his wife Jelka at their home near Fontainebleau, since they seldom came to Paris. She also remained a devoted admirer of Fauré's, although she did complain that he was not always as faithful a friend as he might have been because he tended to allow novelties to distract his

attention to the exclusion of all else. But in the second decade
of the twentieth century the aural distortions which he had
begun to suffer provoked only feelings of sympathy. The way in
which, despite everything, he continued to write sublime music
compensated for a multitude of infidelities. When the writer
Robert d'Humières organized a 'soirée Gabriel Fauré' at
Versailles in the summer of 1910, Winnaretta was among the
first to seize the opportunity to attend. Surrounded by Anna de
Noailles, Lady de Grey, Madame de Saint-Marceaux, Madeleine Lemaire and André Messager, she sat with Fauré at the
edge of the canal in the palace gardens as musicians on a large
boat performed his music for *Caligula*. Then, an invisible
orchestra, hidden in the trees, played the *Sicilienne* from *Pelléas*.
On the boat Fauré accompanied Reynaldo Hahn while he sang
a group of his songs, including *Le Parfum impérissable* and,
appropriately, *Au Bord de l'eau*. Nature seemed sensible of the
occasion: as Reynaldo sang the words '*Au calme clair de lune,
triste et beau*', the moon suddenly appeared above the trees and
cast its pure light on the shimmering waters. The audience was
so moved that, when Fauré's last notes died away, they remained silent for some moments without saying a word.

The Paris première of Fauré's first full-length opera—or
drame lyrique—*Pénélope* on 9 May 1913 was just as moving.
Doubly fascinating for Winnaretta, his mild use of *leitmotivs* was
an interesting, if belated concession to Wagnerian ideas; and
his libretto pleasingly followed the Homeric original, with
which she was very familiar through her Greek studies. The
Paris performance of *Pénélope* was certainly successful, especially
after its rather doubtful première at Monte Carlo two months
earlier and, as part of the celebrations arranged by Gabriel
Astruc for the opening of the fine new Théâtre de Champs-
Elysées, it claimed a lot of public attention for a week or so.
But when followed in the same month by a season of Diaghilev's
ballets, including the controversial premières of both *Jeux* and
Le Sacre, interest tended to be deflected away from it.

However, Fauré was far from being relegated to the older
generation of composers, unable to compete with new arrivals
on the musical scene: he had only recently been giving encouragement to a group of young composers, including Charles
Koechlin, André Caplet, Florent Schmitt and Ravel, when late
in 1909 they decided to found the Société Musicale Indépen-

dante (the S.M.I.) as a positive alternative to the Société
Nationale, which was becoming increasingly reluctant to
perform any work smacking of what it regarded as modernism.
Winnaretta took an active interest in the new society and, at
Fauré's instigation, allowed it to present some of its concerts
at her house. A particularly grand occasion took place there on
11 June 1912 but less pretentious evenings were more common,
as indeed were rehearsal-performances of better known works
such as Fauré's *Requiem*.

But there was an additional reason why Winnaretta was particularly interested in the S.M.I. From the beginning Prince
Edmond's niece, the Princesse Armande de Polignac, had been
associated with it. Armande was almost as remarkable a
woman as her aunt by marriage. A pupil of Gigout, d'Indy
and Fauré, she made an early name for herself as a writer on
music and as a composer of considerable originality. In the
early 1900s she was highly thought of among the young avant-
garde composers. But her works were sufficiently varied in
intensity to suit any occasion. For example, in 1903, scarcely
twenty-seven years old, she was a prime organizer of a new
literary and musical society, called *Élan*, dedicated to publi-
cizing the work of young artists. Her own compositions were
frequently played at its concerts. Meanwhile, in the same year
one finds in the newly-published *Claudine s'en va* Colette painting
a scene in the park at the spa Arriège, in which Claudine
describes to her friends (and her cat Faunchette) the virtues
of the local sulphurous springs, while in the background the
municipal band plays a *Selection from the Dragoons of Villars* and
a *March* by Armande de Polignac. The scope and contrast in
her musical interest can also be detected in her close friendship
with her classmate from the Schola Cantorum, Edgar Varèse,
so ahead of public taste that eventually he had to abandon
France in 1915 and go to America, Armande having organized
the funds for the journey. Once established there, he constantly
urged her to send her works for performance by the International
Composers' Guild, which he all but ran. But that was in the
1920s and by then she had gained a considerable reputation for
herself in France. In 1909 she conducted her first opera *La
Petite Sirène* at Nice. A year later two more operas followed it,
L'Hypocrite sanctifié and *Les Roses de Calife*. A symphony, pic-
turesquely entitled *Les Mille et une nuits*, also made a considerable

impression upon the public, especially since she herself conducted performances of it in Paris and Brussels. In this respect,
she made musical history as the first Frenchwoman, possibly
the first woman ever, to conduct a symphony orchestra in
public.

Winnaretta and Armande enjoyed a remarkable personal
rapport. Armande had been something of a favourite niece of
Prince Edmond's. Winnaretta, who was not much older than
her, shared her husband's affection for her as a person and
respect for her as a creative and executant musician and
showed this in a portrait which she painted of her at her piano.
In itself a fine study in light and shadow, the picture conveys
much of the intensity and vitality of the young musician-
princess. One of the most remarkable things about Armande
was her facility for attracting public attention to her work not
through any of the aggressive ultra-feminism so common in the
1900s but through sheer charm. She was one of the gentlest
figures in what could be a hard world. Her calm nature, her
merry laugh and the incredibly child-like innocence of her
round blue eyes won her more than a forceful personality ever
could.

This could not be said of one young composer whom Winnaretta first met about this time. In 1913, soon after arriving in
Paris, Darius Milhaud frequented the salon of his cousin Xavier
Léons, who delighted in gathering the cream of France's
philosophers under his roof, and as a result he found himself
thrown together with Jacques-Emile Blanche, who, like him,
felt mildly uncomfortable in the company of Léons's serious
friends. Blanche invited him to his house to play piano duets
with his sister-in-law Yoyo and Catherine Lemoine. At the
time Blanche was beginning his portraits of Winnaretta, so one
day he invited her to his home to hear a performance of Milhaud's recently composed Violin Sonata. She had missed its
first performance at an S.M.I. concert a few months earlier
but, hearing it played at Blanche's by the composer and the
violinist Yvonne Giraud, she was enchanted. Standing by
Milhaud at the piano, she turned the pages for him herself.
After that first meeting, she often invited the young composer
to her musical soirées in the avenue Henri-Martin, events
which over the years often featured works by him.

In addition to art, music and ballet, Winnaretta continued

to take an interest in contemporary literature. In 1911 she gave
a substantial sum of money to the Royal Society of Literature
in London so that a prize of one hundred pounds could be
awarded each November to the author of a work of imagination
that had appeared during the previous year. Winnaretta wanted
the prize to be a memorial tribute to her husband because he
had always shown a keen interest in English literature. The
Polignac Prize certainly created some excitement in literary
circles, not always the sort of excitement visualized by her.
From the beginning a source of complaint was that the society's
Academic Committee, which had the task of choosing the
winner, tended to recruit its members from the older generation
of British and American *littérateurs*, men whom the young
writers competing for the prize seldom respected. Their
decisions invariably caused some resentment. Certainly time
showed that the prize-winning writers were not always as
illustrious or immortal as some who failed in the attempt. In
1911 Walter de la Mare was first to win. John Masefield
received the prize in 1912. This caused some resentment. Ezra
Pound, not yet the friend of Winnaretta's he later became, was
annoyed at the committee's decision. He roundly declared that
D. H. Lawrence was a much better poet than Masefield ever
would be and that he deserved recognition for his *Love Poems
and Others*, and so, while James Stephens was receiving the
award for his book *The Crock of Gold* in November 1913, Pound
was sending copies of Lawrence's poems to committee-members
in preparation for the next year. Lawrence was not altogether
happy about the matter. Suspecting that Pound was trying to
repay him for a past kindness, he disliked the idea of being
paraded around by Pound and his friend Ford Madox Hueffer
(or Ford) 'as one of their show-dogs.' Nonetheless, he added, if
they wanted to mention his name in the right places, he could
not object. They did but in November 1914 Ralph Hodgson,
not Lawrence, was the Academic Committee's choice for the
Polignac Prize.

Meanwhile, Winnaretta had been—unwittingly—near the
centre of another difficult situation in the world of literature.
Early in 1914 her old friend and occasional rival Marcel Proust
had attracted sufficient attention with the publication of *Du
Côté de chez Swann* for the editorial committee of the *Nouvelle
Revue Française*, at first lukewarm about his work, to beg him to

allow them to publish the remaining volumes of *À la Recherche*. Proust was delighted: this would mean the fulfilment of one of his dreams. However, he was already contracted to his own publisher Bernard Grasset, to whom, if nothing else, he owed a debt of gratitude for sponsoring his work after three publishers had already refused to touch it. Proust gave serious thought to the problem of how to persuade Grasset to release him from the contract without giving offence and came up with a characteristically devious solution. He asked Reynaldo Hahn to discuss the matter with the Princesse de Polignac in the hope that she could bring her influence to bear upon Grasset, since he was a close friend of hers. If anyone could sway him without antagonizing him, she could. Apart from anything else, Proust added, she was a woman and women always have much more winning ways than men. However, the need to put such an elaborate stratagem into effect did not arise. On 3 April 1914, the day upon which Reynaldo was to visit the princess, Proust received a letter from Grasset asking when his second volume might be ready for publication. Proust decided to make a clean breast of the matter. Abruptly halting Reynaldo in his tracks, he wrote explaining everything to Grasset in the hope that he might magnanimously release him from the contract. But the publisher played so skilfully upon Proust's sensibilities that he agreed to remain with him and, though regretfully, to turn down the *Nouvelle Revue Française*'s desirable offer.

All the while Winnaretta was completely unaware of the rôle of mediator assigned to her. Why Proust should have thought of her is of some interest. Apart for her suitability as a friend of Grasset's, he knew how profoundly she admired *Du Côté de chez Swann*. She had read the book with great enthusiasm soon after its publication in November 1913 and had recommended it to all her friends. She was certainly one of the first to stimulate interest in it in England. In the months before the outbreak of war, the younger members of London's artistic set used to gather at her house in Chelsea to enthuse about Proust's work. Edward Marsh's most vivid memory of the weeks after the declaration of war was of sitting next to the princess while dining at Lady Randolph Churchill's on 16 August. She spoke to him about Proust and gave him a copy of his book. During the following months Marsh steeped himself in it so thoroughly that some years later he was able to give

Charles Scott Moncrieff invaluable help while working on his impressive translation of *À la Recherche*.

But as the European war got underway Proust could only be a diversion from the realities of the political situation. Winnaretta was and always remained practically a-political. A social consciousness and a regard for civilization were her alternatives to political commitment. Governments only too frequently meddled incompetently in matters beyond their grasp. Politicians redeemed themselves only if they had some talent or personal attraction, as did Briand, Herriot and Poincaré. For instance, on 18 January 1913 one finds Winnaretta writing to Madame Poincaré just as she is embarking at Brindisi for Cairo: she has just received the news of Poincaré's election as President and cannot wait to express her joy to him; the wishes of all who love France are fulfilled! In reality Winnaretta was not saying what a good politician or statesman she thought Raymond Poincaré but how much she admired him as a brilliant lawyer and cherished him as a friend.

One occasion upon which she did become vaguely associated with anything political was when Christabel Pankhurst fled from England to Paris in March 1912. As a friend of Ethel Smyth's, she was introduced to Winnaretta as a matter of course. The aim of the Pankhursts' Women's Social and Political Union certainly interested her, although her own concern was with the social rôle of women rather than with political concessions that had to be forced out of sceptical all-male governments. For two years, until the outbreak of war, Christabel Pankhurst (alias Amy Richards) held a conspiratorial court in her flat in the avenue de la Grande Armée. Here she received her lieutenants from England and quite regularly brought them along with her to Winnaretta's house. On one occasion one of her devoted supporters Annie Kenny, an ex-mill girl from Oldham, found herself in the princess's drawing room, completely overcome by its size. 'It was the largest room I ever saw,' she later recalled. 'I felt so tiny.' She was also impressed by the profusion of books around her, particularly when the first that came to hand, a small volume bound in cherry pink leather, turned out to be a translation of Sappho's poems.

Through Winnaretta Christabel Pankhurst met many

Parisian society women who were interested in the suffragette cause and in June 1914, when both Ethel Smyth and Sir Ronald Storrs happened to be in Paris, Ethel brought Christabel to meet him at Winnaretta's. The meeting was successful. The sympathy shown by him for female emancipation inclined Christabel to agree with Ethel that he was indeed 'the one righteous man', although the aggressive Miss Smyth seldom gave opportunities for disagreement. By this time even Winnaretta tended to give her a loose rein, just as long as her headlong careering did not interfere with her own emotional life. She was content to let Ethel drag her off to Saint-Cloud for a game of golf when she had a spare moment in a programme that included visits to old friends, such as Anna de Noailles and Madame Bulteau, and waylaying the Empress Eugénie en route for Cap Martin.

But political undercurrents of much more immediate significance than suffragette demands agitated Winnaretta's world. Indeed, political intrigue and speculation went on around her, sometimes under her own roof, as Europe moved painfully towards war, although she tried to ignore this and concentrate upon preserving a refined way of life. Her concert giving, if anything, became more frequent and more lavish. On 16 June 1913 she had an impressive programme of music played to an impressive audience: a Suite by Bach, Wagner's *Siegfried Idyll*, Brahm's *Mädchenlied* and a *Suite* by Debussy, amongst other works just as unprejudiced nationalistically. But Maurice Paléologue, enjoying a break from his duties at the Quai d'Orsay, found that the last note had scarcely died away before he was button-holed by the Duc de Luynes and his sister the Duchesse de Noailles. What advice could Paléologue give them about Bulgaria? They were both worried about their friend King Ferdinand, who had almost married Madame de Noailles in the late 1880s, since when her feelings for him had not changed. Paléologue could only utter half-hearted reassurances. Ferdinand was playing a very risky game flirting with the Austrians. They should write to him and try to use their influence to wean him away from his Austro-German inclinations for his own good—or he might lose his throne, even his life. Wasted words! During the early war years remembrance of the duchess's charms was not enough to prevent Ferdinand siding with France's enemies—though, according to Proust's

Duchesse de Guermantes, any private soldier's charms might have had more effect.

Paléologue had no sooner left Luynes and his sister to ponder his advice than the Grand Duke Paul drew him aside into one of the adjoining rooms to discuss the Roumanian situation. The grand duke confided in him: his niece the Princess Marie had come to show him a letter from the Roumanian crown prince Carol. It made a very hopeful allusion to the possibility of his marrying a Russian grand duchess. Paul did not say which grand duchess: Paléologue could apparently imagine who she might be. With diplomatic correctness he all but congratulated him on the impending dynastic coup. But he knew that this was no mere family matter. It could prove to be an event of signal importance in maintaining French influence in the Balkans through her Russian allies, especially since the Bulgarians were far from amenable. Grand Duke Paul was as politically aware as Paléologue. He could guarantee that by next day interested members of the government would be given full details of their conversation.

The general significance of the back-stairs diplomacy taking place within earshot was not lost on Winnaretta. It gave her reason to hope for a peaceful solution to Europe's problems. In the meantime, nothing must be allowed to interfere with the routine of a civilized life. Germany's cultural Meccas still summoned the faithful. Italy, France's hesitant ally, could still be visited without fear. In her Venetian palace, almost in defiance of the gods of war, she ignored the cruelty of the age by gathering around her the most brilliant artists of the time. Mann might bring his Aschenbach to Venice to die amid its over-ripe and decaying charms; Frederick Rolfe might die in self-imposed exile from England and the human race in a degree of poverty ill-befitting the Baron Corvo; but at the Palazzo Polignac the keynote was vitality and excellence. A young and impressionable Cecil Roberts sat in the *sala grande* overlooking the canal and marvelled at the succession of great performers whom Winnaretta enticed there to play for her: pianists young and old, Artur Rubinstein and Paderewski, Jan Kubelik and Kreisler, better known then for their violin playing than for their compositions, and, among many more, the singers Melba, Tetrazzini and Caruso. As he watched this magnificent parade, Roberts reflected with passing sadness on how, many years before, his own father had lost his life's savings by buying a faked concession in the Singer Manufacturing Company from a false agent. No wonder he had been over-eager to risk his money on such an investment!

Winnaretta returned to spend the Christmas of 1913 among friends in Venice, an almost sad attempt to savour the traditional enchantment of the season in the timeless atmosphere of that serene city. Lady de Grey celebrated Christmas by giving a grand party. When Winnaretta arrived in her gondola, she found old friends from Paris among the cosmopolitan guests, Henri de Régnier, Gabriel-Louis Pringué and Paul Bourget. The beautiful Principessa Ruspoli was there, attracting attention to her collar of pearls, Marie Mancini's famous necklace, while keeping the company amused with her scintillating conversation. A young Scottish lord, mooring his yacht in the Adriatic, arrived, kilted and attended by pipers, and presented the hostess with two enormous plum-puddings, which reappeared later with blue flames of burning rum, illuminating the darkened dining-room. The bag-pipers, meanwhile, circled the table six times, playing the sad music of their Scottish homeland. Afterwards the windows were opened to let in the sound of church bells ringing and of children singing carols in gondolas.

But, despite the season of peace, thoughts often strayed back to the political situation. As Paul Bourget stood by a window watching the glow of dawn paint the Grand Canal with warm colours, a German prince came up to him and, as if reading his thoughts, tried to reassure him: 'My cousin Wilhelm II likes France a lot.'

Bourget smiled sadly and murmured: 'Behold the announcement of war! This is how the enchantment of the world will end.'

Henri de Régnier joined them at the window and surveyed the scene of marble palaces and untroubled waters bathed in rose and coral hues: 'One must clasp these moments to the heart where they attain the height of beauty and plant a forest of memories. Disillusionment will never be able to penetrate it.'

Chapter 10
War, the Fox and the Philosopher
(1914–1917)

When Germany declared war on France on 3 August 1914 and the same day poured troops across the Belgian border, Winnaretta was staying with friends in Surrey. But for the political situation, at that time of the year she would have been in Bayreuth. For all that, she, like many others, does not seem to have understood how grave the situation was. There were no recent historical precedents to justify the belief that the great powers would not call each other's bluff and quickly settle their differences round a negotiating table. For several weeks she lingered on in England until it became plain that the country was seriously mobilizing for war and that she would have to return to Paris before her way was blocked by advancing German armies. When she arrived there, she was dismayed to find confusion reigning. Many had already fled and many more were preparing to do so. On 5 September, when the French and British began a determined all-or-nothing attempt to check the Germans on the Marne, the thought that the enemy was within sight of the Eiffel Tower precipitated the flight of the last refugees. But Winnaretta stayed on in the city and in fact lent a car to the Rostands, who were making hot foot for the Bordelais with Anna de Noailles and her mother Princesse Rachel de Brancovan. They were in good company: the French government had already retired to Bordeaux and many men and women of fashion, such as Proust, Montesquiou and the Comtesse Greffulhe, had withdrawn to the safety of Cabourg or Trouville.

Like Cocteau's Princesse de Bormes, once the Germans had been checked at the Marne, Winnaretta threw herself whole-heartedly into work that would help sustain the French army in its struggles. What delighted her more than anything was being given the opportunity to help Marie Curie apply the results of her work on radium to treatment of wounded and suffering men at the front. Marie Curie had considerable respect for her and welcomed her help because she was an intelligent woman as well as someone whose open purse made many of her projects possible. Winnaretta also put considerable effort into ventures designed to sustain the *esprit de corps* among the allied nations or to raise funds for the French army and navy. For instance, in the spring of 1916 she was very much preoccupied with the organization of an exhibition of Italian female art, which Madame Bulteau mounted at the Louvre as a manifestation of France's regard for Italy's heroic efforts to check Austrian aggression. Winnaretta joined Anna de Noailles (now returned) in urging the President's wife Madame Poincaré to support the exhibition. Later in the same year the princess was again in contact with Madame Poincaré urging her to support a charity concert which she was organizing at the Opéra; and her band of helpers, the Princesse Lucien Murat, the Marquise de Ganay and the Comtesse Murat, accompanied her to the Elysée Palace to discuss the project. As a close friend of the Poincarés Winnaretta was invariably successful in mustering their support for her charitable ventures.

But there was a more individualistic side to Winnaretta's response to the war-situation. General acts of charity and practical help were very necessary but she soon realized that in the rapidly changing social and economic climate something particular must be done to preserve the civilizing forces of life and help them adapt to the times. When all attention was concentrated upon the tragedy of war she tried to keep in mind the circumstances of her friends in the musical world and did her best to help them survive their difficulties. With remarkable foresight she realized that the days were numbered when composers could write for massive orchestral forces such as those used by Wagner, Bruckner and Mahler. Even without enforced economic stringency, France was likely to react against the large orchestra as being too Germanic. Besides, as a lover of baroque music, she felt that a re-examination of the potential of its orchestral textures might be a profitable exercise, and so she decided to experiment by asking different composers to write short orchestral works for small instrumental groups of around twenty players. She hoped that, once the war was over, she would be able to have these commissioned works performed in her salon. Meanwhile, her commissions would help composers to cope with temporary financial problems caused by the war.

Stravinsky was the one composer most obviously in need of help, since he had little means of supporting himself, far less his wife and children. War had dried up his main sources of income: nothing came from his Russian estates and Diaghilev, more impecunious than ever, had little to spare. Winnaretta knew this. Late in 1915 she wrote to Stravinsky at Morges in Switzerland asking him to call on her when next in Paris. On 29 December he came to conduct Diaghilev's gala performance of *L'Oiseau de feu* at the Opéra and early in January 1916, once the ballet company had left for its American tour, he took the opportunity to visit the princess. Only then did he learn that she was prepared to pay him 2,500 Swiss francs to write something for her. Bearing in mind earlier problems with Fauré, she was careful not to force Stravinsky into accepting work that did not inspire him. She only specified that the work should be orchestral and that the forces employed should be small. She then waited until ideas began to form in his mind before discussing more precise details with him. Stravinsky was delighted with the commission, not simply because the fee was welcome but because it also acted as a spur to a slightly flagging creative urge. At the time he was beginning to feel the strain of working on *Les Noces*, which gave every sign of turning out to be a massive unwieldy work requiring an orchestra of about 150. Winnaretta's request for a small scale work gave him the excuse to abandon the problems of the larger work for the moment and, when he went back to it later, his inspiration returned with redoubled force.

His ideas for the new work formed quickly. He decided to write a burlesque, a semi-acrobatic ballet with a vocal accompaniment. It would be based on episodes concerning Renard the Fox drawn from Alexander Afanasiev's collection of Russian tales. The speed with which Stravinsky's plans for *Renard* emerged is not surprising because he had already turned the idea over in his mind and, while staying in Château d'Oex the previous spring, he had sketched out a duo based on the fable. But the effect of the Polignac commission was decisive. It meant that he had to enlarge the overall action of the work. He also had to consider finding a French libretto for it, since it was to be sung before French audiences. This worried him

considerably because his uncertainty about the language had so
far inhibited him from setting any French text to music. That
problem was soon solved when he returned to Morges and
enlisted the professional help of his friend the Swiss poet C. F.
Ramuz. Winnaretta's commission also had a decisive effect
upon the orchestral score for *Renard*. The limited number of
players involved meant that orchestral textures had to be
exploited to the full. One episode involving a duet for two
barnyard animals in the fable, the Cat and the Goat, called for
the use of an antiquated Russian instrument the *guzla*. Stravinsky decided that by substituting a Hungarian cimbalon he
could imitate the authentic Russian sound required. Then,
instead of using the piano as the foundation instrument, as he
had done in many previous works, he employed the cimbalon
throughout as a *concertante* instrument, and so wove into the
whole work the emotive timbres of Russian peasant music and
the harsh sounds of the animal world. (Stravinsky's effective
use of the cimbalon as an orchestral instrument in *Renard*
encouraged him to employ it again in his *Ragtime*, in which,
again, it unashamedly tried to imitate the sound of another
instrument, the jazz-man's honky-tonk piano. And incidentally
his inventiveness stimulated some Hungarian composers'
interest in using their 'national' instrument in an orchestral
context.)

Stravinsky did not think twice about experimenting with
such an unusual and bizarre instrument in this work for Winnaretta because he knew that musical novelties always appealed
to her and that she was never slow to assess their true significance. Nor did he hesitate to suggest the *Renard* fable as the
subject of the piece. A more conventional patroness might have
objected to a fox dressed up as a nun trying to entice a stupid
cock down from his perch to confess the sins of his outrageous
life as a polygamist with forty wives. Nor did she have any
objection to the rather vicious dénouement where the fox is
strangled, emitting agonized cries as he dies. If in everyday life
she disliked most animals, she was not upset by this tragi-comic
scene in such a fabulous context. What added to the fairy-tale
unreality of the work was Stravinsky's idea of placing the
singers in the orchestra where they sang the dialogue appropriate to the action taking place on the stage but without each
singer being specifically identified with any animal character.

9a Winnaretta acting the
part of a Fury in a
tableau vivant, 1902

9b A portrait of Winnaretta by Jacques-Emile
Blanche, 1914

10a Olga de Meyer, photographed by Baron Adolf
de Meyer, *c.* 1900

10b A Self-Portrait by
Romaine Brooks

11a A Sapphic scene by José-Maria Sert; one of the mural decorations over the pilaster capitals in the grand salon of 57 avenue Henri-Martin, *c.* 1910

11b Violet Trefusis in Italy, *c.* 1930

12a   Winnaretta and
Stravinsky on the
balcony of the Palazzo
Polignac, *c.* 1925

12b   Winnaretta in Venice,
c. 1930

13a Winnaretta and Marie-Blanche de Polignac playing duets for two pianos in Venice, a pastel by Comte Charles de Polignac, *c.* 1930

13b Winnaretta at the organ in her studio, 1933

14 Winnaretta painting a water-colour, 1936

15 Winnaretta with Colette in the garden of her house in Paris, 1938

16a Winnaretta in
England, 1941

16b Dame Ethel Smyth
with Winnaretta in
Surrey, 1942

The use of singers as an addition to the orchestral accompaniment of a mute stage spectacle was certainly original. The balanced integration of the operatic and balletic genres had never before been so perfectly achieved. Certainly, Florent Schmitt had added a soprano chorus to his magnificent ballet score *La Tragédie de Salomé* in 1907 and a wordless choral episode had been woven by Ravel into his score for *Daphnis et Cloë* in 1912 but they were intended to have nothing like the central significance of the vocal writing in *Renard*. It was Stravinsky's example, if anyone's, that Manuel de Falla followed when writing parts for the three singers positioned in the orchestra for his puppet spectacle *El Retablo de Maese Pedro* of 1923, although in 1915 there had been a hint of a similar idea in his ballet score with contralto arias *El Amor Brujo*.

Apart from its influence upon other composers, *Renard* was of cardinal importance in Stravinsky's own career. The need to concentrate upon the potential of a compact performing ensemble presented a host of possibilities which he exploited in later works, partly because of artistic inclination, partly because of continued economic necessity. For example, his brilliant work *L'Histoire du soldat*, which employed a similar small chamber *ensemble*, with the violin as the *concertante* instrument, was in almost every way the direct successor of *Renard*, though ironically *L'Histoire du soldat* was given its public première as well as a private performance in Winnaretta's salon some time before *Renard* was produced in its entirety.

From the beginning Stravinsky's enthusiasm for the *Renard* project was considerable and, despite the initial technical problems, he managed to complete the vocal score by August 1916. The orchestration and the composition of the introductory march were completed early in 1917 and immediately went to press in Geneva. All the time Winnaretta showed a keen interest in its progress and, while Stravinsky was putting the finishing touches to the work in January and February 1917, she came to stay at Lausanne on the pretext of seeing a cosmopolitan assortment of her friends who had sought asylum in neutral Switzerland. Stravinsky's house at Morges was only a short distance away, so she was frequently in contact with him. With the work completed Stravinsky invited her to dine one evening. He came to collect her, bringing her through a still, snow-covered landscape, sparkling in the moonlight, to his house, brightly lit and glowing with the warm colours so much associated with the Ballets Russes. Madame Stravinsky, a delicate woman surrounded by equally delicate children and 'looking like a princess in a Russian fairy tale', had prepared a meal that was a delight to all the senses: 'the table was brilliantly lit with coloured candles and covered with fruit, flowers and desserts of every hue. The supper was a wonderful example of Russian cuisine, . . . composed of every form of *zakousky*, then *bortsh*, tender *sterlets* covered with delicious transparent jelly and served with a perfect sauce, various dishes of fowls and every sort of sweet.' Winnaretta thanked her host for a memorable evening and celebrated the completion of *Renard* by giving him an unusual present, a cigarette holder made of gold and ostrich feathers and shaped like a pipe with a mortice to hold the cigarette upright. It appealed to the extrovert side of his nature.

However, the circumstances under which Stravinsky finished *Renard* were not entirely pleasurable. In January 1917 he learned that the Paris Opéra had mounted a ballet based on part of Maeterlinck's *La Vie des abeilles* with his *Scherzo fantastique* adapted as its score. Both playwright and composer protested at this unauthorized use of their work—or rather abuse, because, Stravinsky maintained, the balletic treatment trivialized it. Although critics praised the end result, he was not easily mollified. The director of the Opéra, Jacques Rouché, knew that Winnaretta was staying in Lausanne at the time and seems to have borrowed Proust's idea of using her as a mediator between himself and the outraged composer because he eventually calmed down and even consented to have 'some bad literature about bees . . . published on the fly-leaf of [the] score, to satisfy the publisher, who thought a "story" would help to sell the music'.

Stravinsky met with more disappointment and frustration, though of a different kind when he tried to introduce *Renard* to the public. Although Winnaretta had sections of the music performed in her salon, the work as a whole was unperformable in a domestic situation. Stravinsky clearly seems to have conceived it as a balletic burlesque in the hope that Diaghilev might add it to his repertoire. But, despite his real fondness for Winnaretta, Diaghilev was enraged by what he regarded as an attempt to usurp his rôle as patron. For several years he refused to allude to *Renard* to either of them. Instead, behind their backs, he dismissed the unheard work with scathing words: Stravinsky was only interested in making money. And what had the princess paid so much for? This *Renard* was just 'some old scraps he found in his dresser drawer'. And so, until Diaghilev's unreasonable petulance dissolved in the heat of an economic crisis five years later, Stravinsky's unique ballet remained in limbo.

While *Renard* was being written, Winnaretta herself experienced something of an economic crisis. On 25 October 1916, she began court proceedings in London with the purpose of restraining the Surveyor of Taxes from assessing her for income tax as though she were resident in Britain. As the facts of the case unfolded during the following months, she was subjected to a deal of unpleasantness. The Surveyor of Taxes had decided that Winnaretta's ownership of the house at 321 King's Road, Chelsea made her liable to pay income tax on her foreign possessions. From the first she had been aware that her little *pied à terre* in London might cost her thousands of pounds a year in income tax and so, acting on the advice of her solicitor, she had arranged to buy the property through her brother Washington Singer and to leave the title in his name, since he was already taxed as a British resident. But after several years, the Surveyor decided that, although Washington was officially the owner of the property, his sister had paid for it, furnished it and subsequently paid all the domestic bills, so her claim that she was in effect a guest in her brother's house was specious. In December 1916 her appeal against the court's ruling was dismissed, leaving the way open for prosecution on a charge of fraud.

On 18 April 1917 committal proceedings opened at Bow Street, where the princess, Washington Singer and her solicitor Alfred Curtis Bird were accused of having conspired together to evade income tax. Although much of the hearing revolved round her and her finances, she herself was not present in court. She remained safely in France while each morning readers of *The Times* were giving enlightening estimates of her income derived from the Singer Manufacturing Company, a variable amount certainly, going from £30,700 in 1908 to £38,700 in 1916 and reaching a peak of £73,300 in 1913. Her annual income from foreign securities over the same period varied between a low £6,000 in 1908 and a high £29,400 in 1913. An expert from Somerset House estimated that between 1898 and 1916 she should have paid at least £38,456 in income tax.

On 25 April the case took on a slightly bizarre turn. The prosecution, faced with the problem of how to prove fraudulent intention, threatened to produce a witness to substantiate the original charges, as well as an additional one under which Winnaretta was summoned for committing perjury in a sworn affidavit. But the court decided to commit only Washington Singer and Alfred Bird. The charges against Winnaretta for criminal conspiracy were not pursued. As soon as Singer and Bird's trial opened on 25 July Frederick Sumpster, a former clerk from Bird's office, appeared in the witness box. He openly admitted having spied upon his employer: he had copied letters from the office letter-book and had listened in to an interview that had taken place between Mr Bird and the princess late in 1913. Using the office speaking-tube, he had overheard the solicitor expressing some disquiet about the legal arrangements that had been made for her house's purchase. Sumpster was asked why he had gone to such lengths. He had long suspected that he might be dismissed from his post, he explained, and was already preparing his plan for revenge. When his dismissal came, Mr Bird had shown himself impervious to his blackmail threats, so he had gone to the Inland Revenue officers, to whom he was already supplying information and, on the payment of a suitable sum, he disclosed all he knew. (And when he left the witness box, he apparently went back to his work as a part-time spy for the government.) Meanwhile, the case continued with legal wrangles about what constituted residence in the United Kingdom but to no avail. When the trial ended on 27 July, Bird was singled out as the guilty man. A fine of £500 was imposed upon him as he stood down still protesting his innocence and defending the honour of a partner who had dealt with the matter before his death in 1910. But the fine involved was a minor matter: with a criminal conviction Bird's professional reputation was ruined. From Winnaretta's point of view, the amount of money that she had to pay the Inland Revenue made her acquisition of a modest house in London seem a very costly self-indulgence.

The court-case and its consequences certainly did not cripple her. Moreover, while in progress, it made very little difference

to her routine way of life. Her friends paid little attention to the
legal battle going on in England. In turn, it in no way affected
her attitude towards the English. On 4 December 1916, while
the second stage of the court proceedings was in progress,
Winnaretta was entertaining guests to dinner, among whom,
Paul Morand noted, was Athelstan Johnson from the British
embassy 'his face shrivelled as though with cold under the ice
of his monocle' but, cold in appearance or not, he was there for
Winnaretta's company and to hear a Borodin quartet played
in her studio after dinner. On 16 December Johnson was again
at Winnaretta's side, this time among guests dining at the
Comtesse du Bourg's. A collection of journalists, diplomats and
general social dilettanti expressed their communal delight in the
outcome of the Pepper Coast Affair; listened intently to Joseph
Reinach's comments on the Chambre's attitude towards
Briand's new ministers; and ruefully shook their heads at the
existence of pro-German feeling in the United States.

On 23 December Winnaretta gave another dinner party.
Many of the same guests came, with the addition of the Greek
minister Athos Romanos and Hélène de Caraman-Chimay and
Anna de Noailles. Cloton Legrand, who was in the habit of
calling on Winnaretta so frequently that she seemed to live
with her, came after dinner. Paris still found their friendship
amusing, laced as it was with their bickering and Madame
Legrand's attempts at point-scoring. Their last quarrel had
caused many to smile: Mme Legrand, despite her poverty,
never let anyone forget that her father had been the Marquis de
Fournès. One day in a rage she had flung at Winnaretta:
'Don't forget that the name Fournès is as good as Singer.' The
princess's reply was abrupt and to the point: 'Not at the bottom
of a cheque!' But on this occasion Cloton Legrand was unusually
quiet as Anna de Noailles, sparkling as ever, managed to find
poetry and romance even in a general discussion on the French
high command—but then rumour had it that Général Mangin
was in love with her. Anna was not quite so happy when the
discussion drifted on to the subject of Foch's illness—retention
of urine, according to some sources. Her comments upon the
competence of his doctors did not deflect minds from the
subject. Joseph Reinach developed the theme and told a story
about Mme Jane Dieulafoy, the archaeologist who had donned
male clothes while excavating Darius's palace at Susa and had

continued to wear them ever since. Affecting masculine habits, at dinners she had insisted on remaining behind to smoke with the men until one day Général Galliffet took her by the arm and said, '*Et maintenant allons pisser!*' Anna's face darkened with disapproval, mainly because she could not compete at such a level, and her relief was apparent when the conversation returned to the foibles of politicians and the follies of Parlement. Reinach commented that the worse enemy of Parlement was Parlement. The public was losing its confidence in it. And Winnaretta added: 'Without Parlement Briand would still be a Saint-Nazaire.'

To Winnaretta politics was only a means to an end, the attainment and maintenance of peace. Otherwise she ignored the subject. But during the turmoil of war political comment, even at her dinner table, was inevitable. The Russian Revolution in March 1917 caused endless discussion and speculation. The Russians living in Paris were paralysed with indecision. Even Diaghilev with his Ballets Russes, bearing the mark of the ancien régime, was uncertain about the future. On 11 May 1917, compromising, he took the easy way out of the problem by beginning a gala performance at the Châlelet with Stravinsky's hastily orchestrated version of the *Volga Boatmen* as a substitute national hymn. While this was being played, a *moujick* in red held up an immense red flag as a standard. Few of the audience applauded the idea. Comte Etienne de Beaumont protested: the *Volga Boatmen* was a death-chant. The older members of the audience shuddered as the red flag reminded them of the Paris Commune. Winnaretta, whose earliest recollections were of her family fleeing from the horrors of war and civil strife in 1870, sat and watched grimly, surrounded by her friends Maurice Rostand, Madame Errazuriz, Valentine Gross and Bakst. They were unmoved by the enthusiasm of Montparnasse's neo-Bohemians with their flannel clothes, shaved necks and dirty finger-nails. Yet, the programme that followed united the audience in a common admiration. *L'Oiseau de feu* preceded a charming *Femmes de bonne humeur*, based on Goldoni with music by Domenico Scarlatti and décor by Bakst. Both contrasted well with the *Contes russes* with music by Liadov and décor by Larionov. The *Polovtsien Dances* from *Prince Igor* finally reassured the audience with its familiar exuberance.

A few days later on 14 May Winnaretta gave a dinner party for guests ranging from her niece the Princesse Jean de Broglie to Jean-Louis Forain and the Baron de Berckheim to André Lebey. Their talk of British mine-fields and of the treasonous behaviour of the Russians distressed her and she turned from the apparently insoluble problems of the political world to discuss with Bakst his work on a production of *Phèdre*, in which he hoped Ida Rubinstein would play. She was equally interested in a forthcoming exhibition of his works at the Fine Arts Club in London, although for the moment London was the last place she wanted to visit. After dinner, as though demonstrating that art was above politics and nationalism, she set a young pianist to play Beethoven's *Appassionata Sonata* and Schumann's *Carnival*.

On 26 May Paul Morand noted that at a dinner given by Winnaretta for the Comtesse Adhéaume de Chevigné, Hugo Rumbold, Forain and Maxime Dethomas the talk centred entirely upon art. The merits of different vintage periods were discussed and Dethomas explained his difficulties in designing the sets for Fauré's *Prométhée* at the Opéra. The sheer size of the stage was inhibiting, as was the management's traditionalist approach to stage-design. But, while Winnaretta's guests discussed their own artistic ideas, they were aware that she was involved in ventures of her own. Stravinsky's *Renard* was on the point of being published and her formative influence upon that work was quite well known. At the same time her friends and acquaintances began gleaning snippets of information about an even more unusual enterprise upon which she had embarked.

For many years Erik Satie's music and life-style had provoked comment in France's avant-garde circles. Winnaretta's friends Debussy, Cocteau and Picasso knew him and kept her informed about his latest escapades. She knew the details of his early career as official composer of Josephin Péladan's Rosicrucian Order and enjoyed what music of his she had heard, sometimes as much as anything for their quaint titles, such as *Morceaux en forme de poire*, Satie's response to one of Debussy's criticisms. Yet, it was Debussy's expression of admiration for Satie, his orchestration of two of the three *Gymnopédies*, that first made Winnaretta think seriously about commissioning a work from Satie. When one of her friends, the singer Jane Bathori, mentioned meeting him on 18 April 1916 at a conference

organized by Roland-Manuel for the Société Lyre et Palette,
Winnaretta asked her to bring him to see her. Jane Bathori
could be trusted to do this with a degree of discretion entirely
lacking in Cocteau, who would have been just as capable of
effecting the introduction.

Over the dinner table the princess took stock of the composer. She watched the flashes of mischievous humour sparkle
in his pale blue eyes behind the characteristic pince-nez. None
of his quaint habits disconcerted her. Seeing how much he
enjoyed one of the items on the menu, a roast tongue, she
pressed him to have another slice. 'Yes, yes, with pleasure,' he
exclaimed. 'But not the head, please, because I loathe calf's
head.'

She was more comfortably amused by the stories of his
experiences as a pupil of Vincent d'Indy's at the Schola Cantorum. In an effort to master the technique of fugal counterpoint he had submitted to institutional instruction but the
liberties he took with the rules made his teachers despair.
'When you are older', they would say, 'you will see what they
are all about.' And Satie added an aside for Winnaretta's
benefit: 'But I am now fifty years old and I still don't understand them.'

Undaunted by this self-confessed inadequacy, she asked Satie
if he would be interested in composing something for her. As
with Stravinsky, she suggested a piece for small chamber
orchestra but this time she had fairly precise ideas about the
nature of the work. At the time her Greek studies had progressed far enough for her to read the tragedies of Euripides and
the *Dialogues* of Plato in the original and she wondered if Satie
was capable of creating a new Greek dramatic form by setting
passages of Plato to music. The idea fired his imagination: only
recently he had read Victor Cousin's new translation of the
Dialogues and, seeing himself as a latter-day Socrates carping
at the injustices and hypocrisy of conventional society, he
readily responded to her suggestion. Her intention, she explained, was that she, with her friends Madame de Wendel and
Madame Argyropoulo, who spoke Greek perfectly, should
recite passages of Plato in turn while music composed by Satie
was played in the background. She obviously had in mind
music similar in function to *musique d'ameublement*, which would
at the same time recapture the striking classical simplicity and

modal textures of the *Gymnopédies*. And in the following weeks she and Satie spent many evenings together discussing the project. At first Satie thought that a set made to resemble a small Empire drawing-room should be used as a background against which the reciters, sitting in armchairs, might declaim the Greek text. But that idea was abandoned: the set went; the reciters were replaced by singers and Cousin's French translation ousted the Greek original. A realization of the initial conception might have proved interesting and, for its day, original, foreshadowing Walton's *Façade*, but what did emerge, a *drame symphonique* for four sopranos and small orchestra, entitled *Socrate*, turned out to be an entirely unique work, a creation with much greater integrity than envisaged at first.

Satie's friends, learning of his work on *Socrate*, were surprised at the unusual seriousness of the subject, while Satie himself so completely identified with it that he was afraid of failing in the task. Moreover, the project was on a larger scale than anything previously attempted by him and even after months of work in January 1917 he confided to his friend Valentine Gross that he had no idea where the work was taking him, although, he added lightly, 'Plato was a perfect collaborator, very gentle and never importunate.' He certainly did not fail: the work, which he conceived of as pure and white like *Antiquity*, emerged as that precisely, Satie's masterpiece, a perfect balance between the spirit of the past and the mind of the present.

Apart from encouraging Satie to write a large scale work worthy of his genius, the Polignac commission for *Socrate* saved him financially for the time being, although, with his compulsion for buying a new umbrella every week, the money did not last much beyond the summer of 1917. But this was not the time for mundane preoccupations. On 18 May, a week after Diaghilev's 'Russian matinée', another gala performance took place at the Théâtre du Châtelet. A ballet entitled *Parade*, an invention of Cocteau's with music by Satie and cubist décor by Picasso, was presented before an illustrious audience, Diaghilev's backers, Misia Sert, the Etienne de Beaumonts, the Comtesse de Chevigné and the Comtesse Greffulhe, side by side with the talented young Poulenc, Auric, Ricardo Viñes, Apollinaire (who had written the programme note), Juan Gris and E. E. Cummings, none of whom, however, contributed anything to the riot of protest that greeted the performance. Outraged

matrons screamed all forms of abuse, ranging from 'drug-takers'
to '*Boches*'. One shouted, 'If I'd known it was so silly, I'd have
brought the children!' Winnaretta, conspicuous by her
presence and lack of visible reaction, was entertained by as
much of the music that was audible, although she knew that,
when the public heard Satie's *Socrate*, the contrast with *Parade*
would cause almost as much of a shock.

But before then one more drama had to be enacted. The critic
Jean Poueigh, who injudiciously wrote a scathing review of
Parade, provoked a response from Satie in the form of a postcard
inscribed with a comment of unequivocal vulgarity. And two
weeks later the composer found himself in court answering a
libel charge. The judge, unimpressed by Cocteau and Apollinaire's arguments about aesthetic pros and cons and irritated
by Satie's turbulent band of supporters, sentenced him to one
week's imprisonment, fined him one hundred francs and
ordered him to pay damages of one thousand francs. Satie's
followers were outraged; Cocteau emerged with a bloodied nose
from a fracas with two policemen; Satie went into a fit of
despair because Poueigh would now be able to distrain his
meagre possessions and because no government-subsidized
theatre would ever touch his music now that he had a criminal
record—though, in truth, he would have died rather than go
near any such establishment! His friends could do little practical
to ease the situation, although a special plea helped to turn the
prison sentence into a suspended one. It was Winnaretta who
came to the rescue with the 1,100 francs required by Satie. She
probably knew that if Poueigh did gain the right to distrain
Satie's possessions, the nearly completed score of *Socrate* would
have been lost. In the event Satie's appeal against the sentence
resulted in the damages being waived by a less testy judge, and
the composer, after meeting his expenses, was left with 888
francs 74 centimes of Winnaretta's loan. He promptly wrote to
her—*chère et bonne princesse*—and suggested that, since present
misfortunes, personal and national, had left him 'destitute of
sols, ducats and other articles of that kind', she might like to let
him keep the remaining sum as an advance on the balance of
his commission money. And no more was said about it.

However, as Winnaretta rescued Satie, while she herself was
being harried by the forces of the law, the general calamity of
war in 1917 began to wear down earlier optimism. America's

entry into the war in April 1917 only seemed to widen the scope of the conflict and no immediate end to the conflict could be envisaged. And so, for the time being, she hesitated to make plans for mounting a production of *Socrate*. Such a seminal work needed to be launched carefully. It also demanded the right audiences and for the moment their interest was elsewhere.

Chapter 11
Peace Returning

(1917–1920)

During 1917 the increasing danger from German attacks on Paris had the effect of flushing Marcel Proust out of his self-imposed seclusion. After years of semi-retirement he began to socialize again with a greater fervour than ever. Almost inevitably he drifted back into the circles most likely to stimulate his senses and titillate his snobbish palate. On 16 December 1916 Paul Morand had been treated to a Proustian meditation on the theme of time past while visiting him at 102 boulevard Haussman: as he mused through a box of photographs from the 1880s and 1890s, Morand saw a spectacular galaxy of Proust's friends, the Princesse Mathilde, Montesquiou, Lucien Daudet as a child, Maupassant on a bicycle, Edmond de Polignac, inseparable from Charles Haas, and Winnaretta in her early twenties, little different from herself at fifty. And soon after that Proust plunged into a new present with old friends. After a gap of about ten years he saw Winnaretta again and their friendship revived, the past forgiven if not forgotten. She welcomed him back as the great novelist whom she had championed from the first. Proust enjoyed her attentiveness and appreciated her attempts to attract him back into the society that meant so much to him, although at first he seems to have doubted her judgment. One evening she invited him to dinner to meet the Abbé Arthur Mugnier. Proust, suspicious of a possible proselytizer, mistook the princess's motives and refused. But during the summer of 1917 he found himself unavoidably rubbing shoulders with Mugnier at parties given by mutual friends, such as Marie Murat, the young Princesse Marthe Bibesco and Paul Morand's Roumanian friend Princesse Soutzo. Proust quickly realized that the abbé was no ordinary priest but a man of great wisdom and sensitivity whose love of God inspired in him an all-embracing selfless love of mankind. There was a blessed simplicity in his message: God, having

created a soul in love, never faltered in that love. Mugnier used
to say that he certainly believed in the existence of Hell because
the Church required him to do so but, he would add, he did
not believe that anyone was there. Proust soon became a close
friend of the good abbé as he helped him to shoulder his burden
of guilt, fear and neurosis; in short, thereafter Mugnier never
ceased to ease his way along the road of personal salvation. His
task as the apostle to the rich and famous was far from easy.
Even after Proust's death he continued to celebrate an annual
mass for him at Saint-Pierre-de-Chaillot until old friends no
longer came. As Mugnier himself would have said, there was
little need: Proust's death had been forgotten because he still
lived in his immortal works.

Seeing them at many social functions, Winnaretta was
pleased by the evident spiritual compatibility of the two men.
For his part, Proust openly regretted being suspicious of her
motives for bringing them together. By December 1917 he was
sending messages of genuine regret refusing invitations to dinner
parties. Comte Robert de Billy asked him to dine along with
Maurice Paléologue, Mugnier, the Comtesse de Chevigné and
Winnaretta but he was too ill to accept. Winnaretta's invitation
to dinner followed by an organ recital in her studio also had to
be declined. Thinking that material solicitude would be less
open to misinterpretation, she sent him a bunch of prodigious
muscatel grapes, which sent him into such raptures that he
immediately wrote her a letter of thanks. Unfortunately during
his illness his letters remained unposted and only with his return
to health did he learn of the omission. His mortification was
intense.

Soon afterwards, in spring 1918, Proust had another *contretemps* involving correspondence with Winnaretta. As the proofs
of *À l'Ombre des jeunes filles en fleur* were coming off the press, he
suddenly decided to dedicate the volume to the 'dear and
venerated memory of Prince Edmond de Polignac', as the
'homage of him to whom he showed so much kindness and who
still admires him . . .' Day after day Proust telephoned Winnaretta to obtain her permission but received no reply. En-
countering Reynaldo Hahn, he soon discovered the reason: she
had left some time before for the Pyrénées. Thereupon he sat
down and wrote her a long, rambling letter in which he protested his sincere desire to publish the dedication. She was not

to heed what enemies said of him. He was anxious not to revive
the bad feelings that had previously marred their friendship. He
assured her that no character in the novel bore the slightest
resemblance to either herself or the prince. *À l'Ombre* could not
provide material for even the most impudent slanderer. To
prove his assertion he then gave her a bland thumb-nail sketch
of the plot and excused himself for it: he would much rather
have written *La Chartreuse de Parme* or the *Brothers Karamazov* as
a more worthy offering to the memory of the prince. He then
urged Winnaretta to reply at once: 'Don't take the trouble to
give me your reasons. Just say "yes" or "no".' If 'no', he would
not lack for other dedicatees. But he sincerely hoped that the
answer would be 'yes'. (At this point he abruptly ended his
letter and cut the final sheet in half as he realized that he had
already written something on the back.)

Winnaretta's answer was a decisive 'no'. And she gave
reasons for her refusal. Proust, unconvinced, immediately
replied in querulous tones: she had taken exactly the opposite
meaning from the one intended. Since she had obviously
misunderstood his real intentions, he would go ahead with the
dedication and await a telegraphed reply from her. He was sure
that she would now be sympathetic to his request and with the
dedication a misunderstanding of twenty years standing would
be laid to rest. But she was unmoved by his pleas and adamantly
refused to give her permission. Offended and disappointed,
Proust at last took the hint and withdrew the dedication. In the
event Winnaretta found nothing in the book that reflected
badly upon her dead husband or herself but ever since the
'Salon' article she had mistrusted Proust's pen, if not himself.
His love-hate fixation with homosexuality and with the foibles
of high society made any personal association with his publications rather undesirable. As a writer Proust was incapable of
respecting confidences; all his observations of man as a social
animal he regarded as valid literary material.

There is possibly another explanation for Winnaretta's attitude. At this point she was slightly sensitive about any publicity
involving family matters because her niece Marguerite (or
Daisy) Decazes had precipitated an unnecessary confrontation
with her husband Prince Jean de Brogile. They had married in
1910, when both were still young, and by 1917 they were the
proud parents of three daughters. But what Daisy did not know,

as many did, was that Prince Jean was interested in men as much as women—if not more so. In 1918, while fighting at the front, he was seriously wounded and, as he lay recovering in hospital, Daisy took the opportunity to examine his correspondence, among which she discovered certain very compromising letters from men friends. Infuriated, she confronted him with them; whereupon, so rumour had it, he simply allowed himself to die. The incident caused a minor sensation, which some felt could have been avoided. The widow, however, did not nurse her grief—or wounds—very long: the following year she married the Hon. Reginald Fellowes, Lord de Ramsey's second son, and as Daisy Fellowes became a by-word for extravagant and skittish behaviour in the Paris of the inter-War period.

Whatever sadness Winnaretta felt about Jean de Broglie's death, she was infinitely more upset by the death of Claude Debussy soon afterwards on 28 March 1918. She had lost a friend; it scarcely mattered that an unappreciative France had lost one of its most significant composers. What added to the tragedy of his death was that in the confusion caused by the Germans' bombing Paris the event passed almost unnoticed. The funeral was chaotic and so unimpressive that a Montmartre housewife, casting a critical eye over the motley handful of mourners behind the coffin, asked who had died and received the scarcely adequate reply, 'A musician.'

Ironically Winnaretta herself could not attend the funeral because at the time she was staying in a cottage at Saint-Jean-de-Luz, which she had rented because Debussy had spent his last summer there and had recommended it with enthusiasm. The house had been built by an English family who, in the heart of the French Basque country, had somehow managed to impregnate it with an English atmosphere. Debussy had been particularly struck by it. 'I always think I'll meet Mr Pickwick on the stairs,' he would say. Winnaretta sensed the same atmosphere, although, as she pointed out, there was nothing particularly English about the appearance of the cottage. It was built in the traditional Basque style and from the colonnade at the front the spectacular view of the plain and mountains was anything but English. And she herself did little to foster the atmosphere. During the rest of 1918 the house virtually became a centre for Debussy memorial events. For much of the time the pianist Ricardo Viñes was also staying at Saint-Jean and Winnaretta took advantage of his presence to give a series of recitals devoted to the music of Debussy and other modern composers whom they championed, particularly Chabrier, Albeniz, Fauré and Ravel. In September 1918 Francis Poulenc, up to his eyes in Red Cross work with Comte Etienne de Beaumont in Paris, wrote to Viñes in almost envious terms about the musical effervescence which he rightly surmised the princess had given social life in Saint-Jean. Whatever her situation, wherever she was, her presence could be counted on to stimulate worthwhile musical activities.

Nonetheless, even the beautiful south-west corner of France began to make her feel restless. She longed for peace and the chance to return to Paris. In the meantime she occupied herself with arranging short trips to see kinsmen in the Gironde and with travelling round the area trying to find interesting things to do. On one occasion the Comtesse René du Temple de Rougemont called in at a local church in Pau, expecting to enjoy a moment of meditative calm, only to find the organ booming out magnificent music. At the console she discovered Winnaretta lost to the world in the music of Bach.

However, the princess was far from being a lotus-eater, using music as an opiate. Rather it was a stimulant to heighten the senses and intellectual awareness. Even during the days of waiting at Saint-Jean she had to have some major musical scheme to occupy her mind. The half-Spanish air of the place gave her an idea; as so often with Ravel, a native of Saint-Jean-de-Luz, she was almost compulsively drawn towards Spain for inspiration. She decided to commission a work from Manuel de Falla and turned to Ricardo Viñes for a formal introduction to him. Although she had met Falla briefly in Paris and had long been attracted by his music, she scarcely knew him as a person, so, following a letter from Viñes with one from herself, she asked him if he would like to write a work for small orchestra and voices, capable of being produced in her house in Paris. As soon as travelling became possible again, she would come to Spain to discuss ideas with him.

Soon afterwards, in November 1918, Winnaretta was able to return to Paris, *en fête* to celebrate the victory. For a time the process of peacetime recuperation and retrenchment pre-occupied everyone. Paris was alive again with friends unseen for many years. The shades of those who had died in the fighting were there too, reminding all that there could be no return to the old days. A vast amount of foreigners from Allied countries thronged the city, new acquaintances and old friends. Immediately the Parisian hostesses resuscitated social activities on a scale worthy of a peace conference city. As early as 20 November 1918 Daisy de Broglie was giving luncheon parties to welcome the visitors. Lady Helen Vincent, now Viscountess D'Abernon, was there with Diana Capel, later Countess of Westmorland, to meet their old friend Winnaretta and the Academician Prince Maurice de Broglie. Count Isvolsky, the former Russian ambassador in Paris, was also invited to stress links with the past and to centre speculative talk on the mysterious fate of the Tsar's family. Had they been murdered or had they escaped? A lot of water had passed under the Russian bridge in the short time since Diaghilev had had the equivocal *Volga Boatmen* played at his Russian gala in May 1917.

With the peacemakers, many others arrived in the spring of 1919 with different ideas in mind. Elsa Maxwell appeared, earnestly bent on socializing on a shoe string. Introduced to the British Foreign Secretary A. J. Balfour, she impulsively invited him to dinner at the Ritz, forgetting that her finances would not stand the strain. An appeal to Lady Colebrooke's good nature resulted in her dinner party being taken over completely: 'Don't worry about the expense. For a proper dinner party there must be eight guests.' Out came a paper and pencil and a list of names was soon made: Lord D'Abernon, Lady Ripon, the Comte Boni de Castellane, the Grand-Duke Alexander, Sir Ronald Storrs, Mrs George Keppel and the Princesse de Polignac—a perfect balance. Elsa Maxwell was disconcerted: among all the guests foisted upon her she only knew Mrs Keppel. But she soon got to know the rest of them, as only she knew how. In fact, later on she was to single out Winnaretta as one of her staunchest friends. She admired her outlook on life, which in Elsa's eyes amounted to originality, simply because, with more money than she could count, she deliberately dressed in a casual manner, often in well-loved but slightly shabby clothes. She shared with Winnaretta a suspicion of women enslaved by their dressmakers and took delight in repeating her version of a story on the subject of her appearance. One day during the war the princess had presented herself at the local *mairie* to hand in a donation for the area's poor-relief fund. As she stood there holding a well-worn handbag containing a cheque for a million francs, the secretary took one look at her old shoes, shabby hat and woollen gloves and motioned her away: 'If you are here for the distribution of free clothes, it's on the first floor.'

The peace conference attracted some more serious-minded women. Christabel Pankhurst re-appeared, bringing her indomitable mother and Mrs Flora Drummond with her. They were intent on lobbying Lloyd George and tackling foreign politicians and statesmen, such as Masaryk and Benes, Aristide Briand and the Australian prime minister Hughes, on the question of women's rights. But they also took time off to revive old friendships. They descended upon Winnaretta to reminisce about Christabel's years of exile in Paris and discuss the furtherance of their feminist ideals.

The suffragettes' society contrasted sharply with the atmosphere of the world which Winnaretta entered when she visited Manuel de Falla soon afterwards. His political views were just as strong, if diametrically opposed to theirs: he was an ultra-Catholic, a royalist and a conservative in the full sense of the word. Winnaretta was highly amused at the way in which he would express indignation when modernist opinions were mentioned or when the voice of democracy made itself heard. But she admired him for his integrity and for the rigorous, near-ascetic life he lived while composing voluptuous music, sparkling with life and colour. And in the summer of 1919 she went to Granada to discuss music not politics. Already in December 1918 they had decided on a suitable subject for the commission. Falla had written to her laconically: 'This subject you will find by reading chapter twenty-six of the second part of *Don Quixote*: the Puppet Show of Master Peter—*el Retablo de Maese Pedro*.' And the reasons why he had chosen this episode from Cervantes were just as concise; more than any other it highlighted the contrast between reality and fantasy: Don Quixote and Sancho Panza, spending the night at an inn, are entertained by Maese Pedro with his puppet-theatre. The story enacted by the puppets is taken from an old Spanish ballad relating the tale of Don Gayferos, one of Charlemagne's knights, who rescues the fair Christian princess Melisandra from the clutches of the Moorish king of Saragossa. So con-

vincing are Maese Pedro's puppets that at the climax of the
drama Don Quixote joins in the conflict on the Christian
knight's side and, flailing his sword to left and right, scatters
decapitated puppets in all directions. For Falla the Don
represented a timeless figure of intransigence, at once tragic
and comic, the personification of the spirit of senseless belligerence, which should have no part in civilized life. And, when
he and Winnaretta discussed the nature of the work, they hit
upon an altogether original idea. It would be an opera of sorts
but the action on the stage would be done entirely by puppets:
those in Maese Pedro's little theatre would be glove puppets,
while the 'audience' of the Don, Sancho, Maese Pedro and his
boy would be fully-articulated marionettes. In this way the
feeling of contrast needed for a play within a play could be
achieved; at the same time an overall feeling of unreality could
be maintained. The vocal parts would be sung by three singers
positioned in the orchestra and the movements of the large
puppets synchronized with the music.

The details of the production and the instrumentation were
largely thrashed out by the composer and the princess during
the few days of her visit. But Falla did take some time off to show
her the sights of Granada. They themselves must have presented
a strange sight as they walked in the streets of the old town:
Winnaretta rock-like and unaffected; Falla, as she herself
noted, 'well below medium height, thin like many Spaniards,
and with his hard, emaciated features and dark, dark complexion, . . . like a figure carved out of walnut or a medieval
saint in discoloured stone.'

One evening Falla took her and his friend the guitarist
Segovia to the gardens of the Alhambra, empty and flooded
with moonlight. Falla chose a place to sit and there they stayed
for hours, listening to the inimitable music of historic Spain that
he asked Segovia to play. Years later Winnaretta reminisced:
'I can never forget the incomparable beauty of those gardens
steeped in music and moonlight.'

El Retablo de Maese Pedro was not easily written. It preoccupied Falla for over four years, during which time he wrote
little else except his *Homenajes* in memory of Debussy. Diaghilev,
pressing him to arrange some of Pergolesi's music as a ballet-
score, met with a refusal (which ultimately was responsible for
Stravinsky's masterly recreation of *Pulcinella*.) Falla spent a lot

of time solving the technical problem of writing music designed
to harmonize with marionette movements. In this he was helped
by the local wonder-child, the poet Federico Garcia Lorca
with whom he had already collaborated by supplying musical
arrangements for puppet-shows given on his parents' estate near
Granada. As a result of their discussions, Falla decided to press
the Princesse de Polignac to commission Lorca's puppet-
makers, Hermenegildo Lanz and Manuel Angeles Ortiz, the
painter, to make the puppets and create the *décor* for *El Retablo*
and she agreed.

Even more significant was Falla's decision to use the harpsichord to achieve a special effect in his score and Winnaretta
encouraged him to use it. The result was the first piece of music
since the baroque era to incorporate the harpsichord into a
score as an orchestral instrument. The distinctive *timbre* that *El
Retablo* gained from it was entirely modern as well as wholly in
keeping with the spirit of Cervantes's age. It added an appropriate dignity to the work, strikingly Castilian in character and
in marked contrast with the Andalusian texture of his previous
compositions. Many of the technical difficulties involved in
writing for the unfamiliar instrument were ironed out for Falla
by the harpsichordist Wanda Landowska while on a visit to
Granada. For some time she had been pressing him to write her
a work for harpsichord and orchestra. But he refused to consider
that project until after the completion of the opera. However,
this did not dampen Landowska's enthusiasm and she insisted
on playing at *El Retablo*'s première in Paris—despite the fact
that she regarded Winnaretta with a degree of veiled hostility:
they were rather too similar in temperament to be bosom
friends.

While Falla continued to work on his commission, Satie
finished his symphonic drama *Socrate* and sent Winnaretta the
manuscript, written in his own exquisite hand. The score was
published in 1919 and a series of first performances of the work
began to take place. The music was first heard in a version for
piano and soprano solo at the princess's house in the avenue
Henri-Martin. Rumours had circulated about a disagreement
between her and Satie on the number of artists to be used. He
had set fragments from three of Plato's *Dialogues*: the 'Portrait
of Socrates', a conversation between Socrates and Alcibiades
from the *Symposium*; 'On the Banks of the Ilissus', a discussion

between Phaedrus and Socrates on aesthetic matters from the
Phaedrus, and the 'Death of Socrates', the poignant description
of the philosopher's last hours from the *Phaedo*; and he had
intended the parts to be sung by four solo sopranos so that,
while the work retained a certain vocal homogeneity, the subtle
contrast in the performers' voices would give some sense of
dialogue. However, the work could be just as well sung by one
singer, because no vocal ensemble was involved. Winnaretta
seems to have pressed for this style of performance not because
of financial considerations but because the use of four sopranos
(to sing the parts of four individual males) would lead to too
much characterization, destroy the narrative *parlando* texture
of the work and, in short, come very near to being a *travesti*
show, which may well have appealed to Satie's mocking sense
of humour but would have affected the audience's objective
assessment of the music.

This private performance at Winnaretta's, for which Satie
played the piano and Jane Bathori sang, was well received.
But when *Socrate* was first introduced to outside audiences, there
was no consensus of opinion about it. Subjected to the scrutiny
of an intellectual audience, it bore up rather well, considering
the strange new genre of music being pioneered. On 21 March
1919, in the cramped conditions of Adrienne Monnier's famous
bookstore 'Les Amis des Livres' at 7 rue de l'Odéon, the
soprano Suzanne Balguerie, accompanied by Satie himself
performed the work before a gathering of friends. Spectacularly
talented, among them were to be seen poets and writers, Paul
Valéry, Francis Jammes, André Gide, Léon-Paul Fargue and
Paul Claudel; artists, Derain, Braque and Picasso; and composers, Stravinsky and most of the group of young musicians
soon to be known as *Les Six*, along with their self-appointed
spokesman Cocteau. As a whole the audience was enthusiastic
about Satie's re-creation of the world of Plato, a work appeal-
ingly classical in spirit rather than neo-classical in the Stravinskian sense. Some, such as Claudel, waxed lyrically eloquent
about it. Paul Valéry, impressed by the sustained unity of the
work with its unclimactic inevitability, described it as 'this
sonorous bath called music'. Only André Gide expressed no
opinion but his musical propensities were well-known: little
written since the death of Chopin interested him.

The first fully public performance did not take place until

138   *The Food of Love*

almost a year later when the Société Nationale de Musique
presented it at a concert in the Old Conservatoire on 14
February 1920. On this occasion the vocal parts were divided
between two sopranos, Jane Bathori and Suzanne Balguerie,
with André Salomon replacing Satie at the piano. The previous
week the *Guide du Concert* had advertised the concert by confronting the readers with a caricature of Socrates on its cover.
Out of his mouth had issued the following injunction, written
in Satie's own distinctive handwriting: 'Those who do not
understand are asked by me to observe the most respectful
silence and to comport themselves in a wholly submissive and
inferior way.' This did produce the desired amount of indignation in some of the audience; but Satie must have been chagrined by the studied lack of interest shown by others: if the
composer thought of himself as a revolutionary, *Socrate* would
do nothing to enhance his reputation.

However this did not stop the Société Nationale from going
ahead with plans to present the first orchestral hearing of
Socrate later that year on 7 June in the Salle Erard. The programme was all Satie, except for an introductory lecture by
Cocteau—and that was on Satie. *Parade* was the first item,
played in a two piano version by Satie himself and Germaine
Tailleferre. *Trois petites pièces montées* came next, followed by
various piano pieces, including the *Gymnopédies* and *Gnossienne*,
played by Ricardo Viñes. Finally, stranger than them all,
Socrate was performed by the soprano Marya Freund, the
famous interpreter of Schoenberg's *Pierrot Lunaire*, with Félix
Delgrange as conductor. The audience's reaction was generally
hostile. Titters greeted certain parts: those unfamiliar with the
life of the historic Socrates, that gadfly of society, scoffed at the
dying philosopher for reminding his friend Crito that they owed
Esculapus a cock; the debt must be discharged. It made the
final pronouncement on Socrates as 'the wisest and most just
of all men' seem a little unrealistic. Many in the audience
booed and the critics wrote even harsher words than before.
Jean Marnold of the *Mercure de France* dismissed it for amounting
to nothing in itself and for plagiarizing from *Boris Godunov* and
Pelléas et Mélisande. The critic of *Le Ménestrel* called it feeble: if
anything the orchestral version showed up the naked, uncon-
cealed and crude poverty of *Socrate* even more than the piano
performance.

At the end of the day the reaction of the younger set of creative artists was all that mattered. More than any other composition, *Socrate* ennunciated an artistic ethic for the 1920s. It implicitly rejected a current style of composition in which an obsession with craftsmanship had begun to mask musical purpose. In *Socrate* Satie reacted against the *écriture artistique*, as represented by Ravel's Piano Trio of 1914, where ingenuity was all that mattered. He deliberately cultivated simplicity and ingenuousness in order to recapture the spirit of music tailored to human proportions. Cocteau's trite booklet *Le Coq et l'Arlequin*, so pitifully negative in its attempt to shock and impress, had nothing like the same significance as *Socrate* for the *Groupe des Six* and most other young composers who plunged into the Parisian melting-pot in the 1920s. Not only its musical language but also its anti-materialist philosophy of the integrity of the individual and its respect for dignity and humanity were very influential. Even the fact that the first more or less public performance took place on the Left Bank under the aegis of Adrienne Monnier helped to polarize artistic life in that quarter in the post-War era. If Satie, through *Socrate*, became the apostle of the neo-Bohemianism of the 1920s, as his patron, Winnaretta was regarded by his disciples as something of a fairy-godmother. She certainly cultivated this rôle in the years to come.

Chapter 12
The Youthful Heart
(1921–1923)

On 16 June 1921 Winnaretta attended a dinner given by Madame Hennessy to celebrate the long-awaited engagement between the Duke of Marlborough and Gladys Deacon. Proust was also there and soon became engrossed in conversation with her, their differences over the dedication of *À l'Ombre* forgotten. Paul Morand, doubly talented as a diplomat and writer, was the subject of the discussion. Proust let drop the comment, 'Paul Morand likes you very much' and was so taken aback by the princess's exclamations of delight that later the same evening he felt obliged to write to Morand asking him not to disappoint her by contradicting what he had said. 'Naturally,' Proust added slyly, 'I refrained from telling her that you were in love with her.'

But why was Proust so surprised at Winnaretta's reaction? Possibly he failed to realize that time for some meant the present projected into the future rather than the past recalled in the present. Winnaretta reacted true to character. Her mind was constantly preoccupied with the process of cultural development. She almost instinctively gravitated towards anything new and talented that showed promise of future greatness. She had long known and admired Morand but he was only just beginning to emerge as a novelist who spoke for the younger generation of the new age. Even allowing for Proustian grandiloquence, for her at the age of fifty-six to be accepted among the up-and-coming artistic set was of supreme importance. Indeed, in her latter years, when she often set the pace herself, she always tried to eliminate consciousness of age and generation-gaps. She possessed a certain timeless quality: she could mix with all types of people but felt most at ease with forward-looking artists whatever their age. A revealing incident occurred some years later. One day she met Reynaldo Hahn in the street and asked him gently why he no longer came to her concerts.

Reynaldo frowned: her musical ventures nearly always contained works by Mozart, Bach or Schubert but they were made to jostle cheek by jowl with the latest works of ultra-modern composers. He tried to make a joke of the matter. 'Until my dying day I shall always hate everything you like in music.' Winnaretta commented that one could not hate Bach or Schubert. And Reynaldo replied: 'Yes, possibly, but you are too fond of the *va de l'avant* and I absolutely cannot stand their ideas.' There was no answer to that, so she took him off to lunch to gossip about the past. Afterwards she turned the incident over in her mind. Why did Reynaldo have such an aversion to the avant-garde? Perhaps their musical aims were too different from his: after all he was proud to be regarded as the 'spiritual heir of Théodore Dubois and Massenet'; or perhaps the reason was that he was no longer very young. She did not stop for a moment to think that he was fully ten years younger than herself.

The princess had always been known to her close friends by the rather girlish name of Winnie. Now she became almost universally known as Aunt Winnie (Tante Winnie, pronounced with an English 'W'); the more reserved called her Princesse Winnie. For many members of France's high aristocracy, she was indeed Aunt Winnie but, while she cherished that expression of relationship, she rather revelled in the affectionate familiarity with which her younger friends used the name. Only on one occasion did she indicate disapproval of its use—though wittily. At a masked ball a young man not noted for his excessive virility (Baron Robert de Rothschild, it has been said) espied the unmistakable figure of Winnaretta dressed as a *dogaressa* and, emboldened by drink, he shouted across the room: '*Bon soir, tante Winnie!*', to which he received the annihilating reply, '*Tante vous-même!*'

During the first years of the 1920s Winnaretta's approach to the young composers of the *Groupe des Six* was cautious. She already knew Milhaud and Poulenc before they were homogenized into a 'group' with Germaine Tailleferre, Arthur Honegger, Louis Durey and Georges Auric, and so tended scrupulously to think of them as individuals rather than as a school. Certainly the intensity of her friendship with them as individuals varied: Honegger and Durey, less gregarious, were not quite so close to her as the others. Much the same was the case with Satie's '*École d'Arceuil*' which emerged a little later. Henri Cliquet-Pleyel and Maxime Jacob never achieved the same level of intimacy with her as Roger Desormière and Henri Sauguet. Nonetheless, they all without exception found her willing to have their latest compositions performed at concerts in her house. But, in the beginning it was apparent that, however different their individual styles of composition, the rising generation of composers, especially *Les Six*, formed a movement of sorts with common aims and artistic philosophies and so Winnaretta hesitated initially to patronize any one more than another by commissioning works that would inevitably bear her own imprint upon them. But she did try to gain them commissions from Diaghilev, who was capable of providing a wider audience for their music than she could with just her salon-set. Since by that time she practically held the purse strings for the Ballets Russes, her wishes did carry some weight in their favour. Diaghilev's production of Poulenc's *Les Biches*, Auric's *Les Facheux* and Milhaud's *Le Train Bleu* in 1924 was the first of a series of balletic triumphs for *Les Six* and their friends.

Winnaretta's complete commitment to the ballet company, that had such distinctive results, came about through a disaster. On 2 November 1921 Diaghilev's full-scale extravaganza production of a traditional *Sleeping Beauty* opened at the Alhambra Theatre in London but, despite critical acclaim, it only lasted for a hundred and five performances, well short of the number required to make the production break even. Once the theatre manager Sir Oswald Stoll had sequestrated the scenery and costumes, Diaghilev found himself back in Paris in the middle of February 1922 with no resources—he had even had to sell his black pearl stud, a treasured gift from Lady Ripon—and with a commitment to mount a Paris season in May. The *Sleeping Princess* as a whole could not be used. At the most a fragment of it, *Le Mariage d'Aurore* could be rescued and that only because costumes from the pre-War production of *Le Pavillon d'Armide* could replace those sequestrated in London. But that did not amount to a season's programme. Then he had an inspiration (or, more accurately, he swallowed his pride) and began to consider the possibility of mounting Stravinsky's *Renard* as a novelty to catch the attention of Paris audiences. Some time before he had heard, or had been made to overhear, fragments of the work sung to a piano accompaniment in Winnaretta's salon but he had pointedly ignored it. Still jealous of the ascendancy which Stravinsky's music enjoyed in Polignac programmes, in time of crisis he did not hesitate to ask her permission to mount the work as a balletic burlesque as originally intended. She gladly gave him the score as well as a large sum of money to enable him to bear the cost of production. Then a final novelty was added to the repertoire, Stravinsky's newly completed opera buffa *Mavra*, based on a story by Pushkin. Winnaretta ended up by paying for its production also. In addition, on 29 May a pre-première presentation of *Mavra* took place at the Hôtel Continental at her expense. Diaghilev wanted to test the reaction of friends to the new work before presenting it to an unpredictable general public at the Opéra on 3 June. *Renard*, which she had breathed life into as early as 1916, never had an integral performance in her house, as originally intended, but became very much public property. As a stage work with masterly choreography by Bronislava Nijinska and décor by Larionov, it was certainly successful when premièred on 18 May but Diaghilev's subsequent coupling of it and *Mavra*, both works of miniature proportions, with works of much grander dimensions, *Petrushka* and *Le Sacre de printemps*, caused them to be dwarfed in the already dangerously grandiose setting of the Opéra. Yet, at the time *Renard* at least was recognized as a unique creation and in 1929, when Diaghilev revived it in a new production with choreography by Serge Lifar, it was entirely successful.

Although Diaghilev's 1922 season as a whole was slightly uneven, the Ballets Russes had been saved for the time being through Winnaretta's intervention. A mood of mild jubilation infected the whole company. After the first night of *Renard* on 18 May the troupe was entertained at a grand supper-party given by Proust's friends Sidney and Violet Schiff. Picasso was there and the young English writer Clive Bell. James Joyce arrived later, drunk and quite incapable of coping with Proust's social chit-chat. In fact, the whole evening was not very happy for Proust. He had earlier tried to make conversation with Stravinsky. Did he like Beethoven? 'I loathe him,' came the impatient reply. 'Not even the late quartets?' Stravinsky growled: 'Worse than the rest!' However sincere Proust's interest in Beethoven might have been, it was certainly not the question to ask a composer with half his mind on the

première of a new work. Moreover, Proust's musical preoccupation coincided unedifyingly with a too superficial current vogue
for the late works of Beethoven. Winnaretta must have been
horrified at this conversation. If only Proust had contented
himself with firing his musical queries at herself, as he usually
did, he might avoid being thought a musical snob. However
she was not out of sympathy with him for long: a few weeks later
on 12 June she encountered him at a party given by Madame
Hennessy just at the point at which they realized that they
numbered among guests who were less than civilized by their
standards. Winnaretta put on a cold, forbidding look of
detachment; Proust shuddered at hearing himself pointed out
as 'the famous Marcel Prévost, who wrote *Les Don Juanes*'. But,
among the more discerning, Proust's fame, indeed his immortality, was not in doubt and, when he died a few months
later, thousands mourned for him. The princess too regretted
the death of a genius but, with a touch of amusement, must
have wondered at the wisdom of playing Ravel's *Pavane pour une
infante défunte* at his funeral: in the circumstances an elegy for a
dead princess was surely a rather tactless choice.

During Proust's last months Winnaretta had distractions
other than his decline. She was still heavily involved with the
fate of Diaghilev's company, which after its life-saving season
in the summer of 1922 was faced with the problem of how to
survive until the 1923 season. Serge Grigoriev, Diaghilev's
right-hand man, suggested the possibility of lending the company to the Monte Carlo Opera, which maintained a small
troupe to take part in its winter season of operas. Fortunately
for Diaghilev, two years earlier, Winnaretta's kinsman and
close friend Comte Pierre de Polignac had surprised all Paris
and delighted his family by marrying Princesse Charlotte, the
heiress of Louis II, the sovereign Prince of Monaco. Winnaretta
had already offered to use her influence with the new Prince
Pierre de Monaco and his wife and they now readily agreed to
help Diaghilev gain a contract from the management of the
Monte Carlo Opera. In fact, Pierre and Charlotte welcomed
this addition to the artistic life of the principality. Once the
arrangement was seen to be successful, they became important
patrons of the Ballets Russes. And until 1929 Diaghilev's contract was renewed annually. Indeed, from that point his company adopted the name of 'Les Ballets Russes de Monte Carlo'.

If Winnaretta was happy to leave the company under the aesthetic aegis of Prince Pierre during the winter months, with the coming of spring she was usually involved in arrangements for its return to Paris. Without ever interfering, she would pay out sums of money to ensure the success of its productions and keep herself in readiness to help it out of the difficulties that invariably arose. In 1923 Diaghilev prepared to stage Stravinsky's *Les Noces*. Rehearsals for the première, to be held at the Théâtre de la Gaieté Lyrique in Paris on 13 June, were begun while the company was still in Monte Carlo but, as the opening night approached, it was clear that the dancers still had not assimilated the music, so Diaghilev suggested that Winnaretta might give a concert performance of it in her house for the benefit of the dancers and the delectation of her friends. She agreed and an impressive concert resulted. A new arrival in the company, the seventeen-year-old Serge Lifar, observed the scene with awe: Stravinsky himself conducts, watched by Diaghilev seated in an armchair, flanked by Bronislava Nijinska and the troupe's leading dancers and surrounded by the cream of musical Paris. Intoxicated by the rhythms of the Russian music, everyone is carried away with enthusiasm and applauds wildly, sure that the ballet will be a triumph. Diaghilev seems quietly pleased and the Princesse de Polignac embraces Stravinsky.

The first public performance of *Les Noces* on 13 June fulfilled predictions of success. Paris audiences, having cut their teeth on *Le Sacre* a decade before, were able to digest this powerful work easily. By contrast, when London audiences saw it three years later, they reacted badly, as they had not with *Le Sacre*; only H. G. Wells tried to refute the critics' judgment by describing it as 'a rendering in sound and vision of the peasant soul'.

The Parisian public possibly interpreted it in less self-conscious terms and their pleasure was all the more uninhibited. On 17 June, the Sunday after the première, the American millionaires Gerald and Sara Murphy, dilettanti artists, occasionally taking a hand in scene-painting for Diaghilev and for Rolfe de Maré's Ballets Suèdois, decided to celebrate the triumph of *Les Noces* by giving a party in a restaurant on board a barge moored opposite the Chambre des Députés. The party turned out to be a personality-studded occasion with a bizarre touch or two. At 7 p.m. the first guest to arrive was Stravinsky, who rushed into the dining-room to inspect the place-cards on the table. Hovering over them as though about to rearrange them, he visibly subsided, apparently pleased to find himself seated on the right hand of the Princesse de Polignac. Then the other guests arrived: the conductor Ernest Ansermet and Georges Auric, Hélène Leon, Edouard Flamet and Marcelle Meyer, who had played the piano parts in the production, the designers Michel Larionov and Natalia Goncharova, the composers Darius Milhaud and Germaine Tailleferre with Cocteau and Picasso in their wake, the editor of the *Dial*, Scofield Thayer, the poet Blaise Cendrars and the high-priest of Dadaism, Tristan Tzara (who was known to feel as much at ease in Winnaretta's salon as in the near anarchic society that he usually frequented); Diaghilev appeared with his brilliant secretary-librettist Boris Kochno. The party was a relaxed impromptu affair which, after dinner, turned into a dance with Ansermet and Marcelle Meyer at the piano supplying the music. At one point Ansermet and Kochno took down a huge decorative laurel-wreath bearing the inscription *Les Noces* and, holding it like a hoop, encouraged Stravinsky to run the length of the room and leap through it. The excitement subsided but it was soon whipped up again by shouted warnings: the barge was sinking! The guests rushed on deck, not suspecting that it was a false alarm concocted by the more impish among them. Winnaretta left with the others as dawn was breaking.

The varied assortment of guests at the Murphys' party was typical of the 'mixed' company from which the princess drew her friends, although in this case love of ballet was a common denominator. Anyone of any interest was immediately invited to her salon. Her house was often referred to as 'the crossroads of the arts'. Indeed, the paths of many great men and women cut across one another there. For example, in the 1920s, Paul Valéry, the poet of infinite sensitivity, became a more and more familiar figure at Winnaretta's and significant friendships resulted from her introductions. Stravinsky first met him at her house around 1922 and subsequently developed a cherished acquaintance with the refined and gentlemanly writer. Another writer, Elisabeth de Gramont, who had just unburdened herself of her husband, the Duc de Clermont-Tonnerre, in favour of Sapphic friendships, often met Valéry at Winnaretta's and would watch him sitting there contentedly listening to a Bach concerto, letting its poetry inspire his own. For her part, the princess actively tried to foster Valéry's reputation. In June 1923, just after her concert performance of *Les Noces*, she arranged for him to give a lecture in her salon and it turned out to be a memorable event, although she herself was a little distressed at the inattention of some of the audience, who were more interested in the buffet than the poet. But she and Valéry persevered and more lectures followed. In late spring 1924 the young Duchesse de La Rochefoucauld, by birth Edmée de Fels, found herself among a learned audience listening to him speak. The occasion left a vivid impression: standing behind a large period desk with the Pannini *Gallerie* paintings as a background, Valéry speaks about Italian art but the subject does not matter; his sheer mastery of language is so impressive. And afterwards in the princess's garden Edmée de La Rochefoucauld meets for the first time the man, 'the prodigious and charming being', of whom she is to make a life-long cult.

Winnaretta herself probably first met Valéry in the house of Madame Lucien Mülhfeld, who, though poor and invalided, presided over a literary salon of such excellence with such authority and queen-like pride that she earned the nickname 'Zénobie'. Over the decades Winnaretta had met among the Mülhfeld protegés writers ranging from Jean Lorrain to Paul Claudel and André Breton (already familiar through Tristan Tzara) to Valéry himself. But possibly Valéry was the one who most easily adapted himself to the atmosphere of Winnaretta's society without committing himself to it entirely or abandoning old friends. Paul Léautaud recorded in his *Journal* a word about Valéry's urbane attitude towards Winnaretta and her multifarious activities. In the office of *Mercure de France* he repeated to Léautaud and Gaston Gallimard an amusing story about her. A woman, speaking of her, had said: 'She is very kind. Is it true? They say that she is a little *pédéraste*.' What some found mildly shocking, Valéry scarcely noticed: Winnaretta and her friends, even the more colourful such as Prince Pierre de Monaco, were an endless source of intellectual stimulation for him.

After *Les Noces* and the Valéry lecture, the third notable event that took place at 57 avenue Henri-Martin in June 1923 was the première of Falla's *El Retablo de Maese Pedro*. The work, which had taken him so long to complete, had advanced him considerably along the road of development as a composer. He had created something that had captured the atmosphere of the past without descending to the level of pastiche: to a baroque style he had added such innovatory *piquances* of melody, harmony and instrumentation that an entirely unique work had resulted. *El Retablo* had already been performed in an orchestral version under Falla's direction in Seville on 23 March. But, before it could be presented in its full stage version in the very much more intimate atmosphere of a drawing-room setting, for which it was designed, long and elaborate rehearsals had to take place. Interested observers watched, fascinated at the developments taking place before their eyes as the date of the première on 25 June approached. Poulenc, for one, was transfixed as he saw emerge a new Falla representing a new Spain, no longer the Andalusia of *El Amor Brujo* but the Castile of Philip III. The audience on the first night were just as enchanted. The thirty minute work, which made great demands upon the skills and talents of puppeteers (among them Ricardo Viñes), the three solo singers, Wanda Landowska at the harpsichord and Madame Henri Casadesus, playing the harp and lute, along with the orchestra of the Concerts Golschmann, conducted by Wladimir Golschmann, so gripped the audience that it seemed to end as soon as it had begun. Through the rapturous applause of an audience *en fête* for the occasion (some of them had even donned Castilian dress) came calls for the work to be repeated. But the artistes refused. A second performance would not be quite so satisfactory, they said.

Thinking nothing of it, the guests left the music room and crowded into the princess's reception rooms to discuss the new work. Everyone talked at the same time, as gossip columnists noted the famous faces among the crowd: passing lightly over the younger generation of talent, Poulenc and Milhaud with an impressionable Henri Sauguet experiencing his first glimpse of the Polignac way of life, they noted Paul Valéry, 'the poet of today clearing a way with gestures of the shipwrecked among the waves of female shoulders', and Henri de Régnier, 'the poet of yesterday', moustaches drooping and proud behind his monocle; Stravinsky, 'a rat among the cats', was with Picasso, surrounded on all sides, and José-Maria Sert beamed with satisfaction after hearing Spanish music, unaware of how it contrasted so markedly in its austerity with the voluptuous opulence of his 'baroque' frescoes in the music room. Some of the artistes joined the crowd and Viñes introduced Wanda Landowska to an admiring Poulenc while she was making a hurried exit.

On the evening of the performance a slight undercurrent of dissatisfaction among the performers was perceptible. Falla, though fêted and praised, was a little disgruntled: *El Retablo*, such a short work, slightly orchestrated, had taken him years to compose and arrange for production. The commission fee seemed small recompense. Moreover, a work in which elements of vision and sound were so interdependent that the music, taken on its own, would lose much of its significance and the spectacle, taken out of the microcosm of a domestic setting into the swamping surroundings of a public auditorium, could not hope to attract wide public interest. Certainly *El Retablo* was well received at its first public performance in a Jean Wiéner concert on 13 November 1923, as it was at subsequent performances throughout Europe, but in later years problems of production spoiled its chances of receiving the attention it deserved as the most significant score in Falla's output. Perhaps forebodings of this sort welled up in the composer's mind later on the evening of 25 June: after all the exclamations of delight had died down and the rose petals showered on him had been brushed off his shoulders, the guests realized that Falla had disappeared. He was only discovered when someone glanced into the darkened music room and saw him sitting alone by the theatre holding one of Maese Pedro's limp puppets in his hand.

If Falla's reaction was tinged with melancholy, some of the performers were openly angry. The Princesse de Polignac had not invited any of them to the select dinner party held before the performance. She had treated them, they claimed, as though she were an eighteenth-century magnate dealing with musical artisans hired for the occasion. That was the reason for their refusal to consider repeating the work. In reality the complaint was less specific than that: having so many ordinary guests to cope with, she had not had enough time to fuss over them as they expected; dinner immediately preceding their performance would have been a technical impossibility.

Winnaretta was very upset about these murmurings of discontent and took immediate steps to appease the most influential ring-leader, Wanda Landowska. The princess discovered an exquisite handkerchief, which she had left on the harpsichord, and next day had it returned to her, hand-delivered in a valuable lacquered box. Implacable, Landowska removed the handkerchief and sent the peace-offering back to her.

However, she had much to thank Winnaretta for in commissioning *El Retablo*. It decisively drew the harpsichord into the orchestral arena where composers could see how well it lent itself to the current interest in exploiting delicate and subtle orchestral textures. Landowska could now take the matter one step further. She harried Falla until he composed his Concerto for harpsichord, flute, oboe, clarinet, violin and violoncello for her as a 'reward' for taking part in the première of *El Retablo*. The Concerto, a magnificent and stimulating work, which owed more than its instrumentation to the puppet-opera, was first performed by her in Barcelona in 1927, although she did have considerable reservations about it because of the strain it placed on her technique. In her treatment of Poulenc, Landowska was more careful. Inspired by the beauty of *El Retablo*, he was eager to write something for her and so, over a period of several years, she coached him in the elements of harpsichord technique and was finally rewarded with the appearance of the sparkling *Concert champêtre*, imaginatively written for harpsichord solo and a richly textured orchestra. First performed in spring 1929, it evoked for listeners gentle images of Watteau's *fêtes galantes* and Fragonard's open-air scenes of aristocratic pleasures. The harpsichord also featured to good effect in his *Suite française* of 1935.

An echo of praise for *El Retablo* found its way into a work of a quite different nature: a friend of Falla's, the poet and statesman Don Salvador de Madariaga, was so impressed by the puppet-opera that he dedicated his *Guía del Lector del Quijote* to 'Manuel de Falla in whose *Retablo de Maese Pedro* the immortal Don Quixote gains a second immortality.'

With the performance of *El Retablo* on 25 June Winnaretta's involvements for 1923 were by no means over. As a whole the year saw great activity among her friends. Morand published his *Fermé la nuit*. Albert Roussel's opera *Padamavati* received its first performance. Remarkable exhibitions of paintings by

Marie Laurencin and the late Henri Rousseau were held at Rosenberg's. Paul Claudel's *Poèmes sur la muraille de Tokyo* appeared. Cocteau published two works, *Le Grand Écart* and *Plain-Chant*. Satie took offence at Poulenc's sending him a baby's rattle fashioned with a head bearing a remarkable resemblance to his own and launched Sauguet, Desormière, Cliquet-Pleyel and Maxime Jacob, his *'École d'Arceuil'* as rivals to *Les Six*— with whom they remained on the best of terms, despite their master. A sensation was caused in March when Grasset thrust the twenty-year-old Raymond Radiguet's novel *Diable au corps* on an astonished public, who admired the youthful author's work despite one critic's reminder that they were called upon to judge a book, not a birth certificate. But it was a death certificate that soon surprised the world. Transported by his mentor Cocteau from his home-from-home in the *avant-garde* bar in the rue Boissy d'Anglais *'Le Boeuf sur le toit'*, Radiguet was taken the round of the salons, where he felt little at ease except among close friends of Cocteau's, such as the Princesse de Polignac. Otherwise that year his time was taken up by *Le Bal de Comte d'Orgel*, which he barely finished before dying of typhoid fever on 9 December. Cocteau's desolation was such that he earned the nickname *'le veuf sur le toit'*, as he set out to ensure that Radiguet lived on in legend.

The year 1923 also saw Rolfe de Maré's Ballets Suèdois at its height. Winnaretta was particularly impressed by music commissioned by Maré from Germaine Tailleferre for a ballet called *Le Marchand d'oiseaux*. The work, with its deliberate archaisms, charmingly reminiscent of Scarlatti, so absorbed her that she immediately commissioned a piano concerto from her. Another novelty mounted by Rolfe de Maré in 1923 was the first American ballet ever written, Cole Porter's *Within the Quota*, which reached the stage of the Théâtre des Champs-Elysées on 25 October, along with another new work, like it, significantly influenced by jazz idioms, Milhaud's *La Création du monde*. Winnaretta knew Cole and Linda Porter quite well since they tended to stay in Venice during the summer while she was there and, when in Paris, they frequented her salon. On one occasion she took the opportunity to introduce Cole Porter to Darius Milhaud and through him Cole subsequently obtained the commission from Maré to write *Within the Quota*, for which Gerald Murphy had produced a scenario and was to provide some striking décor. Although Milhaud had refused to have anything to do with the composition of the ballet, he was, nonetheless, kept busy during the summer of 1923, encouraging Cole to work on what was his first major score and providing him with an obliging orchestrator in the form of that much underestimated composer Charles Koechlin. The result was a light ballet upon the theme of an immigrant's fixation with the American way of life and mythology of instant success with all its symbols, personified in different forms, such as a millionairess, a cowboy and a jazz-baby. A triumph in itself, *Within the Quota* was the proto-ancestor of all American ballets, a genre soon developed by composers, such as Aaron Copeland and Virgil Thomson, and greatly influenced the composition of jazz works on a symphonic scale.

As 1923 drew to a close Winnaretta prepared to go on a cruise to Egypt for Christmas. On an impulse she lifted the telephone and insisted that one of her latest 'discoveries', the pianist Jacques Février, should join her party. Overwhelmed but embarrassed, he refused: he had too many commitments. Winnaretta's telephone worked overtime and before long she had arranged everything so expeditiously that, freed of all his duties, he was soon boarding ship with her guests.

Among the princess's circle he met another 'discovery'— though of a different sort. This was Violet Trefusis, since her tumultuous affair with Vita Sackville-West, a voluntary social exile in Paris. She had met Winnaretta earlier in 1923. From the start the two women had exercised a hypnotic fascination for each other. Reacting against the fixation that she had for her formidable mother, that *grande dame* the Hon. Mrs George Keppel, Edward VII's last *maîtresse-en-titre*, whose intervention in the Sackville-West drama had been decisive, Violet saw in Winnaretta a mother-substitute whose wit and intelligence equalled if not outshone Vita's. For her part Winnaretta was bowled over by Violet's beauty, vivacity and apparent availability, and had begun a determined pursuit of her. She was also encouraged by the acquiescence of Violet's husband Denys Trefusis, who, with full knowledge of their proclivities, had not only introduced the two women but had departed almost immediately afterwards on a long trip to the Soviet Union. Winnaretta saw no obstacle in the way of their happiness, except possibly her year-old involvement with the Roumanian

pianist Clara Haskil and Mrs Keppel's determination to
prevent Violet from courting another scandal. Clara Haskil
presented little problem: Winnaretta already had her firmly
under her thumb. The maternal stumbling-block was almost as
easily circumvented. Winnaretta knew that Mrs Keppel was
only worried about appearances, as indeed she was herself. The
solution was simple: Mrs Keppel and her husband were always
included in Winnaretta's social invitations to Violet.

So it was that the foundations of this new love-affair were laid
as the party—parents included—sailed up the Nile to Luxor.
All social diversions, from tourist-trips to archaeological sites
to bridge-parties on deck, were carefully organized; and
Jacques Février gave endless impromptu recitals on demand.
Indeed, the press-ganged Février turned out to be doubly useful
because Violet soon found that she could use him as a public
foil, flirting with him outrageously in order to distract attention
from her own below-deck activities. But, while Winnaretta was
creating this relationship with its strong bias on the physical
side, at the same time a close friendship was growing up
between her and Février. Their intellectual intimacy was all
the more remarkable in view of the discrepancy between their
ages: the princess was within three weeks of her fifty-ninth
birthday and he was only twenty-three years old.

Chapter 13
The Charmed Circle
(1924–1925)

Although the Princesse de Polignac was effortlessly able to keep pace with all the new artistic ideas of the younger generation, she was in one way a member of a dying breed. By the mid-1920s her life-style, the size of her town-house, the scale of her entertainments and her unstinted patronage of both creative and executant musicians was paralleled by no one else in Paris. Certainly, as that would-be-second-Cocteau Maurice Sachs remarked, the Vicomtesse (Marie-Laure) de Noailles, Lady Mendl, the Comtesse Greffulhe, the Comte Etienne de Beaumont and Winnaretta's niece Daisy Fellowes did manage to keep up splendid establishments but only by dint of limiting the scope of their other activities in a way in which she never did. The day of the great salons was passing. In only a few, such as those of the Marquise de Ludre, Madame Jacques Bousquet and the Duchesse de La Rochefoucauld, could one still hear elevated conversations; in a handful musical offerings continued to be made. But at the Princesse de Polignac's nothing seemed to have changed: all aspects of civilized life were cultivated with a certain moral earnestness and without much attention to the social standing of the participants.

On occasions Winnaretta did exercise a form of discrimination. Nothing had so far blinded her to the fact that some of the purely social members of her audiences still did not appreciate her more recherché activities, and so about once a year she pandered to their old-fashioned tastes and at the same time honoured a cherished soul by inviting them to a special concert of Prince Edmond de Polignac's music. From this memorial act all her musician friends were firmly excluded. The guests usually loved it but Winnaretta's friends suspected that for her part she increasingly found the music dated. Otherwise her maxim was that, if one induced anyone to wear a dinner jacket, he was indistinguishable from the man next to him at table. A

young Maxime Jacob, introduced as an up-and-coming composer by Jane Bathori, went to one of Winnaretta's grand
dinners, to which a 'mixture' of guests had been invited. The
purely chic were not averse to attending her informal soirées but
some refused her invitations to dinner parties because they
knew very well that they might have to rub shoulders with
artists. On this occasion one aristocrat had taken the risk and,
during the course of the meal, honoured Jacob, whom he
clearly did not know, with a whispered confidence: 'One meets
really bizarre people here . . . Artistes!' a little as if he had
spoken of the craze which his host had for monkeys or parakeets.
Maxime Jacob said nothing but, with a touch of paranoia, now
saw things in terms of a social war. Having served himself too
generously with a plateful of venison, prepared in a delicious
sauce, he suddenly realized that, as he continued to eat,
everyone else had finished and was being kept waiting. A
painful social lesson for the inexperienced and over-sensitive
Jacob, he felt better—even avenged—when at the end of the
meal Melchior Marquis de Polignac spilt a full glass of dessert
wine on his dress-coat. His face was a study in impotent rage,
Jacob noted with satisfaction.

The problem with Maxime Jacob was that he completely
misunderstood the implications of the society in which he
found himself. As a friend of Jane Bathori's and as a promising
disciple of Satie's, he was given serious consideration by a
talent-spotting Winnaretta. But it was soon realized that he
was not sufficiently attuned to sophisticated life to qualify for
entry into the select inner circle of her friends. Nor, indeed,
could he see that, when a respectable nobleman cast a doubtful
glance at Winnaretta's artistic friends, he was not criticizing
their cultural propensities but more likely the prevailing moral
climate in which they thrived. Poor Maxime fell between two
Polignac stools and, when he performed his last public act by
abandoning Judaism for Catholicism and becoming a Benedic-
tine monk, many of his acquaintances must have been relieved
to know that he had at last found his niche in life.

The fact was that by the 1920s this inner circle of Winnaretta's friends was composed almost entirely of homosexuals
of both sexes. There were a few very notable exceptions to the
rule: Igor Stravinsky and Germaine Tailleferre, following their
own instincts, had the presence of mind not to object to those

of their friends and they were accepted without awkwardness. Later Nadia Boulanger, aware but impassive, endeared herself by forcing no issues. Otherwise, the homosexual or bisexual element prevailed in an all but overt way. Some of the younger generation could be extrovert about their feelings but they tended to reserve their more outrageous behaviour for the bar-atmosphere of such places as the '*Boeuf sur le toit*'. At the house in the avenue Henri-Martin a greater degree of decorum prevailed. In fact, as far as Winnaretta was concerned, the matter was kept at foundation level. When introduced to someone who seemed likely to fit into the inner circle, her opening words might be: 'You're homosexual, aren't you? Yes? Good, then let's talk about music.'

In effect, homosexuality, though almost a prerequisite for close friendship, provided little more than a relaxing ambiance in a social setting. Winnaretta continued to be non-committal about the more intimate side of her existence. And because she adhered to a well-ordered plan of life, there was seldom much awkwardness or misunderstanding about the nature of the different levels of her friendships. As a result her circle acted as a magnet to those who were willing to play the game according to the rules. For example, Denys and Violet Trefusis were both quickly absorbed into the inner circle, Violet more because of her wit, beauty and inclinations than because of any reputation for discretion and Denys because of his compliance and his genuine ability to talk about music. Indeed, Violet often felt that she was merely tolerated in their musical world: Denys and Winnaretta, like Numa and his Egeria, would rush off together to attend concerts or rehearsals; in the middle of grand dinner parties they would get up and go, with scores tucked under their arms, rather than miss any part of a programme. And in 1929, when Denys lay dying of galloping consumption in the American hospital in Neuilly, Winnaretta's visits seemed to give him most pleasure. 'What did they do?' Violet speculated. 'I can only suppose they talked about music, as I was not encouraged to be present.'

There was another dimension of exclusiveness to Winnaretta's inner circle. There tended to be very little contact between her friends and the devotees of the other dominant Lesbians in the Paris of the 1920s. Women such as Wanda Landowska, Natalie Barney and Gertrude Stein, like queen-bees, consciously rivalled

Winnaretta in their desire to emulate her. Certainly a super-ficial cordiality was maintained between them. But Landowska was too vindictively inclined to steal girl-friends for the sake of doing so; La Barney was too much of an independent-minded Amazon to be very sympathetic, and Gertrude Stein, whom Picasso had introduced to Winnaretta during the War, was not European enough and too grotesquely masculine to be a com-fortable friend. And their respective close friends tended to find contact between the different circles difficult. Their patronesses might waft social courtesies in each other's direction but any devotee, hovering between one or another, could be suspected of multiple disloyalty. In the early days of his stay in Paris the American composer Virgil Thomson seems to have unwittingly provoked such suspicions. Though a close friend of Gertrude Stein and Alice B. Toklas, he was well aware that his career as a composer could be most usefully helped by the Princesse de Polignac, so he recruited Elsa Maxwell as an ally—whose enthusiasm was matched only by her naïvety. Winnaretta seems to have ignored Elsa's heavy hints on the subject and even a promised luncheon date between the princess and the budding composer did not materialize. After making 'six engagements with [Thomson] in three days and failing to appear at any of them', Elsa precipitately left Paris. Jean Cocteau was sym-pathetic and 'offered to write to the princess himself explaining that [Thomson] was not to be judged from [his] acquaintances in café society.' But the young American discouraged this, saying that she had probably never even heard of him. Possibly so. But the truth of the matter may have been that the only acquaintance of his by whom he had been judged was Gertrude Stein and Winnaretta had no intention of opening a dialogue between their two 'realms'.

Another implicit rule of the inner circle was that public scandal should be avoided if at all possible, although, humans being what they are, this was not always easy to ensure. On one occasion Winnaretta arranged a dinner party and musical entertainment in her palace in Venice for an intimate group of female friends. Unfortunately the husband of one of them, an insensitive Englishman, an ex-cavalry major with a propensity for drink and belligerence, resented his exclusion from the party. Eccentrically dressed in a red polo-uniform of Hungarian origin, he attacked the main door of the palace and, when he found it barred, he leapt from his gondola on to the ledge of an unbarred kitchen window. Climbing in, he struck out at the terrified servants and then proceeded to hurl all the elaborate dishes prepared for dinner out of the window into the canal. Winnaretta was horrified, although she succeeded in improvising a cold collation for her terrified and hungry guests, and afterwards, when it came to playing the piano accompaniment for one of their number, a celebrated singer, in her agitation she played some unforgiveable wrong notes. But that was nothing compared with the horror of knowing that all Venice and soon all Paris would be gossiping about the incident. The vindictive major's previous insults paled by comparison with this one: he had written a challenge on a card and sent it to Winnaretta: 'If you are the man you claim to be, come and let's fight!' That approach was, at least, less public, though just as hurting.

But, however much she loathed scandal of this sort, she was not above indulging in a mild joke against herself in public. At a fancy-dress ball given by Madame Cardinal in 1928 she appeared dressed as the dramatist Tristan Bernard, and the outrageously extrovert Marchesa Luisa Casati accompanied her in the guise of his wife Argentina. Francis Poulenc was there too, trying hard to resemble Chéri (a difficult task with his looks) and Colette, more convincing as Léa de Lonval, hovered nearby. Soon afterwards Daisy Fellowes gave a similar ball at which all the guests were to come disguised as famous Parisian personalities. One mysterious figure, dressed in drab black with a shawl over her head, sat resolutely knitting like any *dame des lavabos* with a plate for tips conspicuously placed in front of her. To everyone's surprise she emerged unmasked as Daisy herself. Her daughter the Princesse Isabelle de Broglie was more dignified, though mildly transvestite, as Jeanne d'Arc. The fashionable decorator Jean-Michel Franck wore—with rather too much flair—the gown and jewels of his friend Marie-Laure de Noailles. Winnaretta came face to face with Elsa Maxwell who, like herself, had opted to dress up as Aristide Briand. No one asked the reason for Winnaretta's choice but Elsa left no one in doubt about herself: she enjoyed the chance to wear a soup-strainer moustache—because it suited her quite well.

But there was more to Winnaretta's life in the 'twenties than frivolity, scandal and back-biting. The serious pursuit of a civilized existence was still the only significant motive force in her life. The pleasure cruise that took her and Jacques Février to Egypt for Christmas 1923 ended for her at the Polignac family house at Bouzaréah in January 1924. She had gone there with Germaine Tailleferre so that she could put the finishing touches to her *Concert pour piano*, safe from the distractions of Parisian life. The princess had made it clear that she had commissioned the work because she had been impressed by the Scarlatti-like touches in her ballet *Le Marchand d'oiseaux* and so, when Tailleferre set to work on the Concerto, she retained and developed eighteenth-century textures, indeed so intensely, that the work took many by surprise. Tailleferre, so addicted to impressionism, had unexpectedly, delightfully, returned to a complete musical sobriety, clearly inspired by the Brandenburg Concertos. As Darius Milhaud put it, her Concerto 'leads us back under the great shade of Bach . . .' The source of inspiration was not hard to discover. Winnaretta still preserved an almost embarrassing passion for Bach's music that had grown in early days when certain areas of it were scarcely known and little understood. She had always shrugged her shoulders at the comments of respected friends such as Fauré, who found the fugues boring, and stuck to her own opinion. By the 1920s, having long given up paying attention to any music that did not stimulate her, she frequently insisted upon her guests' sharing with her a diet of Bach's concertos, suites and cantatas, whether they liked it or not. The style cultivated by Tailleferre in her Concerto was a calculated tribute to Winnaretta's taste. In subsequent years other composers, Stravinsky, Igor Markevitch and Poulenc, took up the idea and flavoured works dedicated to the princess with similar Bach-like essences. And not only fellow composers but the general public found Tailleferre's work impressive. The *adagio* received a warm reception when the composer gave it a preliminary airing at a concert on 6 November 1924 and, when the first complete performance took place at a Koussewitzky Concert at the Opéra on 30 May 1925, again with the composer as soloist, the Concerto was received with wild applause. Critics were fascinated by its forceful first movement, in which the two themes were developed simultaneously, one by the piano, the other by the orchestra; they were moved by the finely wrought, suave *cantabile* slow movement and enlivened by the nervous *finale* as is stumbled over *fugato* snatches to an abrupt conclusion.

By coincidence, while Tailleferre was completing her Polignac commission, another of Winnaretta's friends was also composing a piano concerto. Stravinsky put the finishing touches to his Concerto for piano and wind instruments just three months after her on 21 April 1924 and coincidentally it too showed obvious influences from Scarlatti and Bach, particularly in the chattering, *toccata*-like first movement. But Stravinsky had had no thought of Winnaretta's musical tastes when writing it. From the outset he designed it as a work suitable for performance at one of Koussewitzky's concerts and Koussewitzky had decided ideas about it. He wanted Stravinsky to take up a secondary career as a concert pianist and advised him to make his début playing the new work. The date of the première was fixed for 22 May 1925. The concerto would be played at the Opéra in a programme flanked by *L'Oiseau de feu* and *Le Sacre de printemps* but, as the day approached, Stravinsky's nervous tension rose and his confidence faded, so Koussewitzky hit upon the idea of asking Winnaretta to arrange a pre-première hearing of the new work at her house. She readily agreed and a week before the Opéra concert Stravinsky played the Concerto along with Jean Wiéner, who tackled a reduced version of the orchestral part on another piano. The rapturous response of the princess's hand-picked audience contributed enormously to Stravinsky's determination to make a success of the public performance and of his new side-line career. He seems to have appreciated Winnaretta's help and he expressed his thanks by dedicating to her his Sonata for Piano, which he wrote later in the same year.

One of the reasons why Jean Wiéner was called in to help Stravinsky on this occasion was that at the time he was in close touch with the princess because she had just commissioned a work from him, yet another concerted work for piano with a string orchestra. Wiéner had a varied musical background. With a fellow pianist, Clément Doucet, he had helped to make Louis Moysès's night-club '*La Gaya*' a focal point for the youthful avant-garde orbiting round *Les Six*. In 1921, Moysès had opened the even more successful '*Boeuf sur le toit*' and with him had gone Wiéner to supply the music in the form of light American jazz and his own rather derivative compositions. And, more serious, the Concerts Jean Wiéner, which he mounted, impressed music lovers by championing new music across the international board from Gershwin to Schoenberg. Winnaretta got to know him very well in the early 1920s (although he never became one of her closest friends) and often invited him and Doucet to play at her house so that, as Léon-Paul Fargue put it, she could have that 'unbreakable tandem' play a private little Pasdeloup Concert, as though she were a Ludwig II. But there was nothing introverted about the commissioned work that resulted from their friendship. Bearing the intriguing title of *Concerto franco-americain*, it was far too extrovert to be simply a comfortable piece of chamber music.

When Wiéner completed it in 1924, Winnaretta certainly insisted on having it played in her salon, although it was more naturally suited to the concert hall, as its warm reception as a Pasdeloup Concert on 25 October proved. And during the next decade it was frequently repeated in Parisian concert programmes. By contrast, its critical reception was cool. Milhaud thought it too 'popular': although the outside movements were crisp and lively and distinctly influenced by jazz, the second was far too sugary and rather on the light side. Perhaps Milhaud was reacting against jazz elements in others' music, as he was beginning to in his own; perhaps he thought Wiéner's attempt to synthesize French and American musical idioms was as clumsy as his attempt to pay a Franco-American compliment to the princess. The critic of *Le Ménestrel* had a crushing word to say on that subject: though some would say that old France could learn some lessons from young America, this young man—Wiéner—was still in need of some musical instruction from France. But, he concluded, that means little when the dollars flow! If that type of comment was discouraging for Wiéner, for all that his gaucheness had provoked it in the first place, Winnaretta was not very pleased by the unfavourable light case upon her altruistic attempts to foster new music.

In the meantime, during the summer months of 1924, she was influencing the thoughts of another composer. But again it was to be an association that had incalculable consequences. Karol Szymanowski, one of Poland's foremost composers, on his first visit to Paris immediately made himself as much at home among the aristocracy of the Faubourg Saint-Germain as

among the young set surrounding *Les Six*. He met again his
old friend Artur Rubinstein, who played his *Études* op. 4 and
op. 33 to the composer's friends, old and new, and almost
naturally he gravitated into the Princesse de Polignac's circle.
Apart from anything else, she was well known to him as a close
friend of his distinguished fellow-countryman Paderewski. For
her part, she quickly summed up his non-musical propensities,
rather more accurately than Hélène Casella, the wife of the
Italian composer Alfredo Casella, who mistook his good manners and charm for sexual interest and pursued him relentlessly.
Szymanowski found refuge in Winnaretta's house, where his
nature as well as his musical ideas were properly appreciated;
and his irritation at Madame Casella's importunities soon
evaporated.

In the post-War climate of national self-congratulation,
Szymanowski had become interested in Polish folk-lore and,
when he met Winnaretta in 1924, he had a long discussion with
her about it. Already fascinated by East European folk culture
through the Ballets Russes, she suggested that he might write a
specifically Polish work for her. He asked her to explain further
and she outlined a plan: instead of falling back on a folk-tale to
achieve the desired ethnic effect, if he were to write an ecclesiastical work based upon an old Polish text, perhaps Poland's
indigenous culture as well as her renowned religiosity could be
celebrated. A *Polish Requiem* for soloists, choir and orchestra
might be an original idea if a suitable text could be found.
Szymanowski accepted the commission on these terms and
enthusiastically began considering the musical possibilties of old
Polish liturgical pieces. However, by December 1924 he was
beginning to realize that the task was not going to be as simple
as he had imagined. He wrote to Winnaretta asking if he might
delay the work until the following March, excusing himself by
saying that he was anxious to finish composing a concerto,
which he had begun in the meantime. Apparently Winnaretta
was so unperturbed by this that he interpreted it as a sign of
waning interest. Far from it: she had no intention of force-
growing any composer's work or interfering with his artistic
freedom. But Szymanowski's reaction to this was strange: he
went his own way almost completely. Having found no inspir-
ing text for a requiem by mid-1925, he started working upon
an old Polish translation of Jacopo da Todi's poem *Stabat*

Mater. The resulting composition, which found its final form a year later, was one of his most original compositions, combining, as it did, the pure dignified austerity of pre-polyphonic music with the invigorating rhythms and melodies of the Polish tradition. The pervading feeling of the *Stabat Mater* bears a remarkable similarity to the *Symphony of Psalms* which Stravinsky composed four years later in 1930. Possibly some influence from Szymanowski's work may have crept into Stravinsky's. Winnaretta was fascinated by the final result and possible side-effects of her commission, although Szymanowski himself had all but lost touch with her by the time of its first performance in Warsaw on 11 January 1929 and had not even thought to dedicate it to her: a Warsaw industrialist, Dr Bronisław Krystall, paid him to dedicate it to the memory of his wife Isabelle, who had recently died.

But Winnaretta had little time to pay much attention to Szymanowski's vagaries. Very soon after setting the ball rolling with her idea for a *Polish Requiem*, she was involved in commissioning another work that also turned out to be one of its composer's most successful. Darius Milhaud, ten years younger and slightly more vigorous than Szymanowski, had just come to the end of a chapter in his musical development. After *La Création du monde* jazz idioms began to appear more and more threadbare to him, and so Winnaretta suggested that he might write a chamber opera that would satisfy his interest in folk elements in music and also fit in with fashion for classical themes that had followed in the wake of Satie's 'Socrate'. Ideas immediately began to take shape in his mind and soon, with the help of Armand Lunel, a boyhood friend from his native Provence, he worked out a plot based upon the classical legend of Orpheus and Eurydice but transposed into the modern but still timeless setting of the Camargue. Lunel's libretto succeeded admirably in fusing the two elements: his Orpheus is metamorphosed from Ovid's disappointed husband, turned proselitizing pederast, into a local peasant who charms both man and beast not now with a lyre but with a natural talent for healing. The new Eurydice is a wandering gypsy who, out of love, joins him and flees into the mountains far away from disapproving parents. But this heroine also dies, despite Orpheus's medical skills, and is carried to her grave by animals who have fallen under her lover's spell. He then bids farewell

to his lamenting entourage, a bear, a boar, a fox and a reformed
wolf, and returns to his village, only to be torn to pieces by
modern Bacchantes in the form of Eurydice's sisters, who blame
him for causing her death. They learn the truth only after
inflicting this final and fatal misfortune upon him. Lunel's
libretto, aptly entitled *Les Malheurs d'Orphée*, inspired Milhaud to write a work redolent with the sights and sounds of
his childhood experiences. Written at one 'sitting' between 22
September and 2 November 1924, *Les Malheurs* emerged as a
new musical type. Everything was in miniature: the orchestra
consisted of only thirteen players, the scenes were brief and all
the singers, apart from Orpheus and Eurydice themselves,
combined the functions of soloists and chorus; the opera itself
lasted no more than forty minutes in performance time. In this
respect it was the first modern stage work of its type that could
be truly called an opera: *Renard* and *El Retablo de Maese Pedro*
had foreshadowed it but had consciously avoided actor-
singer characterization in an effort to contain any impulse
towards operatic floridity. As far as Milhaud was concerned,
Les Malheurs initiated a period of interest in the chamber opera
as a form: in *Le Pauvre Matelot* and *Esther de Carpentras* he retained the miniature proportions and in *L'Enlèvement d'Europe* of
1927, he achieved record-breaking brevity with an opera that
took only nine minutes to perform.

In the meantime *Les Malheurs d'Orphée* had had its first
performance at the Théâtre de la Monnaie in Brussels on 7
May 1926. Despite the fact that the conductor, Corneil de
Thoran, unduly afraid that the orchestral sound would be too
small for such a large theatre, had doubled the string section
and only succeeded in losing some of the work's agility, the
audience was well pleased with *Les Malheurs* as the partner
on a double bill with Mozart's light-hearted *Il Seraglio*. Milhaud and his wife made the journey to Brussels packed into
a car with Arthur Honegger and his wife amid rugs and suit-
cases. Honegger, enveloped in a huge cape and hat, sat in the
open dickey at the back and slept throughout the journey,
heedless of the rain that poured down on him. Winnaretta
preferred to travel by train, if only to be certain of arriving
in time to witness the birth of yet another unique and influential work which she had been instrumental in bringing into
existence.

In the summer of 1924, while the libretto and score of *Les Malheurs* were still in gestation, Stravinsky's *Sonata pour piano* was also being written with the princess in mind. Returning to his family at Biarritz in June after the Opéra première of the Piano Concerto, Stravinsky immediately began composing it and he continued the work intermittently throughout the summer, while Winnaretta coaxed and encouraged Szymanowski and Milhaud and turned again in the direction of Bayreuth for the first festival since the War. Heedless of recent emnities and of Cocteau's cock and harlequin pronouncements, she stayed to enjoy the full gala programme of the *Ring*, *Parsifal* and *Meistersinger*. She learned about Stravinsky's *Sonata pour piano* when she returned to Paris and, only after he had written the final notes the following October, did she learn—to her delight—that he had dedicated the work to her. Stravinsky had no particular reason for making this gesture. Perhaps a combination of considerations impelled him to do so.

The Sonata was a crisp, contrapuntal work, so clearly linear in conception that anyone—not just the critics—could see in it a decisive turning away from the Russian folk-culture preoccupation that had culminated in *Les Noces*. Here was a distinct return to the mood of Bach's music: the style and texture of the first and third movements paid unmistakable homage to the mid-eighteenth-century baroque genre. That in itself was a tribute to one of Winnaretta's well-known passions in music. The second movement derived its inspiration from an entirely unexpected source: this *adagietto* had a strong flavour of Beethoven about it. Stravinsky had only just begun to revise his damnatory opinion of Beethoven's music, now seeing it in its true light, unobscured by political and national prejudices and overcoming his revulsion at the romanticism of some of its champions. This movement was his way of announcing a magnanimous change of mind, even of making an implicit apology for whatever offence his previous aversion had caused Beethoven-lovers such as Winnaretta. More important, the Sonata as a whole was a potentially risky experiment and, by setting out on a distinctly baroque and classical path, Stravinsky risked being accused of composing a vamped up pastiche as unworthy of himself as of his musical ancestors. By dedicating it to Winnaretta he guaranteed that it would be taken seriously.

She at least would understand and appreciate what he was trying to say; and her opinions counted for something in musical circles. And, of course, the Sonata's dedication was also Stravinsky's way of thanking her for her contribution to the successful launching of his Piano Concerto and of himself as a concert pianist: the proximity of the dates of the Concerto's première and the commencement of the Sonata's composition suggests this, as does the fact that the one was indubitably the parent of the other.

Although Stravinsky gave the Sonata its first performance at Winnaretta's house in Paris, its official public première did not take place until July 1925 at the Donaueschingen Festival, where it met with general approval, spiced with a touch of disparagement from Schoenberg. But its real introduction to the musical world came on 8 September at the Festival of the International Society for Contemporary Music at Venice. Stravinsky, the proud owner of a new Renault, actually drove himself all the way to the Adriatic and sailed the last mile or so to the princess's palace on the Grand Canal. How seriously she had taken his plans to undertake the journey by car is a matter for conjecture. She certainly had qualms about his attitude towards driving. She had only recently encountered him wearing a pair of kid-gloves. 'Where have you been?' she asked, glancing at them. 'I've been out sporting.' The reply was too vague: 'What kind of sport?' 'Motoring!' However, Stravinsky's plaything brought him as far as the coast without mishap. His performance of the Sonata also went without mishap, although he himself expected difficulties from a bad abcess on his right forefinger. He craved the audience's indulgence. No need: at the sound of the first note his finger miraculously healed itself.

But that was not what impressed the audience. They were only conscious of witnessing his transformation into a 'western' composer. According to Gian Francesco Malipiero, the Italian composer and later Stravinsky's biographer, 'the flower of international snobbism' flocked round him afterwards in the Palazzo Polignac. Praises showered upon him. And when someone asked for another cup of tea, in case Stravinsky was still hankering after the ritualistic Russian samovar, all eyes turned towards him to make sure that visions of 'cossacks, sleighs followed by packs of wolves and immeasurable plains covered in snow' were not rising up before a nostalgic exile's eyes. But he was no Proust with his cake-crumbs soaked in a spoonful of tea. The Russian past, if not entirely forgotten, had finally lost all claim to his artistic allegiance.

Chapter 14
The Eternal Inspiration
(1925–1929)

In the 1920s the Venice which Winnaretta had known in her youth was changing. Still timeless, it was, nonetheless, being dragged into the modern world by the noisy, excitable millionaires who, having 'discovered' a haven of civilization, proceeded to acclimatize it to themselves. As she remarked with a shake of the head, 'the Venetians themselves began to feel that their city was being treated as a sort of casino—not the elegant sort we are accustomed to see in Venetian pictures, but a casino like that of Deauville or Monte Carlo.' Some of her friends shared the feeling and commented upon the more apparent decay and decline to be seen around them. Cecil Roberts returned to the city for the first time since the War in the mid-'twenties and was not enchanted by what he saw: the bright new social stars had the wrong sort of lustre and what remained of the old life seemed all the more faded. As the noontide tables at the Café Florian filled up with notables, he 'observed them as figures in a futile pageant, a note of despair sounding off as in Browning's *Toccata*: "Here you come with your old music."'

However, there were contradictory elements in both of these views. Certainly the old faces still to be seen were withered with age and many were soon to disappear. After the War a tired and jaded Réjane (Proust's actress Berma) appeared in Venice and was enchanted by scenes of pleasing familiarity: the Contessa Morosini—whom Kaiser Wilhelm had loved—inseparable from the Princesse de Polignac, a majestic figure, 'seeing all, saying little'; Lady D'Abernon, still beautiful arrived and the Serts, the ubiquitous Misia and her jolly Hans Hals-like husband José-Maria. But Réjane herself never returned to Venice: she left life's stage in June 1920. And Gabriel Fauré too, he paid his last visit to Winnaretta in Venice during September of that year, a venerable old man with such distorted hearing that even the world of music now existed for

him only in his mind as an inner experience. This upset
Winnaretta considerably. Two years later when she attended
the '*Hommage national à Fauré*', a concert given in his honour at
the Sorbonne on 20 June 1922, she was moved by the sight of
him there: 'at the end of the concert all those present turned
spontaneously towards him with overflowing hearts and many
with tears in their eyes; he could neither hear the music nor the
loud applause but he stood there in the balcony looking down
with an unutterably melancholic smile on his handsome face.'
And two years later he too was dead.

But Winnaretta's life in Venice was not entirely taken up
with meditations on death and the decay of generations. Nor
did she and the Contessa Morosini spend all their time sitting
in the Piazza di San Marco, surrounded by pigeons and the
new leaders of the Anglo-Saxon contingent, the Cunards,
Edward and Victor with a skeletal, negrophile Nancy, and
Lady Diana Cooper with her husband Duff, the new wonder-
child of Britain's political nursery. For one thing Winnaretta
was not averse to joining in the parties given by the noisy
millionaires. Each summer in the second half of the 'twenties
the Cole Porters made their presence in Venice a little more
permanent by renting the magnificent Ca' Rezzonico, still
haunted by the shades of the Brownings. They used its enormous grand salon to give costume balls that rivalled the
extravagance of their Parisian counterparts. The princess was
invariably present, mingling happily with the American
nouveaux riches and impresarios, invariably leavened with a
variety of Italian, French and British aristocrats. Elsa Maxwell
was—equally invariably—present, trying to rule her own roost
and, given half a chance, everyone else's. Janet Flanner—
'Gênet' of the *New Yorker*—gave the slightly jaundiced view of
one who was herself too dominating to fit comfortably into that
society: Elsa had, according to her, invented the idea of having
a floating night-club on the Grand Canal and 'her system of
giving people who could afford to pay for it a better time even
in their own homes than they could give themselves was firmly
established'. She certainly arranged balls and other social
events for the uninspired rich but, contrary to the Flanner view,
she was never allowed to give soirées at Winnaretta's *palazzo*.

Regardless of prevailing fashions in entertainment, she stuck
to her old habit of organizing all her musical activities in person,

though some of them did not need much arranging: they just
happened. As Sir Ronald Storrs remarked: 'Hard upon your
welcome to her house in Venice, you would hear an admirable
Schumann Trio or Quartet, in which she might well be taking
part.' Often the other performers were simply drawn from the
guests staying with her. Whether gifted amateurs or top profes-
sionals, they joined forces and made music. Sometimes these
impromptu happenings may well have been slightly contrived.
One summer the young singer Olga Lynn found herself staying
opposite the Palazzo Polignac at the Palazzo Barbaro, which her
friend William Odom had rented. Winnaretta immediately
drew her into her circle, like a protective mother hen, and made
sure that on the next occasion when Cole Porter came to
dinner Olga Lynn was also there, primed and ready to give an
improvised recital, for which Winnaretta herself would 'oblige'
by playing the piano. Cole and Linda Porter were duly ravished
by her singing, Schubert and Fauré seemed so naturally suited
to the unoperatic quality of her voice. The recital ended. Cole
immediately leaped up and insisted that Olga (affectionately
known as 'Oggie') should tour America. And very soon the
American road to fame did open up before her.

However, if Winnaretta had some claim to being mistress of
the unexpected among the Venetian set, she herself conceded
the title to her friend the Marchesa Casati. After the death
of the refined and artistic Comtesse de La Baume, Luisa Casati
took over her house the Casa Dario and there throughout the
1920s gave entertainments which at times were rather too
exciting. During the period of the Ballets Russes her fancy-dress
balls were legendary. Her own costumes were specially designed
by Bakst until his death in 1924. But that was a mere detail. On
one occasion, stepping from her peaceful gondola on to the
house's landing-stage, Winnaretta was confronted by the vision
of La Casati with a tiger stretched out at her feet. She froze—
'like Lot's wife, metamorphosed into a pillar of salt', the more
malicious gossips said—and it took some time to convince her
that the beast had been suitably incapacitated by drugs. Wild
animals and thunderstorms, nature untamed or untameable,
were the only things that terrified her. And she was scarcely
reassured on hearing of similar alarm felt by Venetian citizens
when confronted by a group of guests who had 'kidnapped'
the marchesa's tiger after the party and paraded it in the Piazza

di San Marco. Although this incident provoked an official
rebuke, the residents did become used to the eccentricities of
Luisa Casati and her menagerie. Even Winnaretta could
admire the style of her midday parade in the piazza: in the
words of Cecil Roberts, La Casati would appear 'death-pale,
scarlet cloaked . . . exotic as an Aubrey Beardsley drawing.
She was preceded by a Negro page, who led a doped panther
with a gold collar and chain. It was sheer Tintoretto'—certainly a change from her tiger's first appearance in the streets
of Venice. That was much more reminiscent of Carpaccio's
painting of Saint Jerome returning from the desert with his
'pet' lion, to the horror of his clerical colleagues. And it was
certainly less dangerous than one of her previous goings-on,
when she descended upon Axel Munthe's villa in Capri: she
had proceeded to turn it black with draperies and carpets in
keeping with her own black ensemble, clothes and jewels; even
her hair had turned from red to black (with an intervening
green stage). Only her towering Negro lover had not toned in:
in mocking contrast he had been gilded from head to toe. But
eventually he had collapsed unconscious and was only saved
from death by Dr Munthe's precipitate action in scraping off
the stifling gilt.

The double theme of high style and awareness of mortality
continued to characterize Winnaretta's life in the mid-'twenties.
Light-heartedness was often followed by moments of reflection.
Back in Paris in the late spring of 1925 Maxime Jacob's newly
composed set of songs, *Six Poèmes de Cocteau*, was sung as the
centre-piece of an evening's music-making at Winnaretta's.
Everyone waited expectantly for that particular item on the
programme: verses by Cocteau and music by one of Satie's
protégés was bound to be 'modern' and stimulating. But, so
Jacob claimed, only just before the performance did someone
point out to him a slightly tactless oversight on his part. The
second song *Orageux* contained the curious line '*Prends garde,
ouvrière, la foudre aime les machines à coudre!*' Everyone knew of
Cocteau's facility for investing even the most everyday object
with a poetic significance, and the sewing-machine could be no
exception. But was it not unfortunate that the first performance
of the *Six Poèmes* was being given in the house of a sewing-
machine millionairess? However, it was too late to alter anything or withdraw the work. Overcoming her panic, Jane

Bathori began the cycle but at the end of the offending song she was interrupted by a round of thunderous applause and cries of '*Bis!*' from the more mischievous spectators, such as Henri Sauguet. Winnaretta sat expressionless until the end. She then congratulated the young composer with unaffected warmth. A serene Anna de Noailles fussed over him and Abel Hermant, now a venerable Academician, added a hint of 'official' approval.

One person who was not present at this première was the dedicatee, Erik Satie. Indeed, when the songs were published in 1927, they were dedicated to his memory. By 1925 Satie was already very ill from cirrhosis of the liver. Years of heavy drinking, which had never noticeably affected his lucidity, now showed what damage had been done. He had to forsake his obscure room in Arcueil for a hotel in Montparnasse. But soon Comte Etienne de Beaumont, with Winnaretta's help and unfailing financial support, arranged for him to be admitted to a private room in the Hôpital Saint-Joseph. Cared for by gentle nuns and sustained by champagne and opium-laced medicine, Satie received his visitors, the small band of friends who had survived the years without offending him. The princess, included in the acceptable group, was able to visit him during the early summer months; she watched him decline uncomplainingly until he died in his sleep at sunset on 1 July. Although she had not expected him to recover, she was moved by the death of someone whom she regarded as 'the gentlest and kindest of men, [who was] adored by his friends and . . . pupils' (some of whom, such as Poulenc and Auric, remained devoted to him to the end, despite being officially cancelled from his 'visiting-list'). Winnaretta's reflection on Satie's death was a faint echo of Plato's epitaph on Socrates. And when Sauguet and Milhaud brought back to her an account of the chaotic disorder and poverty of his Arcueil apartment, which only his death had allowed anyone to enter, she appreciated all the more the extraordinary spirit of the man who had lived a life of such material neglect while creating *Socrate*, his masterpiece, a work of such intense spiritual beauty.

Satie's death clearly disturbed Winnaretta. He had been her junior by one year and now his life was over. It focused her mind again on human mortality and made her even more aware that, just as material depravation was a problem in his life, an excess of material possessions was a problem in hers. Death was unavoidable and, when it came, she wanted hers to be like that of her friend John Sargent, who had breathed his last in the April of the previous year: 'for he died in bed in his sleep, his spectacles pushed up over his forehead and in his hands a volume of Voltaire that he had just been reading.' That was a happy death, the last scene in a happy life. But before that was possible for herself, she would have to make sure that her riches had been properly disposed of. And so, after a lot of thought, she invited her trusted friend Maurice Paléologue to Venice in September 1926. On the evening of his arrival she took him on a gondola trip out beyond San Giorgio Maggiore in the direction of the Lido. Only then did she say what was on her mind:

'I wanted to see you in Venice, in my dear Venice, to speak to you of a thing which I have pondered for a long time in my heart. You inspire me with such confidence that I don't hesitate to open it to you to ask your advice. You understand that I owe to my father a considerable fortune. But I am sixty-one-years-old; I am now seriously preoccupied with the arrangements which I have to make for the future of this fortune. I have made a cult of the memory of my father and it is in him above all that I want to find the inspiration for the future use of my inheritance. I need a foundation with which I can associate myself during my lifetime. Instruct me; advise me.'

Paléologue replied that, in view of her own interest in the arts and her father's scientific reputation, the creation of a foundation which could foster and endow artistic and scientific projects might satisfy her generous impulses. In the meantime she might consider sponsoring the activities of the College de France. She acted upon both these pieces of advice. As André Germain put it, she set herself up as the College de France's second protector—after François I. And, after discussing the matter thoroughly with Raymond Poincaré, she had her own institution, known as the Fondation Singer-Polignac, author- ized by special legislation on 25 March 1928 and confirmed as an independent body under Swiss law as the Institut Singer- Polignac on 22 December 1934. Poincaré himself readily accepted an invitation to become the foundation's first president.

Thoughts of death certainly precipitated Winnaretta's decision to shed some of her material responsibilities by institutionalizing her charitable activities in this way. These thoughts also made her resolve to see America, the land of her birth, before old age or death robbed her of the chance. Stravinsky had returned from his American tour with hints of muted enthusiasm, so why should she not explore this area of the world of which she knew nothing? Perhaps she would then be able to understand why the French had the irksome habit of making references to Americanisms in front of her. The blatant ones, such as Jean Wiéner's concoction of the title *franco-americain* for his concerto, were bad enough but the constant sly references to her national origins were insufferable because they were slightly incomprehensible. For example, why had Jean-Pierre Altermann (during his literary youth before humbly taking Holy Orders) prided himself on having recited before her the part of Sir Thomas Pollock Nageoire de l'Echange, meticulously imitating an American accent which, he imagined, sounded like hers? So, as if to clarify her own mind, she decided to cross the Atlantic to see what it meant to be an American and hopefully to dissipate French myths about her American-ness.

But she also used her American trip to make an overt act of defiance against certain elements in French society. In 1926 a moralistic play, entitled *La Prisonnière*, by Edouard Bourdet had been produced at the Théâtre-Femina in Paris. In it the drama of a young woman's struggle with her conflicting loves for her husband and an older woman is unfolded until finally the power of her Lesbian love makes her abandon all to satisfy it. Some socialites were only too eager to suggest that Bourdet's source of inspiration was Winnaretta's Venetian contretemps with her woman-friend's 'betrayed' husband or, more generally, her love-affair with Violet Trefusis, in which Violet's husband Denys played a curiously equivocal rôle. And so, when the princess set out on her much discussed expedition in the spring of 1927, she ostentatiously took with her not only Violet but also Denys Trefusis.

And in some ways, because the visit was so much publicized, it took on some of the appearance of a state visit. The Trefusises had to be fêted in New York by their kinsman Marshall Field, the department store millionaire. In Washington Violet and Winnaretta were invited to visit the White House, though what that taciturn Republican, President Calvin Coolidge, and the gruff and Europeanized princess found to talk about was never revealed. As the man who believed that 'the business of America is business', he was certainly worth cultivating: after all her income depended upon sympathetic attitudes such as his. The party then toured the southern states and, before returning to Europe, visited Cuba where lush exoticism and a Latin atmosphere made a more favourable impression on them than anything on the American mainland. An audience with President Machado must have contrasted markedly with their visit to that austere Presbyterian Coolidge.

Winnaretta's comments on her visit to the United States were restrained, almost ambivalent. Reporters, asking for her impressions, were left to deduce what they wanted from her pronouncement that she had just visited the country for the first time in sixty years and it would probably have to wait another sixty before she returned. Sir Oswald Mosley, a frequent guest at her musical evenings in Paris in the period before his total political commitment, told a more explicit story about her. While staying at Palm Beach's opulent Everglades Club, presided over by Paris Singer, he was delighted to discover the princess there among her brother's guests. The club consisted of a series of pleasant chalets built round a central club-house, to which guests liked to walk each morning for breakfast. But the prevailing calm was broken one morning when Winnaretta was discovered in the entrance hall berating the management in caustic tones: the lavatory in her chalet had broken. 'What is the use of being as nasty as Americans,' she demanded rhetorically, 'if you are as inefficient as Sicilians?' Even allowing for an element of exaggeration in Sir Oswald's tale and for the fact that she had experienced little intellectual stimulation in the plutocratic circles in which she had had to mix, no one could be in doubt that, when she returned to Paris, she came back to the only place she ever regarded as home.

However, there was another reason why Winnaretta was glad to return. She hated to think that the cultural scene in Paris could do without her for very long. The great effusion of money, necessary for the long-term success of the activities of

the Fondation Singer-Polignac, in no way inhibited her personal
patronage of the arts. For one thing she continued to subsidize
Diaghilev's Ballets Russes with the same liberality as before.
On the opening night of the 1925 season Diaghilev had im-
pressed upon the youthful star Serge Lifar the importance of
pleasing the audience. The director of the Opéra, Jacques
Rouché, was there. Rachmaninov was in the audience;
Aristide Briand in his box. Among 'our people'—the only ones
ever allowed backstage—were Stravinsky, Cocteau, Valéry,
Tristan Bernard and Prokofiev, along with the invaluable
Misia Sert and 'Coco' Chanel and, sitting in the front row,
waiting with an eagerness bordering upon impatience, the
Princesse de Polignac. But the diet of novelties that season was
unexceptionable; Auric's *Les Matelots* and Vladimir Dukelsky's
Zephire et Flore. (Vittorio Rieti's more adventurous ballet with
vocal chorus, *Barabau*, was not performed until much later
that year.) And these productions achieved an easy success,
compared with the mounting of Stravinsky's *Oedipus Rex*, with
which Diaghilev soon found himself burdened.

In September 1925, while returning to Nice after the successful reception of his *Sonata pour piano* in Venice, Stravinsky
suddenly decided to write a work in a language suitably distant
from its vernacular origins for it to express a timeless theme
untainted by everyday linguistic associations. The theme he
found in Sophocles' treatment of the story of Oedipus; the
language, dead but undecayed, was to be Latin; and his initial
collaborator-librettist was to be Cocteau. Cocteau could turn
his hand to almost anything creative but Latin verse was one
exception, so, as the first passages of the French text formulated
themselves in 1926, he handed them over to the scholar and
theologian Abbé (later Cardinal) Jean Daniélou, a close friend
(and one better qualified for acceptance in the 'inner circle'
than many ever suspected). Daniélou's Latin translation was a
literary masterpiece in its own right; and, despite his unfamili-
arity with the chosen language, Stravinsky was inspired to
write suitably noble music for it. The result aimed at was an
oratorio-like opera, in which all action was deliberately mini-
mized and the characters purposely depersonalized by wearing
large stylized masks, as in a Greek tragedy.

The composition of *Oedipus Rex* preoccupied Stravinsky
throughout 1926 and the final score was completed by May

1927, almost too late for the production planned for that month to celebrate Diaghilev's twentieth anniversay as a theatre impresario. However, long before this time Cocteau and Stravinsky had run into practical difficulties. Considerable financial backing was required before even the simplest production could be mounted and, contrary to Misia Sert's confident assumption, Coco Chanel showed no enthusiasm about shouldering that particular burden. Diaghilev, who had had to be let into the secret of his anniversary 'surprise' because his company was needed to perform the work, was equally unenthusiastic: he disliked the work at first hearing, calling it *'un cadeau très macabre'*, possibly because he was superstitiously afraid of its morbid subject, or perhaps the oedipal theme touched a tender nerve. So at the beginning of 1927 Winnaretta came to the rescue. Eager to help Stravinsky out of an awkward situation and genuinely captivated by his new, original work, she agreed to sit on the production committee and meet the cost of the enterprise. Even so, it was still not possible to afford the time and money required to mount a full-stage version of *Oedipus* and so a concert performance seemed to be the only answer. The public première was to take place at the Théâtre Sarah-Bernhardt on 30 May 1927, but a few days earlier a private, confidence-boosting preview was organized at Winnaretta's Paris house.

Choir and soloists in evening dress with Stravinsky and Serge Prokofiev playing a two-piano version of the orchestral score met with a muted reaction from the hand-picked audience. But the fully public performance on 30 May, if not exactly disastrous, was far from successful. Otto Klemperer sat with Cocteau and watched Stravinsky (this time as conductor) negotiate unskilfully the difficult passages of his own music. The audience seemed glad to move on to the next work on the programme, *L'Oiseau de feu*, a pleasingly colourful contrast to the sombre, static *Oedipus*. Klemperer, acutely aware of the production's shortcomings, decided that the work was worthy of a full stage production and, by mounting one with the Berlin State Opera in 1928, he ensured that the work lived through its troubled infancy, just as Winnaretta had prevented it from being still-born.

Critics and journalists clearly had trouble fitting the opera into any musical perspective. Janet Flanner tried: it 'was the settled work of a master musician, one who has left his violent youthful *Noces* and *Printemps* behind and, in his middling years, turns to Bach as if finally coming to rational terms with all great musical minds.' And, turning from the fatuous to the trivial, she added, 'The Latin was sung, with Italian pronunciation, to the French audience by Russians. Sophocles' name was on the *Oedipus* program because it seems he once wrote the thing in Greek.' None other than Prokofiev echoed this sneer at its poly-national nature—and rather more bitterly: 'The librettist is French, the text Latin, the subject Greek, the music Anglo-German (after Handel), the performance . . . in Monaco [*sic*], paid for by American money—indeed the height of internationalism.' Though involved in the production himself, Prokofiev seemingly had no qualms about dismissing Winnaretta's contribution as being merely financial and American at that. He had a rather unbalanced view of the influence of French high society upon the musical world. The snobbery of princesses and countesses infuriated him. Their salons blighted the growth of French music. There had been no 'French musician of the first order since the age of Chabrier and Bizet' —so he thought. But Prokofiev was, truth be told, only jealous of the benefits showered upon musicians, such as Stravinsky, who were capable of developing happily in a salon-atmosphere and breathing its air without undue moral discomfort. Domestic to the point of being unaesthetic, Prokofiev demanded that others, and not he, should compromise. He was disappointed and attempted to save his face by denigrating much of what Winnaretta's set stood for in artistic matters. Ironically, it was Diaghilev with his *entourage* of followers who exercised a much more exclusive social and artistic discrimination. Yet his ballet commissions still went to Prokofiev: the revolutionary score *Le Pas d'acier* of 1927 and Diaghilev's last ballet *Le Fils prodigue* of 1929 proved that his complaints were groundless.

Prokofiev certainly did not have to go through the tests that some newcomers to the scene apparently underwent. Diaghilev's cousin, the twenty-four-year-old composer Nicolas Nabokov, found on his arrival in Paris in 1927 that it took several months to earn the acceptance of Diaghilev's 'household'; Roger Desormière, Valichka Nouvel, his administrator, and Boris Kochno. Only then was he introduced to great figures, such as Picasso and Stravinsky, and the more important of Diaghilev's

patrons, Coco Chanel, Lord Rothermere, Misia Sert and the
Princesse de Polignac. And, on condition that he did not
associate with those on Diaghilev's black list, such as Ida
Rubinstein and a newly condemned Jean Cocteau, he might
expect great things.

However, although Diaghilev exercised a possessive tyranny
over his protegés, there was never any doubt about the deep
respect that he and Winnaretta had for each other. The
incredibly young Igor Markevitch, who penetrated Diaghilev's
magic circle about this time, noted this as one of his first
impressions. The sight of them together was distinctive: 'there
was between them . . . a strange affinity; they would appear
to move at reduced speed and advance like two battle cruisers
in a parade.' Nonetheless, by the late 1920s, while continuing
to subsidize his ballet, she was beginning to find his unreasonable restrictiveness rather irksome. And, although she still
allowed him to influence action as a patron, she made a point
of taking an interest in anything new on the musical scene
whatever his view. For example, when Virgil Thomson gave a
concert of his works in the Salle d'Orgue of the old Conservatoire early in 1928, she was there in the audience. From
the musical point of view it was a stimulating occasion, although
Thomson was convinced that a certain non-musical incident
at it claimed more attention. As the programme was about to
begin, Henri Sauguet, annoyed at his painter-friend Christian
Bérard's Cocteauesque desire to go off to smoke opium, brought
his umbrella down on his head with a resounding crack. After
a moment's stunned silence, pandemonium broke loose. Sir
Francis Rose watched as Marie-Laure de Noailles showered
sympathy on the amateur drug-taker, while two princesses,
Violette Murat and Winnaretta, took Sauguet's part. Etienne
de Beaumont, fussy and flustered, tried to restore order among
them. Gertrude Stein and Alice Toklas remained indifferent:
the only side they deigned to take was Virgil Thomson's—and
alas! they were least able to help him as he wanted. And on
28 November 1928, when the 'forbidden' Ida Rubinstein gave
a balletic concert, Winnaretta made sure of having tickets well
in advance—after all, the first performance of Stravinsky's
Baiser de la fée was being given. When she arrived, she discovered Diaghilev, Nouvel and Kochno (who had had difficulty
in obtaining tickets) sitting among their friends, the Beaumonts,

the Serts, the poet Maiakovsky, Picasso and, of course, Stravinsky—the list was endless. Diaghilev tried to divert attention
away from his presence and at the same time implicitly criticize
his friends by saying that the spectacle 'breathed a provincial
boredom'.

But the temperamental genius had not long to live. After a
final successful season in the spring of 1929, he set out for
Germany. On 28 July he went to the Baden-Baden music
festival to hear a work by Hindemith. Winnaretta arrived and
joined his party. She was not at ease: Diaghilev's health
seemed to have deteriorated badly but she could do no more
than discuss her fears with Nicolas Nabokov and his wife. And
Diaghilev had no intention of resting because his trip was partly
a business one. He was bent on cajoling Hindemith into writing
a ballet-score for him and he also wanted to introduce his new
protegé Igor Markevitch to Germany's grand old man of music,
Richard Strauss, so off they went to Munich and almost
inevitably encountered Winnaretta again, attracted there by a
new production of *Tristan*. And that was the last she ever saw
of him. By the time Diaghilev reached Venice, no amount of
well-earned rest could save him, and on 19 August he died
under the jealous gaze of Boris Kochno and Serge Lifar.

Contrary to popular opinion, Winnaretta did not arrange
(and pay for) Diaghilev's funeral: Misia Sert and Coco Chanel
fortuitously were to hand when his end came and they relieved
Kochno and Lifar of the task, which they were emotionally
incapable of carrying out. But, when it came to deciding the
fate of Diaghilev's ballet, Winnaretta was the first person to
whom Nouvel and Lifar turned for advice. Nouvel wanted to
refloat the company but this would have involved Diaghilev's
heirs in raising an enormous sum of around one million francs.
But Lifar and the princess agreed that, for the time being, only
money enough for winding up the company could reasonably
be raised. The dancers were released from their contracts and
many of them found their way into the two off-shoot companies
that bravely tried to continue Diaghilev's work, the Opéra
Russe à Paris and the Ballet de l'Opéra de Monte Carlo,
under the direction of René Blum and later Colonel de Basil.

But, without Diaghilev, the creative genius and drive, which
had made Paris and even Monte Carlo in the 1920s such focal
points of civilization, had gone. If his spirit lingered anywhere,

it was not in those scenes of fevered activity and struggle but in Venice, his last resting place, the timeless city of the waters. On his tomb on the peaceful cemetery isle of San Michele the superscription ran: '*Venise, l'inspiratrice eternelle de nos apaisements.*'

The Princesse de Polignac and friends in Venice, by Philippe Jullian.

Chapter 15
Feeding on the Advancing Hour
(1930–1935)

Diaghilev's death marked the end of an era in artistic history. It also brought to an end a period in Winnaretta's life. After 1929 she patronized ballet much less than before. With advancing years she was attracted more and more by pure music. Opera certainly still claimed her attention but chamber music or unprogrammatic orchestral music occupied a special place in her estimation. New music, newly written or old music newly discovered or refurbished, continued to fascinate her. And this time the collaborator with whom she worked on many of her musical projects was a woman, Nadia Boulanger. Winnaretta had known her for some time; she knew many of her international range of composition pupils; but not until Diaghilev's death did their association begin to blossom in a unique and fruitful way, although there was some overlap between the two periods.

Igor Markevitch had been Nadia Boulanger's pupil for counterpoint (and Vittorio Rieti his orchestration teacher), but it had been Diaghilev who had taken him up as the *wunderkind* of his declining years. In fact, one of his last efforts had been to launch the young composer by having his Concerto for piano and orchestra played on 15 July 1929 as an interval-piece in a ballet programme during the Covent Garden season. To Diaghilev's great disappointment, the London audience was non-committal about it. When it had been given a preview at Winnaretta's house in Paris the reception had been warmer, but the acid test for Diaghilev always had to be the general public's reaction. And even among the private audience in Paris, there had been one dissenting voice: Stravinsky who all but fell out with Diaghilev in his last months over what he considered his inflated estimation of the youthful composer. Stravinsky was uncompromisingly deprecatory, but the princess was prepared to give the boy some practical encouragement when the prop of Diaghilev's moral support fell away. She commissioned him to write another work for piano and orchestra, not necessarily a concerto as such but something along *concertante* lines. The result was his *Partita*, a craftsman-like composition, consisting of three movements, Overture, Choral and Rondo, that skilfully balanced in itself classical and contemporary elements. The title, as well as the music itself was intended to have Bach-like associations designed to appeal to Winnaretta. Published in 1930 the *Partita* was first performed in her Paris house, not by the princess herself, as some believed, but by the incomparable Marcelle Meyer.

And in the decade following December 1931, when the Marquise (Yvonne) de Casa Fuerte launched her adventurous series of concerts of contemporary music, under the name of *La Sérénade*, Markevitch's music figured frequently upon their programmes, thanks (claimed Virgil Thomson, whose music found no favour in the eyes of the *Sérénade* committee because of an imagined vendetta conducted against him by Vittorio Rieti and Markevitch himself) to the Princesse de Polignac and Marie-Laure de Noailles, who mothered him like a foster-child. Virgil Thomson need not have worried. Disappointment acted as a stimulus for him, whereas, for all his encouragement, Markevitch failed to develop as a composer and allowed his youthful facility to be outgrown by a mature genius for conducting. However, of this early association with Winnaretta, apart from the delightful *Partita*, there did remain a close personal bond, which grew stronger as the 1930s progressed. Markevitch himself remarked upon the way in which friendship for her was an organic thing: as a youth all he could see in her was a marble-like coldness; only later did he realize how this hid a great shyness and that underneath was the 'potential of exalted friendship so typically Anglo-Saxon'. Later, when she visited him while recovering from an illness in Switzerland, he discovered the depth and warmth of her affection for him. When she insisted on livening him up by making him play piano duets with her and spiced their music-making with bursts of enthusiasm and uncontrollable laughter, her real nature became apparent.

One thing about which Markevitch never had any doubt was her profound love of music. She pursued her musical ideals with determination, although she often received scant encouragement, even from some of her friends. For example, her obsession with Bach, of which Markevitch was so conscious, still irked many. On 25 October 1930 she held a very elegant soirée and provided a musical menu of three Bach concertos for her guests' delectation. But, noted a young Julien Green, at the end of the second work there was an unseemly rush towards the buffet and a half-sized audience was left to listen to the third concerto—accompanied by competitive noises from the supper room. But worse still: in the middle of that work one of the survivors whispered to her neighbour, 'I detest this contemplative atmosphere'—and without another word they too made for the buffet. Or on another occasion at Winnaretta's, a year later on 11 December 1931, Green had the feeling that some of the audience would have been happier if the musicians had kept quiet in order to let them gossip. One unnamed writer turned to him and confided that he admired those who could distinguish Poulenc from Stravinsky. To him their music had nothing to say. Green ignored him and concentrated upon a magnificent performance of Weber's *Grand Duo Concertant* for clarinet and piano.

Sometimes Winnaretta's preoccupation with music was a source of fun for the less committed. In April 1931, having arranged to give a private performance of Hindemith's *Konzertmusik* for piano, brass and two harps (probably one of its first hearings in France, since it had only been composed in 1930), she became visibly distressed when the harps did not arrive from Pleyel's. The harpists refused to use two chromatic instruments which she had: the music was too difficult for that. But the audience was vastly amused and took in good part her efforts to distract them with songs by Brahms and Strauss sung by an oversized German soprano. When the harps finally arrived, the guests were in too light a mood to cope with Hindemith's music. The salon was too small to contain the overwhelming sound. But, if Julien Green for one was exhausted by this delayed experience, at least his neighbour Serge Lifar was carried away by it. In retaliation Winnaretta occasionally poked fun at her audiences; if they were particularly inattentive to some new work, she would signal to the musicians to repeat it and then turn to her guests and ask which of the two pieces they preferred. Invariably 'the second one' was the favourite. She would just nod reflectively.

If some of the music played at the princess's suffered because its style was unfamiliar, certain new compositions with which she was associated at that time were digested more easily. In the spring of 1932 she made a generous gesture to help two of her young musician friends. She commissioned Francis Poulenc to write a concerto for two pianos and orchestra. If he could finish it in time, she would see that it was performed at the Music Festival to be held in Venice the following September. Poulenc himself and Jacques Février would be engaged as soloists. He accepted the challenge and during the summer, in less than three months—a remarkably short time for one who usually composed orchestral works with painful slowness—a double concerto of the most palatable nature was completed. Light-hearted and carefree, the Concerto for Two Pianos abandoned any attempt at serious musical development to concentrate upon pure melody. The first movement was coloured by Stravinskian rhythms and echoes of Balinaisian gamelan music, which had fascinated Poulenc at the Colonial Exhibition of 1931; the second was characterized by a Mozartian flippancy; and the third was frankly flirtatious. Everything combined to give the work popular appeal. At the première on 5 September Poulenc and Février, playing with the orchestra of La Scala under the direction of Désiré Defauw, had an immediate success. The composition did much to enhance Poulenc's international reputation as a composer, and Février's career as a pianist benefited greatly from the whole experience.

For the rest of September Poulenc stayed on at the Palazzo Polignac enjoying the reaction to his concerto and involving himself in the musical activities of the princess's household. Amongst others Manuel de Falla and Artur Rubinstein were there, and in the morning Poulenc invariably joined Rubinstein to play works for two pianos. Returning from his daily early morning mass, Falla might well be greeted by the strains of his *Nights in the Gardens of Spain*. Sometimes Winnaretta would join in, taking the second piano with Rubinstein or Poulenc. And at one point Elsa Maxwell whisked her off with Rubinstein and a string quartet all the way to the Castello di Vigoleno, at Salsomaggiore near Milan, to visit Madame Jean Hugo (by birth the Principessa Maria Ruspoli and the Duchesse de Gramont by her first marriage). Music-making was the purpose of their visit but, as they drove there through a terrible storm,

the châtelaine stole the show for sheer spectacle 'by illuminating
the entire outline of the castle with torches set in the battlements
and towers' as a guiding beacon for the travellers. The neon
illuminations of Piccadilly and Broadway, thought Elsa, would
have paled beside that display.

But the main concern of the musicians at the Palazzo
Polignac was a serious one. Falla had agreed to conduct a
performance of *El Retablo de Maese Pedro* at the Music Festival,
though only a concert version because of production difficulties.
Even Winnaretta's offer to lend her puppets for it was of little
use since they were too diminutive to be effective in a public
theatre. Nonetheless, the preparation involved was still considerable. Each morning Falla and Poulenc rehearsed at the
keyboard. When full rehearsals took place, Winnaretta usually
persuaded Falla to allow her to be present. What he put into
the making of a performance was fascinating: everything was
under control, although at times the work did claim a little too
much of his attention. At the final rehearsal she was surprised
to see him at the conductor's desk with his face covered in small
pieces of cotton-wool: during the night he had been stung by
mosquitoes and had covered each sting with a little tuft of
cotton-wool soaked in ammonia. By rehearsal time he had
forgotten about them and they remained grotesquely stuck to
his face.

Late in 1932 another composition commissioned by the
princess received an enthusiastic reception at its first performance. A one-movement work, simply entitled *Ouverture*,
by Germaine Tailleferre riveted attention in a concert conducted by Pierre Monteux at the Salle Pleyel on Christmas
Day. The critics practically ignored Alfred Cortot's performance of Chopin's Concerto in F minor, which preceded
it, and extolled the vitality, clarity and homogeneity of the
Tailleferre piece; it was easily one of the most successful of that
year's premières. Tailleferre was still in full possession of her
talent and from the first note the public had loved her new
work.

A third work owed its inception to the Princesse de Polignac
in 1932 and, like Poulenc's concerto, it involved the combination of two pianos. Henri Sauguet had long been accepted
in her circle; his music was often played in her salon. A pupil of
Satie's—and incidentally the grandson of her sister's gardener

at the Decazes's château at La Grave—Sauguet felt a strong
affinity for her and so, when she asked him to write something
for her, he tackled it as though it were a personal gift for her,
something that she might play herself. The work was *Les Jeux
de l'amour et du hasard*, in effect a suite for two pianos; it had five
movements, each one deceptively titled—*Préambule, Poème, Jeu,
Nocturne* and *Sérénade*—and each balanced with the next to
convey all the elaborate emotional contrasts suggested by its
commedia dell'arte atmosphere. On 4 February 1933 the suite was
given its public première at a *Sérénade* concert in the Salle
Gaveau and, with Poulenc and Sauguet himself as soloists, it
met with considerable success. It was often repeated at private
concerts given by Winnaretta, when a variety of performers,
such as Jacques Février or Clara Haskil, might take over from
the original executants. In 1937 it was transformed into a ballet
with the new title of *Le Dompter dompté*. The Compagnie Ballets
de la Jeunesse, as its name suggests, a youthful ballet troupe and
an impecunious one, which could not afford an orchestra, saw
in Sauguet's two piano work great balletic potential and,
provided with a suitable scenario by J. L. Vaudoyer, they
battened on its success.

As she grew older, the Princesse de Polignac seemed to
intensify her musical activities and become, if possible, a more
integral part of cultural life in Paris and so, as if to celebrate her
achievements, early in 1933 a group of her friends decided to
pay her a unique tribute. Under the guidance of Alfred Cortot
on 21 March they presented a special concert at the Salle Pleyel
in which all the music had been dedicated to her and mostly
commissioned by her. The evening began with Cortot conducting the Orchestre Symphonique de Paris in a performance
of Fauré's suite from *Pelléas et Mélisande*. Then followed a complete concert performance of Milhaud's opera *Les Malheurs
d'Orphée*, conducted by the composer. This captivated the public
again with 'its bitter audacity'. The mood relaxed with a crisp
and carefree rendering of Poulenc's Concerto for two pianos,
in which the soloists were the original interpreters, Février and
Poulenc himself. Rather too similar in form to avoid comparisons, Igor Markevitch's *Partita* was given what was its first fully
public performance in Paris and its acid dissonances apparently
surprised and disoriented the public. Only the extreme virtuosity (and extreme youth) of the composer as soloist softened the

reaction. Germaine Tailleferre's *Ouverture* was then conducted by Roger Desormière and, as at its recent première, captivated everyone with its dash, joyfulness and complete cohesion. And finally, the sentimental highlight of the evening was the orchestral version of Ravel's *Pavane pour une infante défunte*, conducted by the composer, who had been specially brought into Paris for the concert. Although this proved to be one of the last occasions upon which Ravel appeared in public, no hint of the tragedy that was soon to blight his career marred the spontaneity of the evening's celebrations. All agreed that it was a tribute worthy of an illustrious champion of music. The programme chronicled musical life in France during one of its greatest periods of development and had subtly spotlighted the part played by her in the process.

But one thing was taken for granted: this process was an open-ended one and her part in it was by no means finished. Three months later the result of another of her commissions received its first performance. Nicolas Nabokov's *Job*, an oratorio for two solo voices, choir and orchestra, was featured on the programme of Georges Balanchine's *Les Ballets 1933* on 23 June during their season at the Théâtre de Champs-Elysées. Using a libretto which his friend the theologian Jacques Maritain had constructed out of the biblical original, Nabokov had created an impressive work. However, most agreed that its first section was too long and too sombre, as it rather monotonously rehearsed Job's tribulations, but its *finale*, in which the new understanding between God and His creature was celebrated in rapturous terms, stimulated the audience's admiration: the Orchestre Symphonique de Paris, with Jacques Février and Jean Doyon as solo pianists, responded to the conducting of Maurice de Abravanel and brought the oratorio to an exultant conclusion. One unusual feature of the production that added considerably to its dramatic impact was the projection at the back of the stage of a series of slides of William Blake's illustrations for the *Book of Job*. The French audience was struck by their forcefulness. Winnaretta, who was already familiar with them, must have been reminded of her husband's pioneering experiments with music and slide projections so many decades before.

In the following year the princess was associated with another new work, this time a more truly balletic one but in its own way as distinctive and unusual as Nabokov's *Job*. This was Stravinsky's *Persephone*, a three act ballet that deviated from convention by incorporating into its score solo arias and choruses, based on a text by André Gide. Another untraditional feature was that the principal rôle was to be mimed, not danced by Ida Rubinstein, who had commissioned the work. As a result it did not have a very propitious infancy. The music, though some of Stravinsky's finest, was difficult, and Gide testily complained of the subjection of his verses to the demands of the music. Stravinsky strongly hinted that the poem of Gide's chosen by Ida Rubinstein was rather old-fashioned. A quarrel between the composer and the producer, Jacques Coppeau, did not help matters.

The first performance at the Opéra on 30 April 1934 was not a success but, according to Stravinsky, it was not as trying as the pre-première run-through which Winnaretta volunteered to give at her house a few days earlier. As he tackled the piano part, Stravinsky found his attention distracted by the way in which René Maison was singing the tenor *arias* in too harsh a voice, while the poet Paul Claudel, no stranger to the art of libretto writing, persisted in glaring fixedly at him. For his part Gide bridled at every note and refused to attend any other performance of the work. Winnaretta was undeterred by adverse reactions. She liked *Persephone* and wanted more to appreciate it, so a few weeks later on 18 May 1934 she boldly coupled it with a Bach *cantata* and some songs by Fauré as the main feature in one of her concerts. How many of the audience did appreciate it is another matter. Even a good-natured Julien Green, who admitted to admiring its 'rhythms of cyclopean power', was critical of the weak, almost loose way in which he thought the work as a whole had been constructed. Ironically, *Persephone* was given a less appreciative reception in Winnaretta's salon than a work such as *Pierrot Lunaire* when performed there about that time. Schoenberg was, generally speaking, not among her favourite composers but by the 1930s the work was fairly well-known to her and her more discerning musical friends.

Meanwhile, another major work commissioned by the princess was going through the process of gestation. She had asked Kurt Weill to write a symphony—his second—for her late in 1932, when he was still living in Berlin under a gathering cloud of suspicion as Hitler's Nazi Party began to dominate

political affairs in Germany. Unshakeably apolitical, she had
watched the turn of events with disquiet, mainly because of the
effect upon the lives of some of her friends. About this time
Elsa Maxwell, in Munich for the Strauss Festival, witnessed an
example of Winnaretta's concern about Germany's predica-
ment. Having noticed her at the opera, Elsa made a point of
going over to speak to her afterwards and found her in the
company of Marie Curie and 'a rather frightened-looking,
middle-aged little woman'. This turned out to be Dr Lise
Meitner, a physicist from the Kaiser Wilhelm Institute in
Berlin. Dr Meitner was brilliant; she was going to split the
atom, Winnaretta informed Elsa, who made no secret of her
lack of comprehension. The princess did not explain further
but with a sage look added quietly: 'Ah! some day you'll know
about it. It is a discovery that is going to change the whole
world'—as it did, but only after Lise Meitner had fled from
Germany, with the increasing virulence of Hitler's antisemitism,
and made her work on the release of atomic energy available to
the Allies. But Winnaretta was not primarily concerned about
political values so much as about their effect upon the arts and
sciences. For the moment the only way in which she could show
her concern was by giving practical help and a sense of purpose
to Kurt Weill during a time of trial.

Weill began writing his symphony in January 1933. At the
end of the month President von Hindenburg appointed Hitler
as chancellor. In March, hounded as a Jew and a composer of
'decadent' music, Weill interrupted his composition and fled to
France, where he set up a temporary home for himself at
Louveciennes. After a further interruption, during which he
undertook and completed a much less exacting commission,
Die sieben Todsünden, he finished the first draft of the symphony
in December 1933 and in February 1934 the full score was
ready. On 11 October the Concertgebouw Orchestra, under the
baton of Bruno Walter, gave it its first performance before a
delighted audience in Amsterdam. The critics, however, were
less enthusiastic. Possibly they expected Weill's return to the
concert hall, which he had deserted almost a decade earlier, to
show less of a marked turning away from the musical textures
of his *Mahagoney* and *Dreigroschenoper* than the Symphony No. 2
did. In fact, here was a quite serious, fully orchestral piece of
music, darkly lyrical throughout and only making some

reference to the composer's recent experiences in its funeral-march-like slow movement. The last movement, lighter and more optimistic, if anything, expressed a feeling of hope for a more trouble-free future. Only after Bruno Walter had conducted the symphony a number of times on both sides of the Atlantic did the critics begin to appreciate it as the noble work of an artist capable of much greater originality of thought than Brechtian philosophy had ever inspired in him. However, as far as Weill was concerned Winnaretta's commission was the last ray of comfort that Europe could give and in 1935 he sailed for more promising American shores.

The year 1934 had seen Winnaretta provide inspiration for another struggling composer, one entirely different from Weill. Aged only twenty-two and still under the tutelage of Nadia Boulanger, Jean Françaix had already gained a reputation as a skilful composer whose originality shone through all his Stravinskian influences. Soon after meeting Françaix through Nadia Boulanger, Winnaretta set him to write a piece for chamber ensemble. He responded by composing his *Sérénade pour douze instruments*, a four-movement work whose lightness of texture and well-balanced instrumentation turned out to have exactly the right proportions for the princess's salon, where it received its first performance later the same year. And small chamber orchestras, similar in balance to the one used for the *Sérénade*, were to become something of a hallmark of Françaix's work in the years to come.

Although Françaix did not become one of Winnaretta's most intimate friends—he was rather too young and shy for that—he enjoyed her patronage throughout the 1930s and benefited considerably from her encouragement. In 1935, for example, when she and Nadia Boulanger were arranging a concert at her house, they pressed Françaix to write three duets for sopranos and string quartet specially for it. The suggested text was derived from Aristophanes and the work had to be composed within fifteen days to be in time for the concert. He accomplished the task within the time limit; the three 'movements', *Les Oiseaux*, *La Prière de Sulpicia* and *Les Grenouilles*, were cleverly written but not until the last moment did he have a chance to hear them performed by the artistes for whom they were intended. Françaix, like everyone else present, found them delightful, although he modestly confessed, mainly because one of the

sopranos (who had begun the concert by singing songs by
Fauré, Debussy and Chabrier) not only possessed an exquisite
voice but was also ravishingly beautiful. This was the Comtesse
Jean de Polignac, by birth Marie-Blanche di Pietro, a Lanvin
heiress, who, after marrying one of Winnaretta's kinsmen, had
become a loved and respected friend, not only because of her
beauty and musical talent but also because she had an un-
exceptionally sweet and understanding nature.

Françaix's *Trois Duos* with their texts taken from Aristophanes
illustrates another facet of Winnaretta's life at this time. Since
learning Greek two decades before, she had kept up her studies
and had applied her classical interests to certain aspects of her
musical life: the choice of texts for *Socrate* as well as for Françaix's duets was an example of this; but also Milhaud's choice
of the Orpheus legend as a basis for the plot of *Les Malheurs
d'Orphée* and Stravinsky's associating her with the initial
productions of *Oedipus Rex* and *Persephone* showed some appreciation of her classical preoccupations. Another point at which
her love of literature and music came together was in her
friendship with the poet Ezra Pound.

Winnaretta first met Pound in Paris in the early 1920s when,
as a composer of the most amateurish and eccentric kind of
music, he had given concerts of his instrumental pieces and
fragments from a rather bizarre opera based upon the life of
François Villon. Whatever she thought about Pound's own
music, she did respect him for his scholarly work on late medieval and Renaissance scores, and for what he did to encourage
musical life in Rapallo, once he settled there after 1924. For
his part, he came to recognize the integrity of her judgment and
discernment in musical matters. He admired and was sometimes amused at her refusal to compromise with inaestheticism
of any sort. Pound chuckled with glee at an incident that
occurred at a concert given by the child prodigy Yehudi
Menuhin in London in spring 1933. Sir Edward Elgar, introduced to the princess, opened the conversation with a conspiratorial whisper: 'Hyperion won.' (The horse backed by him
that day had evidently brought in dividends.) Winnaretta
recoiled slightly, as Pound put it, not being 'deeply impressed
by Ed's dogginess (*sic*)'. She was no doubt even less impressed
by a racing-horse's sporting a name like Hyperion, with all its
classical and Keatsian associations.

In the winter of 1933–34 Winnaretta kept in close touch with Pound as he launched a series of concerts in Rapallo. She even went to visit him there and seems to have spent her time with him discussing music, oblivious of everything else, except the cold. (A month or so later Pound had radiators installed in the hope of tempting her to stay again.) Their discussions centred upon the music of the troubadour Arnaut Daniel and Clement Jannequin, a piece of whose music she sent Pound on her return to Paris, in the hope that it might be sung in one of the Rapallo concerts. But they also ranged as far as the music of William Young, the seventeenth-century British composer of trio sonatas. These too Pound wanted to have performed in his concerts. Winnaretta kept up her association with Pound, until the War intervened, and saw a great deal of him whenever their paths crossed. When in Venice he always came to her concerts and often his *maîtresse-en-titre*, the *virtuoso* violinist Olga Rudge, played at them. With a child's discernment, their daughter Mary Rudge, later Princesse Boris de Rachewiltz, could tell how important the concerts at the Palazzo Polignac were for her mother because of 'her intensive practising beforehand and the elegance of her clothes'.

Another of Winnaretta's poet friends whose interests also strayed into the musical world was Léon-Paul Fargue. A friend of Satie's and a latter-day François Villon, who reconciled in himself his association with the Académie de Goncourt group with his rôle as a poet of Montmartre, glorifying the Bohemian life centred on Rodolphe Salis's '*Chat Noir*' with its famous café-concerts, Fargue found no difficulty in moving in the most exalted artistic circles. Making few concessions to social sensibilities, he expected the Faubourg Saint-Germain to accept him for the Bohemian he was and he succeeded in this. The society of the Comtesse André de Fels or her daughter the Duchesse de La Rochefoucauld, not to mention the Godobeskis, remained open to him.

The Princesse de Polignac was particularly indulgent towards him, although on formal occasions she tried to make him conform to basic conventions for the sake of her other guests. Fargue's neighbour André Beucler was once included in an invitation to dine at her house and on the night before the party found himself sitting behind her at the Opéra. She turned round to chat: after commenting that it must be fun to live so

near the great poet, she asked him to make sure that Fargue
put on a dinner jacket the following evening and arrived in
time, because, as she knew from experience, he was invariably
unpunctual. However, on this occasion Fargue was not simply
late; he did not arrive. News that his washerwoman's frail and
undernourished daughter Ginette had just died arrived as they
were setting out, and Fargue rushed off to comfort the dis-
traught mother. He spared only one moment to send a taxi-
driver with a message explaining their absence to the princess.
Beucler wondered how she would take this, but Fargue reassured him that she would understand: 'Winnie's a broad-
minded woman!' and added that, if he were disappointed at
missing the dinner, he would 'take him to Winnie's another
time. Lots of times. And after dessert there'll always be a pianist
from Transylvania or some such place . . .' And after Fargue
had been to his washerwoman's house and seen the poverty of
the place, his thoughts returned bitterly to the house at 57
avenue Henri-Martin. 'They'll be at dessert by now,' he commented to Beucler. 'At Winnie's, I mean . . . I can see them
round the Dresden china—the glistening lips of pretty girls, the
glistening heads of the learned, as naked baboons' bottoms . . .
Unless, of course, they've already migrated to the grand salon.
And perhaps, by some weird stroke of fate, the Moldavian
pianist is playing some extract from Satie's *Messe pour les pauvres*
or the *scherzo* from Chopin's *Poème de la Mort* in honour of the
beautiful Ginette now being escorted by angels.' But Fargue's
bitterness was directed not at Winnaretta, frugal for all her
riches, but, in true poetic fashion, at the world in which the
washerwoman's child had failed to be 'born under a well-fed
star'. After a bite to eat, Fargue's cheerfulness revived and he
rushed off with Beucler to see if any of Winnaretta's guests had
gone on to the '*Boeuf sur le toit*' where they could find out how
the pianist had acquitted himself.

Fargue's estimation of the princess's character was fairly
accurate. In turn, she had summed him up quite well. Whatever
his shortcomings, she sincerely admired him for his compassion
and humanity as well as for his sparkling wit and ingenuity.
She once asked him to join her on the yacht *Zara* for a short
cruise from Marseilles round the coast of Italy to Venice. He
accepted, apparently undaunted by the party's regimented
sight-seeing programme. He might be told to be ready to leave

the yacht for some place such as Nervi at 9.30 next morning but, without fail, when the launch left with the party, he would still be sleeping off the effects of the countless whiskies consumed the night before. When the party returned in the early afternoon, they would invariably be greeted by the sight of the dishevelled poet, just out of bed and frantically rushing up on deck as if to catch the launch. But, although he saw nothing but the stars in the Mediterranean sky and a whisky bottle on the whole trip, he managed to write a masterly description of the cruise on the *Zara* once he returned to Paris.

Léon-Paul Fargue was very far from letting anything, even whisky, dull his wits. Winnaretta liked to repeat the story of his quarrel with a certain count—dare one say Etienne de Beaumont?—who, though an excellent host, was not renowned for his erudition and was almost notorious for his bad spelling. Their quarrel became so acrimonious that the count challenged the poet to a duel. Fargue accepted with these words: 'Since I have the choice of arms, I choose spelling—you are dead!'

Winnaretta was quite familiar with the way in which poetic licence crept into his everyday life. On one of the last occasions she saw him, she was amused by his news that he had moved from his inaccessible house on the Canal Saint-Martin and had a new apartment in Montparnasse where he pressed her to come to a dinner fit for the gods, prepared by his cook. But she knew that the apartment was in fact one room in the Hôtel Acropolis in the boulevard Saint-Germain where, she commented, she hoped for his own sake he would stay. As an afterthought she added a codicil to her will and left him fifty-thousand francs to ease life for him in his declining years.

Another—more consciously eccentric—poet and writer with whom Winnaretta still associated in the 1930s was Jean Cocteau, despite the fact that in the late 1920s he had come under a slight cloud of suspicion: he was rather too closely associated with the writer Princesse Marthe Bibesco, whose feelings of loyalty to France, her adopted country, Winnaretta regarded with a critical eye, although it had been at her own lunch table that Cocteau and the Roumanian princess had first met some years previously. But worse, Cocteau's period of addiction to opium, for a while, had made him an unreliable friend. And curious side-effects of his addiction lingered on after his cure: in 1930 he published *Opium*, the journal of his cure, in which some strange references appeared. Still pre-occupied with his concept of the Orpheus legend, developed in his poem *L'Ange Heurtebise* in 1925 and subsequently in his play *Orphée*, in *Opium* he elaborated the Heurtebise theme, with all its associations of the Orpheus bisexuality dialectic, in order to include it in this fantasy section: 'The Princesse E. de Polignac bought a house in the country and asked the young under-gardener his name: Raphaël Heurtebise.' And he added a footnote to the effect that marvellous occurrences were caused by some disorder in normal sequences of events and one should not confuse them with minor coincidences. Perhaps so, but what was Cocteau trying to imply about the minor coincidence of Winnaretta's acquiring an under-gardener with such a significant name? Less ambiguous was Cocteau's irritating habit of referring to the amazing likeness between her and Giotto's famous portrait of Dante. He would call her *Mère Dante*, crudely running the words together to emphasize the pun. Yet few ever doubted Cocteau's innate benevolence and she, more than many, was prepared to be charitable about an old friend's uncontrollable verbosity.

About this time one of the friends they had in common, Anna de Noailles, was living out her last days with as much poetry and drama as possible in her apartment in the rue Scheffer next door to Winnaretta's house. By this time the Académie Royale Belge de Langue et de Littérature Française had honoured her, as the Académie Française could not, by giving her a chair. And when she had gone to Brussels to be installed in the Palais des Académies in the presence of King Albert and Queen Elisabeth on 22 January 1922, she had been surrounded by an entourage of women-friends from Paris, her sister the Princesse de Caraman-Chimay, Hedwige, Princesse d'Aren-berg, the Duchesse de Rohan-Chabot, herself a poetess of sorts, and the Princesse de Polignac. Winnaretta certainly admired Anna and almost mothered her during her frequent illnesses, although at times she was not above teasing her about her affected posturings. One thing she took great delight in doing was bringing her face to face with another close friend, Colette, or, as she put it, 'Confronting the thoroughbred with the *percheron*.' According to Violet Trefusis, 'Colette on these occasions would behave like a somewhat grumpy gardener who had been dragged away from his work.' Colette was not keen on Anna's habit of talking about her poetry (of which she had a low opinion) or—invariably—about death. Colette would mutter: 'Death doesn't interest me, not even my own!' Living things, flowers and animals, and the sensuous things of life, food and wine, meant more to her. At times she even managed to interest Anna in them. She once invited her with her sister Hélène to her house and served them with an intoxicating, hot beverage. The sisters were enchanted and went round Paris claiming that Colette had discovered ambrosia, though the drink was a more prosaic concoction of hot Beaujolais flavoured with a suspicion of cinnamon, lemon and sugar.

However, neither of the two sisters had much time left to enjoy the rediscovery of the food of the gods. Hélène de Caraman-Chimay died in March 1929, having placed too much trust in the skill of a faithful but too old-fashioned family doctor —or at least that was the story put about by Dame Ethel Smyth after the news of her death brought her hurrying to Paris. Using Winnaretta's house as a base, she rushed around commiserating melodramatically with all her friends. And the theme of death now became an almost permanent obsession with Anna de Noailles—unlike Colette—particularly her own death. She would never relax; she was never still or silent. Yet, all day, any day, she could be found in the same room, reclining on the same *chaise-longue*, agitatedly inactive and preoccupied with the thought that, before the year was out, she too would be dead. But in the evening she would be whisked off to dine at one of the smart Parisian restaurants where she would dominate the conversation with indefatigable animation until—dying again —she would be ushered home to bed at 2 o'clock in the morning. As Violet Trefusis commented, 'it was comforting to know that she died all day and dined all night'. But in 1933 Anna's prediction was indeed fulfilled: on 30 April she died at the age of fifty-six and was genuinely mourned by a host of friends who had loved her as a clever and sympathetic person and had regarded her façade of twittering affectation and hypochondria as just another engaging characteristic. Winnaretta was particularly upset at losing one of her oldest friends, who in her day had been France's leading poetess.

Anna's death brought Winnaretta closer to Colette, if anything, a friend of even longer standing. Both naturally witty, clever and down to earth, in public they could keep up an

entertaining repartee or a complementary dialogue, their
distinctive accents contrasting delightfully with each other,
Colette's rich, rolling Burgundian and Winnaretta's dry anglicized French. But in private they were even more of soul-mates,
exchanging thoughts or memories of the simple things in life
that delighted them. Over a 'picnic' of hot wine and 'a debauch
of cheese' the princess would settle down comfortably at home
in Colette's house, whereas in her own she often had the
appearance of a slightly embarrassed guest. She would confide
in Colette her longing for a *Walden*-like simplicity of life. She
had bought a shack in the country, she said, and had given an
architect instructions to add a small wing while she was in
Venice. And guess what she had found on her return? She
ground the answer out through clenched teeth: 'The Lououvre!'

However, about this time rustic simplicity was not the only
illusion that Colette and Winnaretta were concerned with
recapturing. In 1932, her literary palate temporarily jaded,
Colette decided to take up another profession. At the suggestion
of André Maginot—of the Line—she developed her natural
facility for making beauty products and set a Salon de Beauté
in the rue de Miromesnil in Paris. A shop at Saint Tropez was
also opened. Colette was only able to do this with the help and
slightly doubtful encouragement of friends. Much of the
required capital came from the banker Daniel Dreyfus, the
Pasha of Marrakesh and Winnaretta. Whatever she thought
about Colette's new job, she was scarcely interested in the
beautician's approach to one's physical features. She was
inclined to believe that Colette's claim, 'The human face was
always my great landscape!' had more of a spiritual than a
purely physical significance.

Chapter 16
The Irreplaceable Maecenas
(1935–1939)

By the mid 1930s the Princesse de Polignac had achieved an almost institutional status in French, indeed in European society. Laudatory descriptions of the rôle played by her in the musical world were numerous: to Poulenc she was 'that irreplaceable Maecenas'; to Maurice Sachs she was the 'champion of the music of today'; to Gabriel-Louis Pringué she was the 'high priestess of music holding a musical academy and giving concerts of high quality.' But she was also still well-known as an artist: as she approached her seventieth birthday, she had caused a mild sensation by mounting a one-man exhibition of her paintings at the Galérie Charpentier in the Faubourg Saint-Honoré. Moreover, she held a place in French high society that was practically unique: without too much exaggeration she was often described as the great-aunt of the French aristocracy. And she was not averse to elaborating the point with the occasional reference to 'my grandmother, the friend of Marie-Antoinette'.

Unfortunately, gossips, sometimes friends misinterpreted her attitude towards her own position as a living legend. Even Stravinsky repeated the story that it was her ambition to have her bust next to Richelieu's in the Louvre. With no generosity and less humour, André Germain embroidered a story about an incident which happened at the requiem for one of her distant Polignac kinsmen. She arrived, heavily veiled in black, and advanced to take a place at the front of the nave, where a pew had been reserved for the immediate family. A nephew, noticing her mistake, in a whisper asked if she would move back a row. But from behind the veils issued that voice which all present recognized: 'In my life, I have often advanced. I have never moved back. But I can walk out.' Whatever the truth of the story, it is certainly more credible than the claim that Germain made in the next breath. Legend had it that the

princess had the Devil at her service. That was how she maintained her control over people's lives. That was how she
managed to rid herself of her enemies. Poor André Germain, he
suffered from the primness and jealousy of the socially impotent.

The worst fault that Winnaretta suffered from in her position
as a cultural arbiter was that occasionally she failed to appreciate immaturity or inaestheticism in others. Questioning her
nephew, the Duc Decazes, about his young son Elie's progress
at the piano, she learned that he was top of his piano class. She
immediately pressed the boy to play something but was clearly
disappointed by the result. The explanation that the young
marquis's piano class consisted of just two pupils only partly
mollified her.

Another revealing incident occurred in June 1936 when she
was invited to a party at Lady (Sibyl) Colefax's house in
London. The guest list was impressive: Earl De La Warr, Sir
Robert Bruce Lockhart, Lord and Lady Stanley, Sir Robert and
Lady Vansittart, the Winston Churchills, the Kenneth Clarks,
Noel Coward, Daisy Fellowes and Harold Nicolson, recording
his impressions for the benefit of his wife. King Edward VIII
and Mrs Simpson were guests of honour. Artur Rubinstein had
been invited to play to the company. Near the piano sat
Winnaretta, listening intently. As Nicolson remarked, 'I have
seldom seen a woman sit so firmly: there was determination in
every line of her bum.' About 12.30 Rubinstein had just
finished his third piece of Chopin and was about to play a fourth
(Winnaretta's foot was tapping impatiently because of the
delay) when the King took advantage of the pause to thank
Rubinstein and announce his departure. But just as he was
leaving, more guests arrived, Lord Berners among others, and
they had to be introduced. Meanwhile, forgetting the King's
presence, Noël Coward sat down at the piano and began to
accompany himself as he crooned a song. The guests gathered
round him. The King abruptly changed his mind and returned
to his seat as Coward redoubled his efforts. After an hour of
Mad Dogs and Englishmen and the like, everyone was in high
spirits. Only then did the King depart. And only Winnaretta
failed to smile throughout the performance. Harold Nicolson
was probably right when he commented that at that moment
the Princesse de Polignac, not to mention Rubinstein, must have
thought the English a race of barbarians.

She may have sympathized with the King and Mrs Simpson, since she was capable of reading more into their apparently blind passion than most could. But she was no respecter of persons on whom inaestheticism reared its ugly head. And after that incident her opinion of the British royal family remained equivocal. The Duchess of Kent, for instance, she admired for the panache with which she organized her married life. The 'knowing' in Paris and London society might relish stories of how the duke's particular friend kept on display in his house a photograph of an attractive woman, who on closer inspection proved to be the duke himself—'in drag'—but a few years later at a social occasion the duchess ruined her reputation for sophistication, at least in Winnaretta's estimation, by asking who 'that fat woman over there' was, as she indicated none other than Myra Hess. She fumed with annoyance.

However, about this time Winnaretta continued to spend a lot of time in England and one of the reasons for this was that she was much in demand by people who did appreciate her both as a link with the civilized world of the past and as an architect of its present. At times this admiration was stimulated by her own interest in the English artistic scene. She followed the activities of the Bloomsbury Group and knew their works. Particularly fond of Virginia Woolf's books, she made a determined effort to meet her. In November 1935 she invited Madame Paul Valéry and Edmond Jaloux to dinner and induced Clive Bell, Virginia Woolf's brother-in-law, to join the party. He was flattered and even more so when he heard what extravagant praise she lavished on her work. After dinner, a niece of the princess mentioned to Bell that one of her aunt's greatest desires was to meet Virginia Woolf and all was instantly arranged. Winnaretta would be in London in two weeks' time, so would lunch at 1.30 p.m. on 12 December be suitable? The encounter took place and the two women instantly felt an affinity for each other.

Virginia welcomed the distraction of Winnaretta's company in the depressing period following the meagre success of *The Years* and subtly tried to tap her as a source of information about the past and about the workings of the human mind. Sitting by the fireside, Virginia would persuade Winnaretta to talk about her youth. She was fascinated by the story of her insistence upon hearing Beethoven's Quartet, opus 131, as a treat on her fourteenth birthday. Its opening bars, Winnaretta confessed, had always been one of the greatest comforts in her life—along with the twenty-third Prelude of Bach's 'Forty-Eight'. Virginia was so impressed that she induced her to write down an account of that memorable birthday. She also found Winnaretta fascinating because of her association with Proust, although there was no secret about how strained their relations had been at times. Virginia was far from discouraged. She pressed Winnaretta to tell her more about him and she was delighted when she sent her one of Proust's letters, which she had recently rediscovered among her papers. A present of gramophone records of Beethoven's Quartet opus 130, accompanied it.

At first sight, the friendship of these two women was surprising: they were both quite dominating characters but, on the other hand, they both had very gentle, shy sides to their natures, which they seemed to bring out in each other. By contrast, Winnaretta's friendship with another English novelist, Rosamond Lehmann, was of a quite different kind. She admired her for having begun her literary career in 1927 by publishing *Dusty Answer*, with its brave—if slightly gauche—treatment of a Lesbian subject. But about the time they first met, she had just written *The Weather in the Streets* and that was a mature masterpiece that confirmed earlier suggestions of promise. While Rosamond's husband, the Hon. Wogan Phillips (later Lord Milford, 'the communist peer'), was fighting in the Spanish Civil War, she often came to Paris and stayed at Winnaretta's house. For one thing she enjoyed the musical activities of the household and the princess was always pleased to have the company of such an intelligent and personable young woman. On occasions her classical beauty could be confusing. Sitting among guests of royal rank at one of Winnaretta's soirées, Rosamond was mistaken by the other guests for the Duchess of Kent. Indeed, according to Jacques-Emile Blanche, there were other mistakes made that evening. One elderly woman, learning that her husband was fighting in Spain, commiserated with her: 'I do hope Franco will win soon and that you'll get him back.' Rosamond's answer was quiet but distinct: 'Oh! he's fighting for the Government.' A long frosty silence ensued.

But Rosamond Lehmann found Winnaretta's less purely social acquaintances entirely unexceptionable. She mixed with them freely: Edouard Bourdet, the dramatist, Jean Cocteau and Louise de Vilmorin, the poetess; and at Marie-Blanche de Polignac's house in the rue Barbey-de-Jouy, she met Christian Bérard, who had just executed his sensational paintings in the dining-room. At Winnaretta's she also met her fellow novelist Colette, who had recently been honoured by being elected to the chair vacated by Anna de Noailles in Belgium's Académie Royale.

The story of Colette's installation at the Académie on 4 April 1936 is well known. Her appearance, wearing sandals designed to show off her bright red painted toenails, to deliver the statutory eulogy on her predecessor, about whose poetry she scrupulously avoided expressing any opinion, caused a sensation. But the whole affair very nearly failed to take place: Colette decided to travel to Brussels by train and her new husband and Winnaretta accompanied her to give her moral support. When they reached the border, a passport official announced that Colette's passport was not in order and refused to allow her to enter Belgium. Cold with indignation, Winnaretta intervened: 'Madame is attending your Académie to give an address. It won't be able to begin without her.' This made no impression on the official, even if he did understand what she said. He still insisted that the passport was invalid. Winnaretta redoubled her efforts. Clenching her teeth more and more tightly in her rage, she growled: 'And I tell you that without Madame there will be no address!' At this the man shrugged his shoulders and passed the responsibility on to a superior, who fortunately proved to be less intractable.

During this period Winnaretta had another boon companion. She had known the *virtuoso* pianist Clara Haskil since about 1922 and since 1927, when Clara's taking up residence in Paris coincided with the closing stages of Violet Trefusis's period of favour, she had been, in effect, the princess's special friend. The trouble with Violet had been that, while she had liked to treat Winnaretta as a mother-figure, she carried the illusion too far; she was too fond of playing the spoilt child. She was also a rich spoilt child and, therefore, unsusceptible to the controlling influence of Winnaretta's purse-strings. Clara Haskil was quite the opposite. Winnaretta used her perpetual indigence as a way of controlling her life and her career, although from 1934 she did guarantee her nominal independence by paying her a monthly allowance of 500 francs—which was increased to 800 francs in 1937—and by installing her in a small apartment of her own in the avenue Malakoff.

Their relationship was strange. On one hand, Winnaretta would try to maintain a tight control over Clara's life; on the other, she would encourage her to be outward-going. She would force her to accept engagements all over Europe and to stand on her own feet as an international artiste. She did not hesitate to introduce her to Lesbian friends who might have become rivals for her affection. One such was the well-known pianist Renata Borgatti, whose incredibly masculine appearance made her an object of wonder even in Paris. Renata had had a passing flirtation with Romaine Brooks in the early 1920s and, a few years later, was rumoured to have a closer relationship with Winnaretta than their two rather dominant personalities might have led one to suspect. However, money was probably a controlling influence in her case also: she was perpetually poor and Winnaretta subsidized her career and later left her a respectable sum in her will. When Clara was introduced to Renata Borgatti in 1932, Winnaretta probably made sure that they became no more than just good friends. That seems to have satisfied Clara, who welcomed a fellow-pianist's support and advice. She was particularly glad to meet through her the famous Swiss piano-teacher Anna Landenhan-Hirzel, whose friend and disciple she became. The effect of this meeting upon her professional life was to prove considerable.

However, what the Swiss teacher could do on the technical side was matched by what Winnaretta did to arrange engagements for Clara on the concert platform and latterly on French and Belgian radio, often despite Clara's reluctance. Painfully shy and oversensitive about her physical appearance, she tried to shun the limelight, allowing fame to slip through her fingers. Winnaretta had no patience with that. She insisted on dragging her round the social and cultural meccas of Paris like a nervous lap-dog. Clara submitted to rounds of socializing at Venice, though she hated the place. In fact, Winnaretta found her rather hard to please. When she took her away from the sophisticated city life for periods in the country at her house in Jouy-en-Josas, Clara was just as disgruntled: now she wanted to be back in the city. By this time Winnaretta had given up trying to follow the changing sequence of moods and simply

ignored Clara's petulance. If she had to leave Jouy to go up to
Paris for the day, Clara would always dress herself for a journey
and wait at the door, hoping to be invited to go along with her.
But Winnaretta would pretend not to notice anything and
would depart with an abrupt, 'I'll see you this evening!' When
business—or pleasure—called her to Paris, she had no intention
of letting Clara get under her feet.

Even in Paris Clara was not always happy. When she
practised at Winnaretta's house in the morning, invariably the
domestics duster and broom in hand would cluster behind the
door to listen in wonder at the force and majesty of the frail
woman's playing. Then the princess would sweep in, scattering
the secret audience and berating Clara for keeping her servants
from their work. But, despite their ups and downs, the two
women's friendship was productive: any career as a top-rank
concert-pianist would have been inconceivable for Clara
without Winnaretta's support, uncomfortable though it was at
times.

While Clara Haskil added lustre to the princess's reputation
as a patroness and as a concert-giver, Nadia Boulanger continued to make a distinctive contribution. Whenever she had a
work that needed championing, she would go to Winnaretta,
who would be sure to arrange a performance of it at her house.
Parisian society began to hear music that had lain forgotten for
centuries. In 1936 Heinrich Schütz's *Resurrection* was itself
resurrected, along with madrigals and motets by Monteverdi.
(These motets so fascinated Poulenc when he heard them in the
Polignac salon that he decided to make a thorough study of
them and as a result he wrote his *Sept Chansons* for unaccompanied
choir.) Boulanger's interests also included Purcell and Jannequin. She performed works by them, as well as by Bach and
Fauré, when, encouraged and financed by the princess, she
founded the Nadia Boulanger Orchestra and began to build up
its international reputation by giving concerts at the Wigmore
Hall in London in December 1936.

Through Nadia Boulanger, the younger generation of composers joined those of the 'twenties in Winnaretta's salon. The
girl composer Marcelle de Manziarly and Dinu Lipatti, newly
arrived from Roumania, were friendly rivals to Jean Françaix.
Lennox Berkeley, as at home in France as in England, was
joined there in 1937 by another Boulanger pupil from Britain,

the Hon. Anthony Chaplin, accompanied by his vivacious wife Alvilde (who was to become the princess's close friend and mainstay during her last years). But possibly an even more dynamic group of individuals was the outstanding band of young singers whom she gathered round her. Marie-Blanche de Polignac, the tenor Paul Derenne, the Swiss tenorino Hugues Cuénod, whose sense of fun was almost as remarkable as his voice, and the bass Doda Conrad, Marya Freund's son, who with Cuénod naturally drifted into the princess's circle of close friends.

Admittedly Doda Conrad's initial contact with her was inauspicious. Having sung at 57 avenue Henri-Martin several times, he was invited to join in one of her exclusive weekend parties at her small house in Jouy-en-Josas. He accepted and, on the appointed Friday evening, the princess's limousine duly drew up outside his apartment. He entered and sat down beside her but to his surprise she said nothing. None of his small talk met with any response; she just sat looking tense and withdrawn. American by birth, Conrad was unimpressed by what he considered the arrogance of an old world *grande dame* and decided that, if the situation did not improve, he would insist on getting out of the car before it passed the last Metro station. However, at that point a spectacular thunderstorm broke out. Suddenly animated, Winnaretta ordered the chauffeur to stop and hurried into the nearest bistro. Brusquely she told him to order coffee and then sat down quite rigid with fear, oblivious of the poor man's embarrassment, as he backed away to sit at a separate table, and of the amazed stares of the other clients. The storm subsided and she immediately climbed into the car again, berating the chauffeur as though it had all been his fault. Then she turned to Conrad and began chatting in a relaxed and charming way. Having seen the timid Winnaretta in a vulnerable moment, he began to understand her as a person. And they became close friends, collaborating with each other, often as much on the business aspects of musical productions as on the artistic side.

It was through Doda Conrad that she was able to arrange with Robert Meyer to finance the Boulanger concerts in London. She also made use of his help in the art world: discussing the work of the Polish artist Mela Muter one day, she suddenly asked him if he knew what had become of her. She was still in Paris, it seemed, still painting but starving. What could be done for her? She would not take kindly to charity, so Conrad must go and buy a small canvas from her on her behalf. He went off on his task but two days later he was being interrogated by Winnaretta on the telephone. What had happened to her picture? It was being framed and would not be ready for another week. And during that time she fretted until the canvas was in her hands, as though afraid that some-one would steal it and deprive her of her enjoyment of it.

But Conrad and his friends learned to put up with Win-naretta's penny-pinching: they realized that, abstemious with such essentials as food and drink, she often forgot that the young people flocking around her had healthy appetites. She would lavish money on concerts of the highest quality but spend only a tiny fraction of the amount upon catering. But the more ingenious among her devotees soon learned how to reach the buffet tables first and make quick inroads into what food was provided. However, that was only a minor, often amusing irritation that was easily outweighed by the sense of privilege felt at being the princess's house-musicians in all but name. When, for example, one had the experience of singing Fauré's *Cinq Mélodies de Venise* in the Palazzo Polignac with the dedicatee as one's accompanist, as Hugues Cuénod did, Winnaretta's mild other-worldliness was of little consequence. And, when she discovered the Hungarian pianist Lili Kraus practising in a hotel in Lausanne, she instantly paid her a large fee to give a recital to her party in a specially hired room and then intro-duced her to a singer as his ideal accompanist, as she did to Doda Conrad, her thoughtfulness in things that mattered was very apparent. But this caused less excitement than when she commissioned a work and specified that the composer should take into account her singer-friends' special qualities of voice: in 1936 she asked Jean Françaix to write a chamber opera in which parts could be created for Cuénod and Conrad. After some thought, they decided upon a comic subject, based upon a *libretto* which Françaix would create out of Alain-René Le Sage's fantastic story *Le Diable boiteux* (incidentally, on the cen-tenary of the première of a ballet by that name, produced at the Paris Opéra on 1 June 1936 with Fanny Elssler in the leading rôle.) However, Françaix's work suffered a few inter-ruptions and so it was not until 1937 that he managed to put

the finishing touches to his jewel-like opera, whose sparkling
music for the two solo voices and a miniature orchestra of solo
instruments, consisting of woodwind, limited brass, harp,
percussion and strings, admirably suited Le Sage's amusing
tale of magic and light immorality. Nadia Boulanger conducted
the first performance in the princess's salon and shortly afterwards the opera was broadcast in the United Kingdom.

Jean Françaix was scarcely twenty-five when he completed
Le Diable boiteux. Although his musical style was not revolutionary, he represented the newest generation of French composers
with whom the princess was associated. The death of Maurice
Ravel at the end of 1937 confirmed this feeling of her commitment to the eternal present. She had long cherished warm
feelings for Ravel and, even after he went into semi-seclusion
at Montfort l'Amaury some distance from Paris, she had kept
up the friendship by visiting him periodically at his charming
Louis-Philippe cottage. The last occasion upon which she saw
him was when he was induced to come to the Concert of
Dedications given in her honour in March 1933. This touched
her profoundly because she knew by that time that he was
suffering from some nervous disorder, although not until some
time later did she realize the seriousness of his condition.
When she heard the news and followed the progress of his fatal
illness, she could not help reflecting upon an incident which
occurred after that concert. A small group had joined her and
her friend the Princesse Illinsky (the Grand-Duke Dmitri's
American-born morganatic wife) for dinner, during which she
noticed that Ravel was deep in conversation with Madame
Illinsky. What could they be discussing? Not music surely,
since she had no ear for music and the name Ravel probably
meant nothing to her. Ravel explained: 'Oh! we are talking
about death.' Winnaretta was surprised, especially since their
conversation had been punctuated by outbursts of hilarity.

Winnaretta did not share Ravel's carefree attitude towards
death. She was certainly alarmed when he himself died, and
she became all the more upset and worried when she began to
suffer from angina about that time. She reacted very testily
whenever an attack of giddiness came in the middle of some
social event and interfered with her pleasure. But she was also
acutely aware that they had more serious implications. So in
1938 she decided to make a final will in order to dispose of the

remainder of her property. Between July 1938 and April 1939, when the last codicil was signed, she had to concentrate upon making complicated arrangements for disposing of pictures, precious musical manuscripts, houses, books and furniture, not to mention the residue of her money, from which she left countless bequests. A codicil dealt with the problem of what should be done about the mortgage created in her name in order to enable the Duc d'Ayen to purchase the family château at Maintenon from his father the Duc de Noailles. She wiped out the debt, a very simple and generous solution, which unfortunately led to much litigation in the Noailles family a decade or so later. The paintings and objets d'art left to the Louvre made an impressive list but for the most part the gifts made in the will were of a personal nature.

Her real legacy had already been made and was already bestowing benefits upon humanity through the Fondation Singer-Polignac. During the 1930s much was accomplished. Gérard Bauër's work in the field of art and music was financed. Laboratories at the College de France were created. André Mayer was given support in arranging a conference on natural history. In 1937 a conference on the subject of hormones took place and prizes were awarded to two physiologists Pol Bouin and Paul Ancel for their work in this field. In 1939 a conference on the subject of astrophysics was held. Archaeological expeditions to Greece were subsidized and money went to help restore Hagia Sophia in Istanbul. In the following decades hundreds of bequests were made to encourage executant musicians, composers and creative artists. The Musée Gauguin was set up in Tahiti. Work on the properties of the halucenogenic mushroom was financed. The Institut Océanographique received the invaluable gift of a ship (named the 'Winnaretta Singer') to help with its underwater studies. The cost of a six-year expedition to study the coral reef of New Caledonia was sustained by the Fondation. The purchase of a mobile laboratory for the Institut Pasteur's work in Dakar was made. These constituted only a fraction of the work made possible because of the princess's bequest.

In the 1930s Winnaretta did not feel that the activities of the Fondation absolved her from taking an active personal interest in deserving causes. How much money she gave away simply and quietly no one will ever know. But, apart from sitting on a

number of charitable committees, she could not conceal what
she did when financing the construction of Salvation Army
hostels in Paris and modernizing workmen's dwellings in the
city. The work of the Society for the Preservation and Re-
habilitation of Young Girls in Paris also received money and
encouragement from her. In addition, especially later in the
1930s, she began to give away some of her possessions to friends
and family, as though disburdening herself of worldly encum-
brances, which nonetheless she wanted to be appreciated and
cared for. One day soon after their marriage in 1937 the Marquis
Elie Decazes and his wife were invited to his great-aunt's: she
had a gift for them. It turned out to be the full-length portrait
of her, painted by Sargent when she was the Princesse de Scey-
Montbéliard. She pressed it upon the young couple and insisted
that they should take the enormous canvas away with them
there and then. A taxi was called and only with difficulty was
the sentimental gift borne off.

However, the princess's days were only occasionally darkened
by morbid or nostalgic preoccupations. She herself tended to
laugh at life's born pessimists; she would show scarcely veiled
irritation at the type of person who was always complaining.
One day one of her guests in Venice was an Italian who whined
for hours on end about the amount of taxes he had to pay. As
the complaints flowed, the adjectives and superlatives redoubled
in strength, piling one on top of the other—*ingiusto, eccessivo,
pesantissimo, esageratissimo!* 'The government has put taxes on
everything. I wonder what it will think of putting them on
next.' The princess's voice, calm and terse, rang out: 'On
adjectives!'

Ill-health scarcely inhibited the inveterate traveller in
Winnaretta. Venice still saw as much of her as ever. She still
surrounded herself there with guests, family and friends,
especially those with musical talents. In fact, one of the last art
representations of Winnaretta was executed by her kinsman
Comte Charles de Polignac, a pastel drawing made while she
was playing piano duets with Marie-Blanche de Polignac.
Frequently she would go herself to meet her guests at the new
station, Santa Lucia, in her little white motor-boat, 'The Rose
of Devon'—generally known as '*le bidet de la princesse*'. Some
certainly did not expect to be collected by her in person.
Alvilde Chaplin, arriving one morning with her cousin Angus

Menzies, after having sat through an overnight journey from Salzburg, was disconcerted to find Winnaretta waiting with '*le bidet*'. Her dusty appearance and her *lederhosen* did not go down very well with her hostess. But times were becoming troubled. Yet in the summer of 1938 the princess did manage to organize one last major expedition before the outbreak of war. This was a cruise to the Greek islands. Among the guests whom she took with her to share in her classical interests, perhaps the most illustrious, possibly also the youngest, was her fifteen-year-old kinsman Prince Rainier, heir-in-line to the throne of Monaco.

After staying in Venice for the remainder of the summer of 1938 and witnessing the Munich Agreement of 29 September, she turned away from the political situation with a feeling of despair and concentrated upon the only thing that retained any significance for her, the arts. Early in 1938 she had commissioned Francis Poulenc to write another concerto for her. What she had in mind was a work for organ and small orchestra, something reminiscent of Handel's organ concertos, that could be played comfortably on the organ in her music studio. Poulenc's ideas took shape quickly but he wrote the concerto fairly slowly, as he worked out a complex musical structure of great density, based upon an elaborate and skilful development of a single theme. The theme itself resembled, or rather hinted at, the opening of Bach's *Fantasia* in G minor, which a few years earlier the princess had scribbled on photographs of herself seated at her organ and had given to some of her friends. But Poulenc's concerto, once it had taken its final shape after a lot of work and a series of consultations with Winnaretta, bore more resemblance to a *fantasia* by Buxtehude, although its episodic changes of mood and *tempo* concealed under a rhapsodic veneer much greater formal control than was immediately apparent. The concerto's orchestration for strings and timpani only was as original as it was simple, deliberately so in order to achieve a proper balance between the orchestra and the organ in the princess's studio. With these instrumental forces Poulenc achieved a new dramatic, almost Gothic ecclesiastical sound: as he said, it was 'Poulenc on the way to the cloister, very fifteenth-century.' This surprised everyone who heard the first performance and thrilled many of them.

The Organ Concerto was completed in August 1938 but it

had to wait for some time before it could be put into rehearsal and fitted into concert programmes. In the meantime, the princess continued to delight Paris with her regular soirées and, when on a trip to London in November, she encountered Reynaldo Hahn, she even arranged for him to play for a party of her guests. The event coincided with a Buckingham Palace party, to which England's political best had been invited, but Winnaretta's little concert attracted many of the uninvited, including the aged courtesan Maxine Elliot, whose days of intimacy with the royal family—to be precise, the King's grandfather—were long past. At least in Reynaldo's traditional programme she could relive scenes of Edwardian frivolity, which, like her priceless beauty, had long since faded to no more than a memory. Back in Paris a more novel and sensational event took place in Winnaretta's salon that winter, a balletic recital given by the Indian dancer Ram Gopal. Still very young and at the beginning of his career, he fascinated some of the guests as much with his beauty as his dancing. However, it was Poulenc's Organ Concerto that was the real highlight of the 1938–39 season. The first performance, attended by the flower of musical life in Paris, took place as planned in Winnaretta's music studio with the Orchestre Symphonique de Paris under the baton of Roger Désormière. The organ was played by Maurice Duruflé, himself a noted composer associated with Olivier Messiaen and André Jolivet's group 'Jeune France'. Some time later, on 21 June 1939, the *concerto* had its first public performance at a *Sérénade* concert in the Salle Gaveau. However, it was given a rather rough reception by the critics: Poulenc had taken a wrong turning. What had happened to his old charm and spectacular expertise in handling the sonorities and rhythms so characteristic of the composer of *Les Biches*? The concerto had no unity of thought behind it. The sooner Poulenc got back on the rails again and produced some new, seductive *Bestiaire* the better. Winnaretta did not agree and if anything, these meaningless phrases stimulated her to encourage Poulenc to continue the logical process of his musical development.

One other composer caused something of a stir under Winnaretta's aegis during that final pre-War season. As a seventeen-year-old prodigy Dinu Lipatti had arrived to take up his studies in Paris in 1934. After a while he had been accepted by

Nadia Boulanger as a composition pupil. She had also taken over the job of directing his budding career as a concert pianist. Through her, Lipatti had been introduced to Winnaretta, who took him to her heart. He soon became a familiar figure among the talented young in her salon. One reason for his quick acceptance was that he immediately captivated his compatriot Clara Haskil with his simple charm—something which few men succeeded in doing. They were both sensitive and shy people, as well as incredible *virtuosi*. The princess recognized what a perfect artistic match they made. She encouraged them to play duets together in private and had them play at her soirées. On occasions she also joined Lipatti at the keyboard. His acceptance was complete: he joined in the intimate weekend parties at her house in Jouy-en-Josas, to which only the privileged few were ever invited.

Winnaretta was so enthralled by Lipatti as a pianist and interested in furthering his career as a composer that, as the summer vacation of 1939 approached, she decided to give a grand 'going-away' concert dedicated to him. The programme was all Lipatti: the music had come from his own pen and he played all the solo parts. Winnaretta engaged the Orchestre de la Société des Concerts from the Conservatoire to play with him under the baton of his mentor Charles Münch. The evening was a great success as much among the *chic* society Parisians as the artistic set who flocked to her salon to hear the talented Roumanian.

Intended as a farewell concert for a young prodigy, it was a happy occasion but, with the clouds of war gathering threateningly over Europe, some of those present must have wondered if it would prove to be a farewell to an era, to a whole way of life.

Chapter 17

The Pebbled Shore
(1939–1943)

On 10 August 1939 Winnaretta's youngest brother, Franklin Morse Singer, died in the American Hospital at Neuilly. And, as she prepared to follow his remains to England, she cancelled arrangements to open the Palazzo Polignac in Venice for the summer. Accompanied by Alvilde Chaplin and Prince Pierre de Monaco, she arrived in Torquay in time to join the small group that gathered round the Singer family vault at noon on 21 August. For a few days after the funeral she stayed on in Devon among her family. Prince Pierre, a rare and trusted confidant, returned to France soon afterwards. Since Winnaretta had no commitments for the summer and was feeling slightly jaded, she decided to spend a few more weeks in England to take a cure. And it was during that time that Hitler's armies swept into Poland and, on 3 September, Britain and France declared war on Germany.

On 19 September she wrote to Poulenc in Paris to thank him again 'for so many beautiful hours of music and for having composed for [her] the Concerto of Venice and that of Paris, whose profound beauty haunted [her]'; and she went on to say that for the moment she had yielded to her family's persuasion to stay in England but hoped soon to be able to return to Paris. Meanwhile, by a quirk of fate, she found herself in the country where the Franco-Prussian War had driven her as a young child. Although she longed to be back in France, she did feel at home in the Devon countryside; there were even some friends from Paris in the area: Audrey Norman Colville (to whose memory Poulenc dedicated his *Hyde Park* in 1945) lived in a ravishing house nearby, although she did spend much of her time rushing around in a Red Cross ambulance.

As months passed and hostilities between the enemy countries intensified, Winnaretta realized that an immediate return to France was inadvisable and so she left the uneasy calm of life

in Devon to take up residence in a small four-roomed flat in
Mayfair, at 55 Park Lane. Alvilde Chaplin, whose husband was
serving in the Royal Air Force, joined her there for the sake of
companionship. And it was here that they listened on the radio
to the succession of disastrous events of May and June 1940.
The invasion of the Netherlands and Belgium and the evacua-
tion from Dunkirk, they were ominous setbacks. France fell and
all hope faded as Pétain signed an armistice with Hitler on 22
June. Winnaretta then knew that all possibility of returning to
Paris had disappeared. Stranded in England like a refugee, she
felt that her whole world had collapsed in ruins around her.
However, although she was afraid and unwell, she distracted
herself by thinking of the plight of others and of the practicalities
of living rather than abandoning herself to despair. What was
happening to her friends in France? Some of them, such as
Darius Milhaud and Colette's husband, were Jewish and might
expect scant consideration from Nazi conquerors. Others must
have been badly hit financially. Cloton Legrand had lived in
straitened circumstances before the war but now her position
would be intolerable. Little did the princess know that Cloton
would be reduced to burning bundles of a lifetime's letters from
admirers, including Maupassant, for warmth when her fuel ran
out. The days when she had almost too regularly dropped in to
play bridge or just to chat, and often bicker with Winnaretta
(sitting glancing unobtrusively at her watch as the minutes
passed) now seemed enviable. But her own position was not
exactly easy. Her main sources of income had been cut off; she
had brought little with her from Paris other than the luggage
needed for a short trip, and so all but the simplest life-style was
impossible. Moreover, she had the anxiety of wondering what
had become of her property and possessions in France, although
she did make an attempt to forestall the worst happening: she
knew a diplomat from the London embassy of a neutral South
American country and, through him, contrived to send a
postcard by way of Chile to the Duc Decazes in Paris. The
German authorities, imagining that she had taken refuge in a
neutral country and not in enemy England, left her Paris house
untouched. Only one of her own paintings, a copy of a Carpaccio, at Jouy-en-Josas, was damaged: it came out of the war
with a bullet-hole in it. But she certainly had no idea what was
happening in France, and so her worries remained.

Apart from worry, boredom was her main affliction. Having
no concerts to arrange and unable to commission new works
herself, she had to find other means of distraction. She went to
what concerts there were in London; the National Gallery
recitals organized by Myra Hess were a godsend. Throughout
this period she continued to play the piano, still taking lessons
to keep up her technique. Sometimes, tired of solitary music
sessions, she would go to the Wigmore Hall studios and persuade
pianists practising there to play duets with her in an effort to
recapture the joy of shared music-making. She still tried to
keep up with the world of organ music and, in fact, soon became
a close friend of the organist of Westminster Abbey, William
McKie, who became a devoted admirer of hers. Art also provided distraction and solace. A steady stream of canvases and
water-colours came from her brush while she was in London
and whenever she travelled down to Devon for short periods.
But reading was her main diversion. She demolished the novels
of E. M. Forster and explored the corpus of English literature
from the eighteenth century onwards, as she had not done
before. Her friends were hard put to it to keep her supplied with
suitable reading matter. And when she was wearied with reading, she would go to the bookshop in Curzon Street, run by
Heywood and Lady Anne Hill almost more as a rendezvous
for literary friends than as a bookseller's. Nancy Mitford, who
all but managed the shop, was very taken by her and would sit
and chat with her for hours. Her initial impression of the
princess was that of 'an old, sad exile' but she soon came to
admire her for her intellect and for her command of witty
repartee that never deserted her even in her most disconsolate
moments.

However, about this time Winnaretta did have one major
preoccupation. Her friends began to insist that she should write
her memoirs. She had already attempted to reminisce on paper
before the outbreak of war when Virginia Woolf asked for an
account of her fourteenth birthday. But she had found that so
difficult that a secretary had had to do the writing. Now, with
no amanuensis, she yielded to Sir Ronald Storrs's suggestion
that she should record her impressions on a phonograph so that
he could have them transcribed. But this did not prove to be
very successful. Eventually she tackled the task herself, writing
down clouded memories of incidents ranging over her whole life,

as she recalled them. Only a very small portion of her experiences were recorded in this way and she gave the manuscript to Raymond Mortimer, who rewrote and reshaped her prose, cutting it drastically and doing his best to decipher a handwriting so execrable that it was the cause of an unbelievable number of mistakes. However, her 'Memoirs', though brief, incomplete and wholly lacking in structure, did contain many valuable sense impressions of half a century and more of social history. After her death, Cyril Connolly was happy to publish them as an article in his literary journal *Horizon*.

Meanwhile, though bored for want of distraction and still hankering after life in Paris, Winnaretta did not lack social contacts in London. Despite wartime conditions, she daily met and socialized with old friends: Lady Crewe, Lady D'Abernon, Lady Diana Abdy, the Dowager Lady Rumbold (the wife of one of Prince Edmond's cousins), Mrs George Keppel and, next door in the Dorchester Hotel, that mixed blessing Lady (Emerald) Cunard. Violet Trefusis made periodic appearances in London, after fleeing from France as the Germans approached Paris. Daisy Fellowes had also left France to live at Donnington near Newbury. She visited London when she could tear herself away from her latest hobby, breeding a special kind of black sheep. Still elegant and handsome, she was now slightly less high-spirited. For one thing, she had suspended her practice of crossing herself as she turned away with a shudder from advertisements for Singer sewing-machines—the main, but for her too mundane source of her fortune. By contrast, Winnaretta still continued to give Singer shops a friendly wave and a greeting: '*Bonjour!*', even though after the fall of France her income from Singer shares was cut off.

Winnaretta still saw something of Dame Ethel Smyth, as domineering as ever, despite being an octogenarian. The princess usually had to bow to her will and visit her in Surrey rather than meet her in London. Ethel would make sure that she kept her promises to come by making the arrangements in writing through Alvilde Chaplin. She would outline a tempting lunch menu: cutlets, savoury eggs, junket and choice wines; and give travel instructions, all the time referring to Winnaretta as 'Herself' or, in a postscript reminding her to return a book on the Vic Wells, as the '*Principessa*'. Winnaretta submitted quietly and probably enjoyed seeing Dame Ethel, despite her still untamed temper and extreme deafness. However, one afternoon of shouting into her ear-trumpet was all that she could stand. But, back in London, she was always pleased when she came across Ethel's friends, particularly the writer Maurice Baring. They developed a great admiration for each other: he even went so far as to say that she was 'the wittiest woman in Europe'.

Another friend whom she occasionally saw was Lord Berners, diplomat, composer, writer and general eccentric (a tame word employed by those who were lost for a more descriptive one). She had known him since the days when he had associated with Diaghilev's Ballets Russes and had often accepted invitations to stay at his house at Faringdon, where he kept up a grand style with his aristocratic young friend Robert Heber-Percy. Winnaretta was glad to see something of Lord Berners, if only as a link with the past, while he welcomed her for her dry, humorous approach to life even at its low wartime ebb.

A younger composer, Lennox Berkeley, was re-introduced to Winnaretta by Alvilde Chaplin and entered her circle of London friends. He still found her formidable, almost forbidding, but soon he realized that, once conversation progressed beyond the small-talk stage, she would relax. Anything intellectual interested her, the more philosophical the better. She certainly enjoyed having a composer of the younger generation—and one from the Boulanger stable—around her again. Unfortunately there could be no question of her commissioning a work from him nor of his writing anything to dedicate to her, at least not until the war had ended.

Not long after his return to England in 1942, Benjamin Britten met the princess. A lunch party, arranged at the Café Royal with the tenor Peter Pears and Alvilde Chaplin, gave her a fair insight into the composer's mind and philosophy of life. She followed his career with keen interest, apparently so much so that rumours circulated about his writing a work for her. But the truth of the matter was never revealed.

Yet there was a strange irony in Winnaretta's position in wartime London. Whereas she was almost exclusively interested in the work and ideas of the up-and-coming avant-garde of the musical and literary world, she found that they were often more interested in her as someone who had known the talented great of previous generations. Proust, something of a bête noir in his own lifetime, became even more so two decades after his death. On 25 February 1943 she entertained Stephen Spender to dinner, as one of England's more notable poetic veterans of the Spanish Civil War, but his conversation seems to have centred not on his own work but on Proust's. And, as usual, Winnaretta attempted to discourage discussion, this time by telling a less than complimentary story about him. Proust liked to play at being the great man by engaging a taxi, riding in it for a hundred yards or so and tipping the driver 100 francs just to impress him. Unfortunately for him, Winnaretta added, this could give rise to unfortunate misinterpretations.

About this time James Lees-Milne, the art historian and one of the National Trust's mainstays, was tackling *À la Recherche* and longed to question the princess about Proust. But he had to wait for the right moment. At a party at Sibyl Colefax's on 13 May, he made a point of talking to her rather than to his friends, Harold Nicolson and Desmond Shawe-Taylor, but for the moment he had to confine himself to swapping pleasantries about the other guests. They laughed roundly at each other's confession of complete ignorance of the identity of most of the others; and the Proustian element was confined to the level of Lees-Milne's silent reflection: there was 'something godlike about her and . . . very Faubourg Saint-Germain'; the princess, sitting solidly, unmoving on the same sofa all evening, looked 'rather like a large Buddha'. But she was not quite so impassive when he went to dinner with her on 22 July. The other guests, a fellow art historian, John Pope-Hennessy, Winston Churchill's niece Clarissa and one David Horner, whom (the others believed) Winnaretta had invited under the impression that he was E. M. Forster. However, he turned out to be the slightly less than young man who lived with Osbert Sitwell and he proved to be as capable as any of them of holding his own in a conversation on the subject of the English novelists. Almost inevitably the French novelists infiltrated the discussion and once again Winnaretta was confronted with the shade of Proust. Her guests soon learned, if they did not already know, that she had not particularly cared for him. Why? He was far too hypersensitive. He could read an insult into even the most innocuous remark and then the unwitting offending party might expect to receive a volley of recriminating letters from him. Moreover, he was always in love, invariably unrequited, and used to pour his sorrows out on his increasingly impatient friends. He was almost as impossible when he was happy; he would 'toss money to servants as though it were chicken food'—his version of the grand style. After that Winnaretta had to soften the image slightly for his English admirers. As a young man, she admitted, he had been handsome and had had 'melting brown eyes'. And, of course, she admired him as a writer and had been delighted to learn that in England before the First World War—when only *Du Côté de chez Swann* had been published and was little known in France outside the Faubourg Saint-Germain—there was already a thriving Proust 'fan-club'. She then seized the opportunity to dispel rumours that Proust had modelled Madame Verdurin on her. There was no connection whatsoever: the confusion had arisen because in those pre-War days she and her English friends had amused themselves at her King's Road house by taking the names of the characters from La Verdurin's salon: Professeur Brichot, Dr Cottard, Odette de Crécy and the rest; she, of course, had had to be 'the Mistress' herself.

A sequel to this dinner party occurred a few days later on 30 July when James Lees-Milne went to tea at Emerald Cunard's. Winnaretta arrived in high glee and told the assembled company how he had come to dinner and afterwards had sent her a present of *Tom Jones*, not just an ordinary copy but 'a rare edition of two volumes of priceless value'. When he heard this, Lees-Milne, who had obtained it through Nancy Mitford from Heywood Hill's Bookshop, went stiff with fear at the thought of 'how much that villainous Nancy would charge . . . for this book'. But Winnaretta was delighted with the gift and highly entertained by Fielding's rumbustious hero.

During the autumn of 1943 Winnaretta's health deteriorated. Her angina attacks became more frequent and the drugs which she took seemed less effective. However, this scarcely inhibited the social life which she had built up around herself. In fact, if she ever had to cancel a dinner party, it was because of the indisposition of one of her guests, such as a considerably younger Clarissa Churchill on 6 October. The following day, as planned, the princess braved the rigours of a grand reception given by Henry ('Chips') Channon for Field-Marshal Wavell and his wife. There were 105 guests to be greeted or avoided: Freya Stark and Eve, the daughter of her old friend Marie

Curie, the Duke of Alba and his seventeen-year-old daughter Tana, beautifully poised and detached, Loelia Duchess of Westminster and Daisy Fellowes, and political friends Leslie Hore-Belisha and Harold Nicolson. Violet Trefusis was also there, 'grandly got-up in an 1860 affair'. Even the host Chips Channon did not hesitate to repeat Hore-Belisha's comment that 'it was the most glamorous party since the war'. However, when the blackout fell at seven o'clock, there was rather too general a rush to find taxis, and in the confusion that followed Winnaretta was forgotten and had to sit on the porter's chair in the front hall for an hour before a vehicle came for her. Meanwhile, people milled around, chatting and making dates.

One of the dates arranged by Winnaretta herself was a dinner party on 4 November. Among the guests, for whom Alvilde Chaplin cooked dinner, was Sir Paul Dukes, as an authority on Russia responding with interest to the views of a table companion, a Norwegian woman, who had arrived, after tea with King Haakon, full of misgivings about Russia's designs on Norway. David Horner, no longer cast in the rôle of E. M. Forster, had also been invited and was 'croaking like a cheap gramophone'. Sitting beside James Lees-Milne, the princess made isolated contributions to the conversation 'in a deep voice and trenchant manner, ending each sentence with a French epithet'—which was often difficult to understand. One guest, however, had no difficulty: the Prince Marc de Beauvau-Craon, who had just succeeded in escaping from France, knew her of old from her Paris days. He unfolded stories of life in France under German occupation, the lack of facilities, the German monopoly of cultural life in Paris, the phenomenal cost of a meal at *Maxime*'s, the internecine rivalry between the Wehrmacht and the Gestapo and the pillaging of art treasures by the invaders. Prince Marc had seen Germans deliberately destroying his cousin's Van Dycks and Rubenses because of his refusal to collaborate. The news was alarming and allowed little room for hope. For Winnaretta life in London must have seemed pleasant by comparison, despite its privations and despite her fear of air-raids (during which she would sit on a three-legged stool in the corridor outside her flat waiting terrified until the all-clear sounded.)

On 24 November the princess gave another dinner party with Alvilde Chaplin, who took the opportunity of James

Lees-Milne's early arrival to express her anxiety about her health: recently she had been having as many as twenty angina attacks in a day. But when she entered the room, she looked quite well. 'Her remarkable face, like some mountainous crag, was sunset pink.' And during the dinner her mind was very alert. Most of the time she spent talking to Lees-Milne about Sir Kenneth Clark's latest series of lectures. Perhaps, wondered the princess, if she wrote to him, he would send her a copy of his script of the most recent one, which she had missed. The conversation moved on to E. M. Forster, for whom she had become a self-appointed champion. And, before Lees-Milne slipped away for fire-watching duty, the talk had come round to Proust again. His concept of England and the English, Winnaretta maintained, was derived entirely from his study of Ruskin at the time when he was working on his translation of *La Bible d'Amiens*. Continuing the English theme, she added an anecdote about the Duke of Marlborough's surprise at the sight presented by Proust at a dinner party given for him in Paris: he arrived, 'pale and ill, wearing a long seal-skin dressing-gown down to his ankles'. That had been the last occasion upon which Winnaretta had seen him.

And that was almost the last occasion upon which the princess herself was seen. Next day, Thursday 25 November, she lunched with Sir Edward Marsh and Raymond Mortimer and they chatted pleasantly about the irrepressible genius of Benjamin Britten. When Winnaretta left, Marsh reflected upon how remarkable she was—'a very great lady, intelligent and cultivated to the last degree . . . She got handsomer and handsomer as she grew older.'

In the evening she went out to dine with Sibyl Colefax. Those present, including Sir Ronald Storrs and James Pope-Hennessy, found her lively; and she stayed until eleven o'clock, listening on the radio to the first part of *The Rescue*, a poetic drama based on the story of Homer's *Odyssey* by Edward Sackville-West with an orchestral score by Benjamin Britten. Storrs accompanied her home in a taxi but, on the way, she began to feel unwell. He waited with her in the entrance hall of her block of flats, where she sat for a while trying to recover. As soon as she was well enough, she went upstairs. But, once there, her condition took another turn for the worse. Alvilde Chaplin sent for a doctor, who, though he could do little to help, joined her vigil by the princess's bedside. At 2 a.m. she had a severe heart-attack and died.

At first light, despite her grief at the loss of a beloved friend, Alvilde Chaplin began tackling the task of arranging a funeral worthy of her. A death-mask should have been made but, finding this distasteful, Mrs Chaplin had an original idea: she asked Sir Kenneth Clark if he knew of anyone who might make a death-bed sketch of her. And he suggested that Thomas Monnington, the Royal Academy's bright young man, might undertake the commission. He did and the result was a sketch that admirably captured her serenity and striking handsomeness, which death had done nothing to diminish.

On the morning of Wednesday, 1 December, a requiem mass was celebrated at the Church of the Immaculate Conception in Farm Street. It was a very solemn and moving service, attended by a host of friends and acquaintances, as well as a number of diplomatic representatives. William McKie had eagerly agreed to provide the organ music, as a labour of love, almost an act of homage. Before the requiem he played Chorale Preludes by Bach and during it Peter Pears joined him to sing Mozart's *Ave Verum Corpus*, the *Benedictus* from Bach's Mass in B minor and the moving *In Paradisum* from Fauré's *Requiem*. Afterwards, as the princess's friends dispersed, 'talking quietly and lovingly about her', William McKie played the Saint Anne's Fugue, which she had always greatly admired.

Then the last stage of the Princesse de Polignac's mortal journey began. Her remains were transported by train to Torquay where, mourned by a handful of close friends and her family, they were laid to rest in the Singer family vault, beside her revered father and the husband whom she had admired and loved so much. Her name was inscribed upon the white marble of the tombstone under the German epitaph which she herself had chosen for Prince Edmond forty-two years before:

'Blessed in faith, blessed in love.'

Bibliography

Since the Princesse Edmond de Polignac directed that most of her papers should be destroyed after her death, very little manuscript material relating to her life has survived. However, unpublished documents in private hands, particularly those of the Marquise d'Argenson, Mrs James Lees-Milne and the heirs of Charles Koechlin, have proved invaluable, as have collections in various archives and libraries, especially the *Papiers Montesquiou* and the *Papiers Poincaré* in the Bibliothèque Nationale, Paris; the *Monk's House Papers* in the University of Sussex; manuscripts relating to the life of Frederick Delius in the Delius Trust Archive, London, and the Grainger Museum in the University of Melbourne; and legal documents relating to the Singer family in Somerset House, London.

The following list of published works is limited to those containing primary source material used in this present biography:

Astruc, Gabriel, *Le Pavillon des fantômes*, Paris, Grasset, 1929.

Auric, Georges, 'Une Oeuvre nouvelle de Satie', *Littérature*, no. 2, April 1919.

Balsan, Consuelo Vanderbilt, *The Glitter and the Gold*, London, Heinemann 1953.

Barker, Richard, *Marcel Proust*, London, Faber and Faber, 1958.

Barrès, Maurice, *L'Oeuvre de M.B.*, Paris, Au Club de l'honnête homme, 1965–68.

Bathori, Jane, 'Erik Satie', *Les Lettres Françaises*, May–June 1966.

Bauër, Gérard, [Guermantes], 'Les Mots et leur usage', *Le Figaro*, 18 July 1966.
                  'Une Initiatrice de la musique contemporaine', *Le Figaro*, 28 Nov. 1944.

Bazin, Germain, *The Louvre*, London, Thames and Hudson, 1957.

Bell, Clive, *Old Friends*, London, Chatto and Windus, 1956.

Bell, Quentin, *Virginia Woolf. A biography . . . Mrs Woolf 1912–1941*, vol. II, London, Chatto and Windus, 1972.

Beucler, André, *Poet of Paris. Twenty Years with Léon-Paul Fargue*, London, Chatto and Windus, 1955.

Bibesco, Princesse Marthe, *Le Confesseur et les poètes*, Paris, Grasset, 1970.

Billy, André, *L'Epoque 1900*, Paris, J. Tallandier, 1951.

Blanche, Jacques-Emile, *Mes Modèles*, Paris, Stock, 1928.

    More Portraits of a Lifetime, London, Dent, 1939.

    Portraits of a Lifetime, London, Dent, 1937.

    La Pêche aux souvenirs, Paris, Flammarion, 1949.

    'Quelques Instantanés de Marcel Proust', *La Nouvelle Revue Française*, vol. 20, 1923.

Boyer, Ferdinand, 'L'Abate de Canillac e G.P. Pannini', *Urbe (Revista Romana)*, July–August 1948.

Bramsbäck, Birgit, *James Stephens*, Upsala, Lundequist, 1959.

Brandon, Ruth, *Singer and the Sewing Machine*, London, Barrie and Jenkins, 1977.

Bril, France-Yvonne, *Henri Sauguet*, Paris, Seghers, 1967.

Bronowicz-Chylińska, Teresa, *Karol Szymanowski*, Kraków, Polskie Wydawn, 1961.

Brown, Frederick, *An Impersonation of Angels*, London, Longmans, 1969.

Buckle, Richard, *In Search of Diaghilev*, London, Sidgwick and Jackson, 1955.

    Nijinsky, London, Weidenfeld and Nicolson, 1971.

Campodonico, Luis, *Falla*, Paris, Le Seuil, 1959.

Carassus, Emilien, *Le Snobisme et les lettres françaises de Paul Bourget à Marcel Proust, 1884–1914*, Paris, A. Colin, 1966.

Carley, Lionel, *Delius, the Paris Years*, London, Triad Press, 1975.

Casella, Alfredo, *Strawinski*, Brescia, La Scuola, 1951.

Castellane, Comte Boni de, *Comment j'ai découvert l'Amerique*, Paris, Crès, 1924.

Cattaui, Georges, *Marcel Proust*, Paris, Julliard, 1952.

Channon, Sir Henry, *Chips. The Diaries of Sir H.C.*, London, Weidenfeld and Nicolson, 1967.

Chase, Gilbert, *The Music of Spain*, New York, Dover Publications, 1959.

Chéron, Raoul, 'Necrologie', *Le Gaulois*, 13 August 1901.

Clarac, Pierre, and Ferré André, *Album Proust*, Paris, Gallimard, 1965.

Clermont-Tonnerre, Elisabeth de Gramont, Duchesse de, *Marcel Proust*, Paris, Flammarion, 1948.

Souvenirs du monde, Paris, Grasset, 1966.

'Un Grand Poète', *Les Oeuvres Libres*, nouv. sér. no. 8, 1946.

Years of Plenty, London, Cape, 1932.

Clouzot, Marie-Rose, *Souvenirs à deux voix de Maxime Jacob à Dom Clément Jacob*, Toulouse, Privat, 1969.
Cocteau, Jean, *The Journals of J.C.*, London, Museum Press, 1956.
　　My Contemporaries, London, Owen, 1967.
　　Opium. The Diary of a Cure, London, New English Library, 1972.
　　Portraits-Souvenir 1900–1914, Paris, Grasset, 1935.
Cohen, Harriet, *A Bundle of Time*, London, Faber and Faber, 1969.
Colette, *Journal à rebours*, Paris, Fayard, 1941.
Collet, Henri, *Albéniz et Granados*, Paris, Alcan, 1926.
　　'Erik Satie', *L'Esprit Nouveau*, no. 2, 1920.
Corpechot, Lucien, *Souvenirs d'un journaliste*, vols II–III, Paris, Plon, 1936–37.
Cossart, Michael de, 'Princesse Edmond de Polignac: Patron and Artist', *Apollo*, vol. CII, no. 162, August 1975.
　　'Ravel, the Pavane and the Princess', *Musical Opinion*, vol. 97, no. 1159, May 1974.
　　'Stravinsky and the Princesse Edmond de Polignac', *Durham University Journal*, new ser. vol. 36, no. 2, June 1975.
Curtiss, Mina, *Bizet and his World*, London, Secker and Warburg, 1959.
D'Abernon, Helen Viscountess, *Red Cross and Berlin Embassy*, London, J. Murray, 1946.
Dean, Winton, *Georges Bizet. His Life and Work*, London, Dent, 1965.
Debussy, Claude, and Louÿs, Pierre, *Correspondance, 1893–1904*, Paris, Corti, 1945.
Degand, Léon, and Rouart, Denis, *Claude Monet*, Genève, Skira, 1958.
Demarquez, Suzanne, *Manuel de Falla*, Paris, Flammarion, 1963.
Desaymard, Joseph, *Emmanuel Chabrier d'après ses lettres*, Paris, Roches, 1934.
Drew, David. 'Preface', in Kurt Weill, *2 Sinfonie*, Mainz, Schotts, 1966.
Dujardin, Marie, 'Marcel Proust à Venise', *Le Figaro*, 10 October 1931.
Duncan, Isadora, *My Life*, London, Gollancz, 1968.
Edel, Leon, *Henry James. The Middle Years, 1884–1894*, London, Hart-Davis, 1963.
Faral, Edmond, and Heim, Roger, *Les Heures de musique à la Fondation Singer-Polignac, 1951–1966*, Paris, Fondation Singer-Polignac, 1966.
Fargue, Léon-Paul, *Dîners de lune*, Paris, Gallimard, 1952.
　　Méandres, Genève, Milieu du Monde, 1946.

Fauré, Gabriel, *Catalogue de l'Exposition G.F.*, Paris, Bibliothèque
        Nationale, 1963.
        Catalogue de l'Exposition G.F., Paris, Bibliothèque
        Nationale, 1974.
        Lettres intimes, Paris, Grasset, 1951.
Février, Henry, *André Messager*, Paris, Amiot-Dumont, 1948.
Flak, Micheline, 'Thoreau et les français', *Europe*, July–August 1967.
Flanner, Janet, *An American in Paris*, London, Hamish Hamilton,
        1940.
        Paris was Yesterday, 1925–1939, London, Angus and
        Robertson, 1973.
Fouquier, Baron Marcel, *Jours heureux d'autrefois*, Paris, Michel, 1941.
Fouquières, Comte André de, *Cinquante Ans de panache*, Paris, Horay,
        1951.
        Mon Paris et ses parisiens, vol. I, Paris,
        Horay, 1953.
Gauthier, André, *Manuel de Falla*, Paris, Seghers, 1966.
Gavoty, Bernard, [Clarendon], 'À la Mémoire de la Princesse de
        Polignac', *Le Figaro*, 9 December 1965.
        Clara Haskil, Genève, R. Klister, 1962.
        Louis Vierne, la vie et l'oeuvre, Paris, Michel, 1943.
Georges-Michel, Michel, 'La Mort de Serge de Diaghilew et la fin
        des Ballets russes', *La Revue Musicale*, no. 110, December, 1930.
Germain, André, *La Bourgeoisie qui brûle*, Paris, Sun, 1951.
        Les Fous de 1900, Paris, Plon, 1954.
Gilbert, Martin, *Sir Horace Rumbold*, London, Heinemann, 1973.
Gill, Brendan, *Cole*, London, Michael Joseph, 1971.
Goncourt, Edmond and Jules de, *Journal*, vol. XX, Monaco,
        Imprimerie Nationale, 1956.
Goudeket, Maurice, *Près de Colette*, Paris, Flammarion, 1956.
Green, Julien, *Journal 1928–1958*, Paris, Plon, 1961.
        Journal 1926–1934. Les années faciles, Paris, Plon, 1970.
Grigoriev, S. L., *The Diaghilev Ballet, 1909–1929*, London, Constable,
        1953.
Gunn, Peter, *Vernon Lee. Violet Paget*, London, O.U.P., 1964.
Hahn, Reynaldo, *Notes*, Paris, Plon, 1933.
        Thèmes variés, Paris, Jadin, 1946.
Halicka, Alice, *Hier. Souvenirs*, Paris, Pavois, 1946.
Hall, Richard, 'Princesse Winnie', *Opera News*, vol. 34, nos. 9–10,
        1969–70.
Harcourt, Eugène d', 'Un Prince Musicien', *Le Figaro*, 9 August
        1901.
Harding, James, *The Ox on the Roof*, London, Macdonald, 1972.
Haskell, Arnold, *Ballet Russe*, London, Weidenfeld and Nicolson,
        1968.

Haskell, Arnold, *Diaghilev. His artistic and private life*. London, Gollancz, 1955.

Hassall, Christopher, *Edward Marsh. Patron of the Arts*, London, Longmans, 1959.

Hell, Henri, *Francis Poulenc*, London, J. Calder, 1959.

Helleu, Paul, *Catalogue de l'Exposition P.H.*, Paris, Bibliothèque Nationale, 1957.

Hermant, Abel, *Souvenirs de la vie mondaine*, Paris, Plon, 1935.

Heyworth, Peter, ed., *Conversations with Klemperer*, London, Gollancz, 1973.

Hier, Florence, *La Musique dans l'oeuvre de Marcel Proust*, New York, Columbia University, 1933.

Hofmann, Rostislav, *Serge Prokofiev*, Paris, Seghers, 1963.

Howe, Henry, *Adventures and Achievements of Americans*, Cincinnati, Howe, 1959.

Hugli, Pierre, 'Il y a cent ans naissant Erik Satie', *La Gazette de Lausanne*, 14 May 1966.

Hugo, Valentine, 'Le Socrate que j'ai connu', *La Revue Musicale*, June 1952.

Ingres, Jean-A.-D., *Catalogue de l'Exposition Ingres au Petit Palais*, Paris, 1967.

Jaloux, Edmond, *Les Saisons littéraires*, vol. II, Paris, Plon, 1950.

Jean-Aubrey, G., '*El Retablo* by Manuel de Falla', *The Chesterian*, new ser. no. 34, October 1923.
  'Gabriel Fauré, Paul Verlaine et Albert Samain ou les tribulations de *Bouddha*', *La Revue Musicale*, Numéro spécial G. Fauré, 1945.

Jeanneret, Albert, 'Socrate', *L'Esprit Nouveau*, no. 9, July 1921.

Jourdan-Morhange, Hélène, *Ravel et nous*, Genève, Milieu du Monde, 1945.

Jullian, Philippe, *Dreamers of Decadence*, London, Pall Mall, 1971.
  Edward and the Edwardians, London, Sidgwick and Jackson, 1967.
  Robert de Montesquiou, a Fin-de-Siècle Prince, London, Secker and Warburg, 1965.

Jullian, Philippe, and Phillips, John, *Violet Trefusis*, London, Hamish Hamilton, 1976.

Koechlin, Charles, *Gabriel Fauré*, Paris, Alcan, 1927.

Landowska, Wanda, *Landowska on Music*, New York, Stein and Day, 1964.

Lanjean, Marc, *Jean Françaix, musicien francais*, Paris, Contact Editions, 1961.

Laplane, Gabriel, *Albéniz, sa vie, son oeuvre*, Genève, Milieu du Monde, 1956.

Larnac, Jean, *La Comtesse de Noailles*, Paris, Sagittaire, 1931.

La Rochefoucauld, Edmée, Duchesse de, *Images de Paul Valéry*, Strassbourg, Le Roux, 1949.

Lawrence, D. H., *The Letters of D.H.L.*, London, Heinemann, 1932.

Léautaud, Paul, *Journal Littéraire*, vols IV–V, Paris, Mercure de France, 1957–58.

Lees-Milne, James, *Ancestral Voices*, London, Chatto and Windus, 1975.

Lemaitre, Georges, *Four French Novelists*, London, O.U.P., 1938.

Lifar, Serge, *À l'Aube de mon destin*, Paris, Michel, 1948.

    Ma Vie. From Kiev to Kiev, London, Hutchinson, 1970.

    'Misia', *La Nouvelle Revue des Deux Mondes*, March 1975.

    Serge Diaghilev, London, Putnam, 1940.

Lipatti, Anna, *Dinu Lipatti: la douleur de ma vie*, Genève, Perret-Gentil, 1967.

    La Vie du pianiste Dinu Lipatti, Paris, La Colombe, 1954.

Long, Marguerite, *Au Piano avec Gabriel Fauré*, Paris, Julliard, 1963.

Lynn, Olga, *Oggie. The Memoirs of O.L.*, London, Weidenfeld and Nicolson, 1955.

Maciejewski, B. M., *Karol Szymanowski. His Life and Music*, London, Poets and Painters' Press, 1967.

McKibbin, David, *Sargent's Boston*, Boston, Museum of Fine Arts, 1956.

Malipiero, Gian Francesco, *L'Opera di G.F.M.*, Bologna, Edizioni di Treviso, 1952.

    Strawinsky, Venezia, Cavallino, 1945.

March, Harold, *The Two Worlds of Marcel Proust*, London, O.U.P., 1948.

Markevitch, Igor, *Point d'Orgue. Entretiens avec Claude Rostand*, Paris, Julliard, 1959.

Markiewicz, *'Stabat Mater' Karola Szymanowskiego*, Katowice, 1963.

Marks, Elaine, *Colette*, New Brunswick, Rutgers University Press, 1960.

Marsh, Edward, *A Number of People*, London, Harper, 1939.

Marsh, Edward, and Hassall, Christopher, *Ambrosia and Small Beer*, London, Longmans, 1964.

Mauclair, Camile, 'Les Salons littéraires à Paris', *Revue des Revues*, vol. 28, 1899.

Maurois, André, *Le Monde de Marcel Proust*, Paris, Hachette, 1960.

Maxwell, Elsa, *I Married the World*, London, Heinemann, 1955.

Mila, Massimo, ed., *Manuel de Falla*, Milano, Ricordi, 1962.

Milhaud, Darius, *Études*, Paris, Aveline, 1927.

    Notes without Music, London, D. Dobson, 1952.

Missoffe, Michel, *Gyp et ses amis*, Paris, Flammarion, 1932.

Mitchell, David, *The Fighting Pankhursts*, London, Cape, 1967.

Montesquiou, Comte Robert de, *Le Chef des odeurs suaves*, Paris, G. Richard, 1893.

Monteux, Doris, *It's All in the Music*, London, William Kimber, 1966.

Morand, Paul, *Journal d'un attaché d'ambassade, 1916–17*, Paris, Table Ronde, 1948.
    Le Visiteur du soir, suivi de quarante-cinq lettres inédités de Marcel Proust, Genève, La Palatine, 1949.

Mosley, Sir Oswald, *My Life*, London, Nelson, 1968.

Mount, Charles Merrill, *Monet*, New York, Simon and Schuster, 1966.

Myers, Rollo, *Emmanuel Chabrier and His Circle*, London, Dent, 1969.
    Erik Satie, London, Denis Dobson, 1948.
    Ravel: Life and Works, London, Duckworth, 1960.

Nabokov, Nicolas, *Old Friends and New Music*, London, Hamish Hamilton, 1951.

Nectoux, J.-Michel, *Fauré*, Paris, Le Seuil, 1972.

Nicolson, Harold, *Diaries and Letters, 1930–1939*, London, Fontana, 1971.

Nijinsky, Romola, *Nijinsky*, London, Gollancz, 1933.

Oleggini, Léon, *Connaissance de Stravinsky*, Lausanne, Foetisch, 1952.

Orledge, Robert, 'Cole Porter's Ballet *Within the Quota*', *Yale University Library Gazette*, vol. 50, no. 1, 1975.

Pahissa, Jaime, *Vida y Obra de Manuel de Falla*, Buenos Aires, Ricordi, 1947.

Pahlen, Kurt, *Manuel de Falla und die Musik in Spanien*, Olten, Walter, 1953.

Painter, George, *Marcel Proust*, 2 vols, London, Chatto and Windus, 1959–65.

Paléologue, Maurice, *Journal, 1913–1914*, Paris, Plon, 1947.

Peyrefitte, Roger, *L'Exilé de Capri*, Paris, Flammarion, 1959.
    The Jews, London, Secker and Warburg, 1967.

Pierre-Quint, Léon, *Marcel Proust*, Paris, Kra, 1935.
    Proust et la stratégie littéraire, Paris, Corrêa, 1954.

Piroué, Georges, *Proust et la musique du devenir*, Paris, Editions Denoël, 1960.

Polignac, Hedwige, Princesse François de, *Les Polignac*, Paris, Fasquelle, 1960.

Polignac, Prince Louis de, ed., *Hommage à Marie Blanche, Comtesse Jean de Polignac*, Monaco, Jaspard, Polus et Cie, 1965.

Polignac, Winnaretta, Princesse Edmond de, 'Memoirs', *Horizon*, vol. XII, no. 68, August 1945.
    'Mes Amis Musiciens', *Revue de Paris*, August–September 1964.

Popovitch, Olga, *Catalogue des peintures du Musée des Beaux-Arts de Rouen*, Paris, 1967.

Porel, Jacques, *Fils de Réjane. Souvenirs, 1895–1920*, Paris, Plon, 1951.

Poulenc, Francis, *Correspondance, 1915–1963*, Paris, Le Seuil, 1967.
    Emmanuel Chabrier, Paris, La Palatine, 1961.
    Moi et mes amis, Paris, La Palatine, 1963.

Pound, Ezra, *The Letters of E.P., 1907–1941*, London, Faber and Faber, 1951.
    Literary Essays of E.P., London, Faber and Faber, 1954.
    Pound/Joyce . . . the Letters of E.P. to J.J., London, Faber and Faber, 1967.

Pourtalès, Guy de, *Richard Wagner*, London, Harper, 1935.

Pringué, Gabriel-Louis, *Portraits et fantômes*, Monaco, R. Solar, 1951.
    Trente Ans de diners en ville, Paris, Edition Revue Adam, 1948.

Proust, Marcel, *Autour de soixante lettres de M.P.*, Paris, Gallimard, 1929.
    Correspondance Générale, vols II–VI, Paris, Plon, 1931–36.
    Letters of M.P., London, Chatto and Windus, 1950.
    Letters to his Mother, London, Rider, 1956.
    Lettres à Madame C., Paris, J. B. Janin, 1947.
    'Le Salon de la Comtesse Aimery de La Rochefoucauld', *Cahiers Marcel Proust*, no. 3, Paris, 1971.
    [Horatio], 'Le Salon de la Princesse Edmond de Polignac: musique d'aujourd'hui; échos d'autrefois', *Le Figaro*, 6 September 1903.

Quennell, Peter, ed., *Marcel Proust, 1871–1922*, London, Weidenfeld and Nicolson, 1971.

Rachewiltz, Mary, Princesse Boris de, *Discretions*, London, Faber and Faber, 1971.

Radnor, Helen, Countess-Dowager of, *From a Great-Grandmother's Armchair*, London, Marshall, 1927.

Régnier, Henri de, *L'Altana ou la vie vénitienne*, 2 vols, Paris, Mercure de France, 1928.

Roberts, Cecil, *The Bright Twenties*, London, Hodder and Stoughton, 1970.
    The Growing Boy, London, Hodder and Stoughton, 1967.

Rose, Sir Francis, *Saying Life*, London, Cassell, 1961.

Rostand, Maurice, *Confessions d'un demi-siècle*, Paris, Jeune Parque, 1948.

Roy, Jean, *Darius Milhaud*, Paris, Seghers, 1968.

Rubinstein, Helena, *Je suis esthèticienne*, Paris, Le Conquistador, 1957.

Rumbold, Sir Horace, *Recollections of a Diplomatist*, 2 vols, London, Arnold, 1902.

Sachs, Maurice, *Au Temps du Boeuf sur le Toit*, Paris, Nouvelle Revue Critique, 1948.

        La Décade de l'illusion, Paris, Gallimard, 1950.

St John, Christopher, *Ethel Smyth*, London, Longmans, Green, 1959.

Sarkany, Stéphane, *Paul Morand et le cosmopolitisme littéraire*, Paris, Klinchsieck, 1968.

Satie, Erik, *Catalogue de l'Exposition*, Paris, Bibliothèque Nationale, 1966.

Schaeffner, André, *Stravinsky*, Paris, Rieder, 1931.

Schneider, Marcel, *Henri Sauguet*, Paris, Ventadour, 1959.

Scott, John, *Genius Rewarded or the Story of the Sewing Machine*, New York, Caulon, 1880.

Secrest, Meryle, *Between Me and Life*, Macdonald and Jane's, 1974.

Seroff, Victor, *Maurice Ravel*, New York, Holt, 1953.

        The Real Isadora, New York, Dial Press, 1971.

Servières, Georges, *Gabriel Fauré*, Paris, Laurens, 1930.

Shattuck, Roger, *The Banquet Years*, London, Faber and Faber, 1958.

Siohan, Robert, *Stravinsky*, London, Calder and Boyars, 1965.

Smyth, Ethel, *As Time Went On . . .*, London, Longmans, Green, 1936.

        Beecham and Pharaoh, London, Chapman and Hall, 1935.

        What Happened Next, London, Longmans, Green, 1940.

Sokolov, Lydia, *Dancing for Diaghilev*, London, John Murray, 1960.

Spycket, Jérôme, *Clara Haskil*, Lausanne, Payot, 1975.

Steegmuller, Francis, *Cocteau*, London, Macmillan, 1970.

Stein, Gertrude, *The Autobiography of Alice B. Toklas*, London, Bodley Head, 1933.

Storrs, Sir Ronald, *Orientations*, London, Nicholson and Watson, 1943.

Stravinsky, Igor, *Chroniques de ma vie*, Paris, Denoël et Steele, 1935.

Stravinsky, Igor, and Craft, Robert, *Conversations with Igor Stravinsky*, London, Faber and Faber, 1959.

        Dialogues and a Diary. London, Faber and Faber, 1968.

        Expositions and Developments, London, Faber and Faber, 1962.

        Memories and Commentaries, London, Faber and Faber, 1960.

Stuckenschmidt, Hans, *Maurice Ravel*, London, Calder and Boyars, 1969.

Suckling, Norman, *Fauré*, London, Dent, 1946.

Sutton, Denys, *James McNeill Whistler*, London, Phaidon, 1966.

Szymanowski, Karol, and Smeterlin Jan, *Correspondance*, London, Allegro Press, 1969.

Tansman, Alexandre, *Igor Stravinsky*, New York, Putnam, 1949.

Tauman, Léon, *Marcel Proust, une vie et une synthèse*, Paris, Colin, 1949.

Templier, Pierre-Daniel, *Erik Satie*, Cambridge, Massachusetts Institute of Technology Press, 1969.

Thomas, Louis, *L'Esprit de Montesquiou*, Paris, Mercure de France, 1943.

Thomson, Virgil, *Virgil Thomson*, London, Weidenfeld and Nicolson, 1967.

Thoreau, Henry David, *Walden; or, Life in the Woods*, New York, New American Library, 1953.
  'Walden ou la vie dans les bois', tr. Winnaretta Singer, *La Renaissance Latine*, vol. II.iv–III.i, December 1903–January 1904.

Tiersot, Julien, *Un Demi-Siècle de musique française, 1870–1919*, Paris, Alcan, 1924.

Tintori, Giampiero, *Igor Stravinsky*, Paris, Le Sud et A. Michel, 1966.

Tomkins, Calvin, 'Living well is the Best Revenge', *The New Yorker*, 28 July 1962.

Torres, Eduardo, 'El Retablo de Maese Pedro', *La Vida Musical*, vol. I, no. 4, April 1923.

Trefusis, Violet, *Don't Look Round*, London, Hutchinson, 1952.

Trend, John, *Manuel de Falla and Spanish Music*, New York, Alfred A. Knopf, 1934.

Tyler, Parker, *The Divine Comedy of Pavel Tchelitchew*, London, Weidenfeld and Nicolson, 1969.

Vallas, Léon, *Vincent d'Indy*, vol. I, Paris, Michel, 1946.

Varèse, Louise, *Varèse, a Looking-Glass Diary*, vol. I, London, Davis-Poynter, 1973.

Vernet, Lawrence, 'Marcel Proust admirateur imprévu de Thoreau', *Europe*, 1969.
  'Actualité de Thoreau', *France Amerique: Revue des Nations Américaines*, 1968, 3e trimestre.

Vlad, Roman, *Stravinsky*, London, O.U.P., 1960.

Wagner, Richard, *My Life*, London, Constable, 1911.

White, Eric Walter, *Stravinsky. A critical survey*, London, John Lehmann, 1947.
  Stravinsky's Sacrifice to Apollo, London, Hogarth Press, 1930.

White, Eric Walter, *Stravinsky. The Composer and his Works*, London,
          Faber and Faber, 1966.
Wolfensberger, Rita, *Clara Haskil*, Bern, Scherz, 1962.
Young, Mahonri Sharp, 'Thief of Souls', *Apollo*, vol. 92, no. 111,
          May 1971.
Young, Percy, *Stravinsky*, London, D. White, 1969.
Zayed, Georges, ed., *Lettres inédités de Verlaine à Cazals*, Genève, E.
          Droz, 1957.

Index

236

Index

Billy, Comte Robert de, 129

Bird, Alfred Curtis, 119–20

Bizet, Georges, 39, 89, 178

Blake, William, 188

Blanche, Mme Antoine, 42

Blanche, Jacques-Emile, 42, 58, 77–78, 101–2, 106, 202

Blum, René, 180

Blumenthal, Georges, 78

Bolm, Adolph, 93

Bonnières, Robert de, 19, 33

Borgatti, Renata, 204

Bouchor, Maurice, 34

Boulanger, Général Georges, 41

Boulanger, Nadia, 156, 182, 191, 205–6, 208, 213

Bourdet, Edouard, 174, 203

Bourget, Paul, 23, 59, 112

Boyer, Isabelle Eugénie, *see* Singer, Mrs I.

Boyer, Jeanne-Marie, Lady Synge, 11–12, 68

Boyer, Louis-Noël, 6

Boyer, Pamela, 6, 12

Brahms, J., 50, 110, 184

Brancovan, Prince Constantin de, 76

Brancovan, Princesse Rachel de, 54, 69, 70, 78, 113

Braque, Georges, 137

Briand, Aristide, 93, 109, 121–2, 134, 158, 176

Brigode, Comtesse de, *née* Gramont, 23

Britten, Benjamin, 218, 222

Broglie, Princesse Isabelle de, 158

Broglie, Prince Jean de, 130–1

Broglie, Princesse Jean de, *see* Fellowes

Broglie, Prince Maurice de, 133

Broglie, Abbé le Prince Paul de, 42

Brooke, Lady, Ranee of Sarawak, 40

Brooks, Romaine, 94, 100–1, 204

Brown, Horatio, 79

Browning, Robert, 168, 169

Bulteau, Mme 'Toche', 84, 87, 91, 110, 114

Burne-Jones, Sir Edward, 40

Calmette, Gaston, 103

Campbell, Mrs Patrick, 62

Camposelice, Duc de, 10–11

Camposelice, Duchesse de, *see* Singer, Mrs I.

Capel, Diana, 133

Caplet, André, 104

Caracciolo, Duchesse di, *née* Sampayo, 94

Caraman-Chimay, Prince Alexandre de, 69, 75

Caraman-Chimay, Princesse Alexandre de, *née* Hélène de Brancovan, 69, 74, 78–9, 84, 86, 87, 91, 121, 196–7

Cardinal, Mme, 158

Caro, Elme, 23

Carol, Prince, of Roumania, 111

Carpaccio, Vittore, 31, 171, 215

Carriès, Jean, 26

Caruso, Enrico, 111

Casadesus, Mme Henri, 148

Casa Fuerte, Marquise (Yvonne) de, 183

Casati, Marchesa Luisa, 158, 170–1

Casella, Hélène, 162

Castellane, Comte Boni de, 23, 133

Castellane, Comtesse Jean de, 93

Cendrars, Blaise, 146

Cervantes, M. de, 134, 136

Chabrier, Emmanuel, 26–9, 43, 132, 178, 192

Chaliapin, Feodor, 92, 102

Chanel, Gabrielle, 176–7, 179, 180

Channon, Sir Henry, 220–1

Chaplin, Hon. Anthony, 206, 215

Chaplin, Hon. Mrs Anthony, *née* Alvilde Bridges, 206, 210–11, 214–215, 217–18, 221–3

Chaplin, Arthur, 1

Charles X, 38

Chausson, Ernest, 26–7, 34, 49, 54

Chevigné, Comtesse de, 93, 123, 125, 129

Chopin, F., 19, 54, 65, 91, 137, 186, 194

Churchill, Clarissa, 219, 220

Churchill, Lady Randolph, 62, 108

Clairin, Georges, 31

Clark, Edward, 3–4